THE middle east

OPPOSING VIEWPOINTS®

Other Books of Related Interest

Opposing Viewpoints Series

Africa
American Foreign Policy
The Breakup of the Soviet Union
Central America
Eastern Europe
Global Resources
Islam
The New World Order
Terrorism
The Third World
War
Weapons of Mass Destruction

Current Controversies Series

Europe
Hunger
Interventionism
Iraq
Nationalism and Ethnic Conflict

At Issue Series

Ethnic Conflict
The United Nations
U.S. Policy Toward China

THE middle east

OPPOSING VIEWPOINTS®

Mary E. Williams, Book Editor

David L. Bender, *Publisher*

Bruno Leone, *Executive Editor*

Bonnie Szumski, *Editorial Director*

David M. Haugen, *Managing Editor*

OPPOSING
VIEWPOINTS®
SERIES

Greenhaven Press, Inc., San Diego, California

Library of Congress Cataloging-in-Publication Data

The Middle East : opposing viewpoints / Mary E. Williams, book editor.
     p.   cm. — (Opposing viewpoints series)
     Includes bibliographical references (p.   ) and index.
     ISBN 0-7377-0132-3 (pbk. : alk. paper). —
ISBN 0-7377-0133-1 (lib. : alk. paper)
     1. Middle East—Politics and government—1945– . 2. Religion
and politics—Middle East. 3. Middle East—Foreign relations—
United States. 4. United States—Foreign relations—Middle East.
5. Arab-Israel conflicts—1993–   —Peace. I. Williams, Mary E.,
1960–   . II. Series: Opposing viewpoints series (Unnumbered)
DS63.1.M5426 2000
956.04—dc21   99-10881
                                                                       CIP

Greenhaven Press, Inc., P.O. Box 289009
San Diego, CA 92198-9009

"CONGRESS SHALL MAKE NO LAW...ABRIDGING THE FREEDOM OF SPEECH, OR OF THE PRESS."

First *Amendment* to the U.S. Constitution

The basic foundation of our democracy is the First Amendment guarantee of freedom of expression. The Opposing Viewpoints Series is dedicated to the concept of this basic freedom and the idea that it is more important to practice it than to enshrine it.

CONTENTS

WHY CONSIDER OPPOSING VIEWPOINTS?

"The only way in which a human being can make some approach to knowing the whole of a subject is by hearing what can be said about it by persons of every variety of opinion and studying all modes in which it can be looked at by every character of mind. No wise man ever acquired his wisdom in any mode but this."

John Stuart Mill

In our media-intensive culture it is not difficult to find differing opinions. Thousands of newspapers and magazines and dozens of radio and television talk shows resound with differing points of view. The difficulty lies in deciding which opinion to agree with and which "experts" seem the most credible. The more inundated we become with differing opinions and claims, the more essential it is to hone critical reading and thinking skills to evaluate these ideas. Opposing Viewpoints books address this problem directly by presenting stimulating debates that can be used to enhance and teach these skills. The varied opinions contained in each book examine many different aspects of a single issue. While examining these conveniently edited opposing views, readers can develop critical thinking skills such as the ability to compare and contrast authors' credibility, facts, argumentation styles, use of persuasive techniques, and other stylistic tools. In short, the Opposing Viewpoints Series is an ideal way to attain the higher-level thinking and reading skills so essential in a culture of diverse and contradictory opinions.

In addition to providing a tool for critical thinking, Opposing Viewpoints books challenge readers to question their own strongly held opinions and assumptions. Most people form their opinions on the basis of upbringing, peer pressure, and personal, cultural, or professional bias. By reading carefully balanced opposing views, readers must directly confront new ideas as well as the opinions of those with whom they disagree. This is not to simplistically argue that everyone who reads opposing views will—or should—change his or her opinion. Instead, the series enhances readers' understanding of their own views by encouraging confrontation with opposing ideas. Careful examination of others' views can lead to the readers' understanding of the logical inconsistencies in their own opinions, perspective on why they hold an opinion, and the consideration of the possibility that their opinion requires further evaluation.

EVALUATING OTHER OPINIONS

To ensure that this type of examination occurs, Opposing Viewpoints books present all types of opinions. Prominent spokespeople on different sides of each issue as well as well-known professionals from many disciplines challenge the reader. An additional goal of the series is to provide a forum for other, less known, or even unpopular viewpoints. The opinion of an ordinary person who has had to make the decision to cut off life support from a terminally ill relative, for example, may be just as valuable and provide just as much insight as a medical ethicist's professional opinion. The editors have two additional purposes in including these less known views. One, the editors encourage readers to respect others' opinions—even when not enhanced by professional credibility. It is only by reading or listening to and objectively evaluating others' ideas that one can determine whether they are worthy of consideration. Two, the inclusion of such viewpoints encourages the important critical thinking skill of objectively evaluating an author's credentials and bias. This evaluation will illuminate an author's reasons for taking a particular stance on an issue and will aid in readers' evaluation of the author's ideas.

As series editors of the Opposing Viewpoints Series, it is our hope that these books will give readers a deeper understanding of the issues debated and an appreciation of the complexity of even seemingly simple issues when good and honest people disagree. This awareness is particularly important in a democratic society such as ours in which people enter into public debate to determine the common good. Those with whom one disagrees should not be regarded as enemies but rather as people whose views deserve careful examination and may shed light on one's own.

Thomas Jefferson once said that "difference of opinion leads to inquiry, and inquiry to truth." Jefferson, a broadly educated man, argued that "if a nation expects to be ignorant and free . . . it expects what never was and never will be." As individuals and as a nation, it is imperative that we consider the opinions of others and examine them with skill and discernment. The Opposing Viewpoints Series is intended to help readers achieve this goal.

David L. Bender & Bruno Leone,
Series Editors

Greenhaven Press anthologies primarily consist of previously published material taken from a variety of sources, including periodicals, books, scholarly journals, newspapers, government documents, and position papers from private and public organizations. These original sources are often edited for length and to ensure their accessibility for a young adult audience. The anthology editors also change the original titles of these works in order to clearly present the main thesis of each viewpoint and to explicitly indicate the opinion presented in the viewpoint. These alterations are made in consideration of both the reading and comprehension levels of a young adult audience. Every effort is made to ensure that Greenhaven Press accurately reflects the original intent of the authors included in this anthology.

INTRODUCTION

"There has been enough destruction, enough death, enough waste. And it's time that together we occupy a place beyond ourselves, our peoples, that is worthy of . . . the descendants of the children of Abraham."

—King Hussein of Jordan

The twentieth century has been a turbulent time for the Middle East. Ethnic conflicts, political and economic instability, territorial rivalries, religious disputes, and war have marred the region that has often been referred to as the cradle of civilization. An examination of one of the area's most challenging issues, the Arab-Israeli conflict, reveals the fragility of peacemaking efforts in the region.

Most of the Arab world objected to the establishment of Israel as a state within the Palestinian region in 1948. From that point on, territorial disputes between Israel and its Arab neighbors resulted in several wars during the last half of the twentieth century. In addition, the status of the Palestinian Arabs living in Israeli-occupied areas—many of them descendants of refugees of the 1948 Arab-Israeli war—remained uncertain.

International alliances further complicated tensions in the Middle East. For many years, the Arab-Israeli conflict was enmeshed in the cold war rivalry between the United States and the Soviet Union. U.S. military aid to Israel was counterbalanced by Soviet military aid to Syria and the Palestine Liberation Organization (PLO). With the support of opposing superpowers behind them, conflicting parties in the Middle East had no real incentive to work together to resolve disputes. In the late 1980s, however, the decline of the Soviet Union and its new rapprochement with the United States left its former Middle East allies stranded without economic and military backing. These allies then sought new links with the United States and the West.

Many historians agree that it was largely due to U.S. and Western influence that Arab-Israeli relations took a new turn in the 1990s. In October of 1991, delegations representing Israel, the Palestinians, Jordan, Syria, Egypt, and Lebanon met in Madrid, Spain, to discuss the Arab-Israeli conflict. This was a momentous occasion, because it was the first time that Israel and its Arab neighbors, excepting Egypt, had directly talked with each other.

These discussions did not result in any formal accords, but instead set up the framework for future talks.

In February of 1993, Israeli and Palestinian negotiators participated in secret talks in Oslo, Norway. These talks focused on implementing eventual Palestinian self-rule by withdrawing Israeli troops from the Gaza Strip and the town of Jericho. The Palestinian Authority, led by Yasser Arafat, was to govern these areas. In September 1993, Arafat and Israeli prime minister Yitzhak Rabin met in Washington, D.C., to sign this historic Oslo agreement. The Oslo II accords of September 1995 and the January 1997 Hebron accord handed some Israeli-occupied West Bank territory over to full or limited Palestinian rule.

Each of these accords, however, has been met with setbacks

that have threatened to derail the peace process. In 1994, violence broke out in the West Bank and Gaza as Jewish settlers resisted the government's efforts to hand territory over to the Palestinians. Wanting to ensure security for Jewish settlements in Israeli-occupied areas, Israel kept postponing the promised troop withdrawals. In November 1995, Rabin was assassinated by an Orthodox Jew unhappy with the Oslo accords. Palestinian militants, angered by the territorial stalemates and with what they perceived as an overly accommodationist Palestinian Authority, assailed Israel with hundreds of terrorist attacks, including some suicide bombings, in 1996 and 1997.

Palestinian officials continued to demand a final settlement that would lead to the establishment of a Palestinian state encompassing Gaza and most of the West Bank. In January of 1998, however, Prime Minister Benjamin Netanyahu's cabinet declared that large parts of the West Bank would remain permanently under Israeli control. While Palestinian representatives claimed that Israel's decision thwarted the legitimate aspirations of the Palestinian people, Netanyahu's supporters argued that Israel needed to ensure the security and safety of Israelis. The peace negotiations seemed to have reached a permanent impasse.

At Maryland's Wye River Conference Center in October 1998, U.S., Israeli, and Palestinian negotiators jumpstarted the deadlocked peace process. Israel agreed to hand over more West Bank land in exchange for Palestinian promises to conduct a serious antiterrorism program. Moreover, Israel is required to release 750 jailed Palestinians and to provide "corridors of safe passage" for Palestinians traveling between Gaza and the West Bank. The Palestinians, in turn, must forbid all appeals to violence, outlaw weapons possession, and allow the United States' CIA to oversee their counterterrorism program. In addition, the Palestine National Council has agreed to delete from its charter all language calling for the destruction of Israel.

Whether the breakthrough at Wye is a major turning point in the road to Middle East peace—or a mirage leading to another dead end—remains to be seen. The authors in *The Middle East: Opposing Viewpoints* examine the region's tensions as well as its potential for peace in the following chapters: Why Is the Middle East a Conflict Area? How Does Religion Affect the Middle East? What Role Should the U.S. Play in the Middle East? How Could Peace Be Advanced in the Middle East? The wide-ranging viewpoints in this volume can help readers better understand the issues facing the Middle East and gain insight into the difficulty of attaining peace in the region.

CHAPTER 1

WHY IS THE MIDDLE EAST A CONFLICT AREA?

CHAPTER PREFACE

The Middle East has long been a center of ethnic, religious, and political rivalries. One issue that illustrates the persistent nature of these conflicts is the Arab-Israeli dispute. After World War I, Palestine, a region of land southeast of the Mediterranean Sea, came under British administrative rule. At this time, Palestine was populated by Arabs—Muslims and Christians—and Jews, who comprised 10 percent of the population. The number of Jews in Palestine increased, however, after the Nazi Holocaust of 6 million European Jews during World War II, which bolstered efforts on the part of Zionists to establish a Jewish homeland in Palestine. In 1947, the United Nations voted to divide Palestine into Jewish and Arab states—a decision that was rejected by neighboring Arab nations. Jewish nationalists proclaimed the establishment of the state of Israel in 1948, accepting the boundaries delineated by the UN resolution. The armies of Egypt, Iraq, Jordan, and Lebanon immediately invaded Israel, but were defeated in 1949.

Subsequent wars between Arab nations and Israel erupted in 1956, 1967, 1973, and 1982; and in 1987 and 1996, widespread civil violence broke out in Israel. Much of this conflict stems from the unresolved issue of the Palestinian Arab refugees. After 1948, large numbers of Palestinians fled Israel—some uprooted by war, some fearing for their safety in a new Jewish state, and some fleeing from extremist groups on both sides. Most of these refugees—and their descendants—are living in camps in the Israeli-occupied areas of the West Bank, the Golan Heights, and the Gaza Strip (territories won during the former wars). Palestinian demands for Israel to release this land to Palestinian authority and Israeli efforts to protect Israel from Palestinian militant violence are a continuing source of friction among several Middle Eastern nations.

The Arab-Israeli dispute is not the only cause of conflict in the Middle East. The region's role as a vital supplier of oil increases its potential for political, territorial, and economic strife. From 1980 to 1988, territorial and religious animosities between Iraq and Iran erupted into the region's bloodiest twentieth-century war, resulting in more than one million casualties. Recently, the international community has become increasingly concerned with the possibility of a buildup of biological, chemical, and nuclear weapons within feuding Middle Eastern nations. These and other sources of tension are analyzed by the authors of the following chapter.

| "The discovery of oil was a curse: the desire for material gain replaced old values of loyalty, honor and respect for tradition."

OIL PROFITS HAVE CREATED CONFLICT

Lawrence G. Potter

In the following viewpoint, Lawrence G. Potter argues that financial profits from oil and natural gas reserves have led to conflict in the Middle East. Western nations have sometimes interfered with Middle Eastern politics to procure oil assets, Potter points out. Furthermore, oil revenues enabled Persian Gulf countries to modernize rapidly, which destabilized the region's traditional cultures and value systems. After the discovery of oil, monarchs and ruling sheikhs provided financial security to citizens and to religious institutions in return for their political loyalty. Presently, however, the region's population is increasing while oil revenues are remaining stable. Faced with burgeoning unemployment and decreasing economic benefits, many people in the Gulf are demanding greater say in government while maintaining potentially divisive ethnic and religious loyalties. Potter is a professor of international affairs at Columbia University.

As you read, consider the following questions:

1. What is the "rentier mentality," according to Potter?
2. According to the author, why did Britain and the U.S. overthrow the Iranian government in 1953?
3. In Potter's opinion, why do the governments of Gulf states feel a need to create a sense of national identity?

Excerpted from Headline Series no. 315, *The Persian Gulf in Transition*, by Lawrence G. Potter, published by the Foreign Policy Association (1998). Reprinted with permission from the FPA, 470 Park Ave. So., New York, NY 10016.

The Persian Gulf is a 600-mile-long arm of the Indian Ocean, which separates the Arabian peninsula from Iran. (Since the 1960s some Arab states have referred to the Persian Gulf as the Arabian Gulf, in an attempt to give it a new identity and belittle Iran.) The Gulf is surrounded by Iran, the predominant state in terms of population, and seven Arab countries: Iraq, Kuwait, Saudi Arabia, Bahrain, Qatar, the United Arab Emirates (UAE) and Oman. The Gulf is bounded by the Shatt al-Arab waterway in the north, which forms the frontier between Iran and Iraq, and the Strait of Hormuz in the south, which connects it to the Gulf of Oman and the Indian Ocean. The strait, which is 34 miles wide at its narrowest point, is the choke point of the Gulf: some 30,000 vessels, mostly oil tankers, pass through it each year. The possibility of its closure by Iran has long been a nightmare for Western oil importers and defense planners.

The Gulf states contain some 116 million people, representing many ethnic, religious, linguistic and political communities. A major cleavage pits Arab against Persian. Arabic, a Semitic language, is spoken in Iraq and the countries of the peninsula, whereas Iran has an Aryan heritage, and its main language, Persian (Farsi), is an Indo-European tongue. Persians regard their cultural legacy as richer than that of the Arabs, although their religion, Islam, was founded by an Arab, the Prophet Muhammad.

Muslims (followers of the Islamic religion) are split into two major sects, Sunni and Shiites. The two differ over who was legitimately entitled to lead the Islamic community after the death of Muhammad in A.D. 632. The Sunnis, who predominate, believe that the community should choose its own leader. Shiites, who are a majority in Iran, believe leadership is vested in the family of the Prophet. Sunni Islam has historically been associated with bestowing legitimacy on the power of rulers; Shiite Islam, with opposition, martyrdom and revolt.

THE PRESENT IMPORTANCE OF THE GULF

The present importance of the Gulf stems from its energy deposits. Sixty-five percent of the world's known oil reserves are located in the Gulf countries, which produce over a third of the world's daily output. (By comparison, North America holds 8.5 percent of the world's reserves.) Saudi Arabia ranks first in reserves, with 259 billion barrels, followed by Iraq (112 billion), the UAE (98 billion), Kuwait (94 billion), and Iran (93 billion). The cost of oil production in the Gulf is the lowest in the world: it currently ranges from fifty cents a barrel in Saudi Arabia to $2 in offshore wells in the UAE. The Gulf is also rich in natural gas, with Iran and Qatar holding the world's second- and third-largest reserves, respectively. . . .

The modern strategic importance of the Gulf dates from the mid–nineteenth century, when three great empires confronted each other there: British India, czarist Russia and Ottoman Turkey. The British established political control over much of the Gulf in the early 1800s and kept it for 150 years. A tradition of outside involvement persists today.

After World War I, the political map of much of the Middle East was redrawn. The Ottoman Empire was replaced by modern nations, including Turkey, Iraq and Saudi Arabia. The small Arab shaikhdoms on the western shore of the Gulf were under British protection until 1971 (in the case of Kuwait, 1961). Iran was never a colony, and for much of the nineteenth and twentieth centuries Britain competed with Russia for influence there.

The oil revenues that began to accumulate after World War II enabled the Gulf states to modernize, and, by the 1960s and 1970s, to provide generous entitlement programs for their citizens. The state became what political scientists call a "rentier" one: the income from oil accrued directly to the ruler, who provided for his citizens' economic security in return for their political loyalty. This arrangement bought time for the tribal shaikhs who had been in power before the discovery of oil. It also led to the growth of a "rentier mentality" among the citizenry, who felt a sense of entitlement to riches, whether they worked or not.

DOMESTIC CHALLENGES

All of the Gulf states must contend with rapidly rising populations. In 1950, their combined population was estimated to be some 24 million; today, it is around 116 million and is projected to rise to 209 million by the year 2025. In Iran, a population of 35 million at the time of the revolution in 1978 had swollen to 60 million by 1996. The rate of population growth, however, has not been accompanied by an equivalent rise in oil revenues, the main source of government income. Today, the oil monarchies can no longer afford the generous social programs they instituted in wealthier days. Unemployment is now a widespread problem, and millions of jobs must be created in the next 15 years. At the same time that countries cut benefits, they are confronted with demands for more say in government.

The holiday from reality is over in the Gulf monarchies, both politically and economically, according to oil economist Vahan Zanoyan. To survive, the governments must forge a new social contract that allows for greater political participation. The question is whether the rulers are willing to make the changes needed, especially if their monopoly of power is threatened. It is not clear that Gulf monarchies are ready to confront their problems: "Surprisingly little indigenous discussion takes place regarding the future of the area," according to scholar Anwar Gargash of the UAE. "No regionwide consensus or outlook is emerging, and no Gulf perspective is crystallizing regarding the future state of affairs.". . .

OIL AND SOCIAL CHANGE

The story of the Persian Gulf in the twentieth century is the story of oil—the exploration, discovery and export of petroleum—and the effect this has had on traditional societies. The vast revenues that suddenly accrued to the fortunate Gulf states led to far-reaching economic changes, but on the Arabian peninsula, few political ones. Indeed, the oil revenues, coupled with British support, enabled monarchies, which were overthrown in most other Middle Eastern states after World War II, to survive and thrive in the Gulf.

Oil was first discovered in southwest Iran in 1908. In 1914, on the eve of World War I, the British government, which needed oil for its warships, assumed control of the producers, the Anglo-Persian Oil Company. Oil was discovered in commercial quantities in Iraq in the Kurdish region in 1927, in Bahrain in 1932, and in Saudi Arabia and Kuwait in 1938. Before World War II, Iran was the leading oil exporter in the Middle East, and its refinery at Abadan was the largest in the world.

Oil operations in a country were usually controlled exclusively by a single company, often a joint venture or partnership. Such an arrangement discouraged competition and prevented overproduction, which would lower prices. Britain initially tried to prevent the Gulf shaikhs from signing agreements with non-British companies, but eventually American firms won concessions in Bahrain, Kuwait and Saudi Arabia. The British refused the United States permission to open any consulates in the area, however, until 1950, when the first one opened in Kuwait.

PETROLEUM COMPANIES

The most famous petroleum partnership was the Arabian-American Oil Company, known as Aramco, which was granted a concession by King Ibn Saud in 1933. "If the first pillar of the Saudi state has been the Wahhabi Islamic religious movement," writes historian J.B. Kelly, "the second has been the Arabian-

American Oil Company. . . . The company has served the house of Saud as guide, confidant, tutor, counselor, emissary, advocate, steward and factotum." Aramco aimed to be a model company, not only seeing to the training, health care and housing of its workers, but also building roads, hospitals and water pipelines for the surrounding community. Its expatriate workers were housed in enclaves that resembled suburban America.

Accelerated Modernization

[The Middle Eastern] oil countries . . . went through an accelerated process of economic modernization without any significant change in their political and social forms of government. Thus the Saud dynasty in Saudi Arabia and the al-Sabah family in Kuwait (and other families of sheikhs in the Gulf) were transformed from heads of tribes to heads of the richest countries in the world. Economic and political control remained in the hands of those same traditional strata (as their base was broadened and their life-styles were changed); and while some of those dynasties, as in Kuwait, managed to carry on a relatively enlightened policy of social investment, control and supervision of resources remained in the hands of the traditional rulers.

Shlomo Avineri, *Dissent*, Spring 1991.

After World War II, major changes took place in the oil industry. Iran had long complained that Britain was too stingy in the compensation it paid: in 1950, the oil company paid Iran 16 million pounds in royalties and made 100 million pounds in profits from its Iranian operations. When Aramco agreed in 1950 to share profits with Saudi Arabia on a 50-50 basis, Iran wanted a similar agreement. The (now renamed) Anglo-Iranian Oil Company, however, would not agree to profit sharing. Matters came to a head when Iran's prime minister, Mohammad Mossadeq (1951–53), nationalized the company. For Britain, this was a great humiliation and meant the loss of a key economic asset. Mossadeq's government was overthrown in August 1953 and the shah, Mohammad Reza Pahlavi, was restored to power in a countercoup that was organized by U.S. and British intelligence.

Thereafter, although Iran retained sovereignty over its oil, it struck a new agreement with a consortium of oil companies to operate the concession. The British share was reduced to 40 percent and American companies received an equal stake. (It was not until 1973 that Iran took full control of its oil operations.) A major consequence of the Iranian crisis was that companies across the Gulf, especially in Kuwait and Saudi Arabia, stepped up production. At the same time new commercial quantities of oil were discovered—in Qatar and Abu Dhabi in 1960, in Oman in 1963, and in Dubai in 1969.

THE IMPACT OF OIL

The development of the oil industry set in motion many changes. Between World Wars I and II, it began to open up the Gulf to the outside world at the expense of British control. For the first time, local rulers struck commercial deals with oil companies and gained a secure source of income independent of any British subsidy.

The Gulf area was also becoming more important as an international communications and transportation hub, with British airlines securing landing rights to stop over on the way to India. (Traditional ties with the subcontinent, though, were becoming less important than relations with the greater Arab world.) With increased oil exploration came more pressure to delineate boundaries. This led, after World War II, to the protracted Buraimi oasis dispute between Saudi Arabia (backed by the United States) and Oman and Abu Dhabi (backed by Britain) over boundaries in the southeastern part of the Arabian peninsula, which was believed to contain oil. In 1952, Saudi troops occupied part of the oasis. Arbitration failed, and in 1955 the Saudis were evicted by forces from Abu Dhabi and Oman under British command. Not until 1974 did Saudi Arabia relinquish its claim, in return for a strip of territory giving it access to the Gulf east of Qatar.

Oil proved to be a mixed blessing. It provided salvation to Bahrain in the 1930s, when the economy collapsed along with the pearl industry. In the postwar period, it paid for the rapid modernization of Iran and the Arab monarchies, some of which enjoyed very high per capita incomes. In the 1960s and 1970s, the Arab Gulf states began providing their people free education, health care and housing. But there was also a downside. Even the shah of Iran, in a 1973 interview with the Italian journalist Oriana Fallaci, was ambivalent about the value of Iran's great resource: "So much has been written about the curse we call oil, and believe me, when you have it, on the one hand it's a blessing but on the other it's a great inconvenience. Because it represents such a danger. The world could blow up on account of this damned oil."

The modernization process, which lasted for centuries in the West, has been compressed into decades in the Gulf countries, putting a great strain on traditional societies. Saudi Arabian novelist Abdelrahman Munif, in the first volume of a monumental trilogy in Arabic entitled *Cities of Salt*, describes a Bedouin village's tragic encounter with American oil prospectors. The author's theme is that the discovery of oil was a curse: the desire for material gain replaced old values of loyalty, honor and respect for tradition. "The tragedy is not in our having the oil," he said in an interview, "but in the way we use the wealth it has created and in the future awaiting us after it has run out." The availability of huge oil revenues, he believes, corrupted political leaders and turned Saudi Arabia into a repressive state.

The Need to Create National Identity

Governments of the states created in the Gulf in the twentieth century—Iraq, Saudi Arabia, Kuwait, Bahrain, Qatar and the UAE—keenly feel the need to create a sense of national identity. Governments of Iraq, for example, have long promoted the idea that ethnic, religious and linguistic differences are irrelevant, since all its citizens are Iraqis. (Some fear that Iraq is now undergoing a process of "retribalization," in which people are returning to primordial loyalties of clan, family and religion.) In the Arabian peninsula, governments have tried to create a historical memory and national symbols to elicit loyalty and reinforce the legitimacy of the rulers. Governments have emphasized their cultural heritage (turath) by carrying out archaeological excavations and building new museums in places such as Doha (Qatar) and Dubai (UAE). The challenge in all the Gulf states has been to reconcile traditional forms of rule with modern forms of political expression.

On the Arabian side of the Gulf, Islam and tribalism have traditionally provided legitimacy to the ruling families. In Saudi Arabia, their close association with Wahhabi Islam has given the Al Saud rulers a status that other Gulf monarchs lack. However, Islam and tribalism, which had previously acted as a check on the rulers, now have been adapted to serve them, according to political scientist F. Gregory Gause III. The rulers have made the clerical establishment dependent upon the state by financing it, something that never happened in Shiite Iran. The tribes are now under effective state control, although the ruler makes a public display of his fidelity to tribal institutions, such as the majlis [a tradition that allows anyone to approach the ruler to seek redress of his problems] and shura [a consultative form of government]. "What most Westerners see as a 'traditional' political culture is in fact a construction of recent decades, in which rulers employ a political language redolent of Islamic and tribal overtones to convince their citizens of the legitimacy of their political system," notes Gause.

Over the past century, the traditional way of life in the Arab Gulf states has been irrevocably changed, due in large measure to the British intervention and the rise of the oil industry. External and internal forces have served to reinforce the power and wealth of one segment of the population, the ruling shaikhs. Because of the way in which the modern states were formed and boundaries arbitrarily delimited, tribal and family loyalties and religious, linguistic and ethnic identities in many cases are more important than country citizenship. These are at the root of many of the present tensions in the region.

"More people are making more political demands in the [Persian] Gulf states than ever before."

POLITICAL DISCONTENT CAUSES CONFLICT

F. Gregory Gause III

The growing demand for political representation precipitates conflict in the Middle East, contends F. Gregory Gause in the following viewpoint. In Saudi Arabia, for example, Islamic activists have criticized the regime and have demanded more participation in government. The Saudi government responded to this criticism by arresting the activists and by executing a citizen with alleged connections to the opposition movement. Other Persian Gulf nations are facing similar popular demands for representative government and for greater freedom of expression, Gause maintains. This burgeoning political dissent is fueled by economic troubles, growing populations, increased educational levels, and tension among various Islamic sects. Gause is an assistant professor of political science at the University of Vermont in Burlington.

As you read, consider the following questions:

1. For what reasons have Islamic activists criticized the Saudi government, according to Gause?
2. In the author's opinion, what is ironic about the rise of Islamic opposition in Saudi Arabia?
3. Why has political activism in Kuwait not been plagued by violence, in Gause's opinion?

Excerpted from F. Gregory Gause III, "The Gulf Conundrum: Economic Change, Population Growth, and Political Stability in the GCC States," The Washington Quarterly, vol. 20, no. 1 (Winter 1997), pp. 145–65. ©1996 by the Center for Strategic and International Studies (CSIS) and the Massachusetts Institute of Technology. Reprinted with permission of MIT Press Journals.

The bombings of U.S. military facilities in Riyadh, Saudi Arabia, in November 1995 and Dhahran, Saudi Arabia, in June 1996 not only took 25 American lives; they also exploded the carefully crafted image of domestic tranquility within the kingdom that both the Saudi and the U.S. governments have portrayed to their own populations and to the world. The reaction, at least in parts of the U.S. media, was to go to the other extreme. Comparisons abounded with the Shah's Iran, with all the subconscious associations of massive street demonstrations and embassy hostages. Reassured by experts that the two cases are very different, and that the Saudi regime looked secure, U.S. media attention shifted to the tragedy of TWA Flight 800 [which exploded in mid-air in July 1996] and the bombing at the 1996 Summer Olympic Games in Atlanta.

Yet, the situation in Saudi Arabia and its Gulf Cooperation Council (GCC) partners—Kuwait, Bahrain, Qatar, the United Arab Emirates (UAE), and Oman—deserves more than this superficial scrutiny. Saudi Arabia in 1996 is not Iran in 1978, but the story does not stop there—the Saudi Arabia of 1996 is also not the Saudi Arabia of 1976, and that is more to the point. Things have changed in the kingdom, and in the Gulf as a whole, creating a new set of political challenges for the six monarchical rulers upon whom the United States has based its regional policy. The welfare states built in the 1970s, with seemingly limitless resources for very small populations, are now strained by high population growth rates and flat oil prices. Indigenous middle classes, created by state education and employment policies, expect remunerative employment and increasingly seek an outlet for their hopes of political participation. It is the working-out of these changes in society at large, more than the bombers of Riyadh and Dhahran, that present the long-term threat to the domestic stability of the Gulf states.

ISLAMIC POLITICAL DISSENT

The Riyadh and Dhahran bombings did not emerge out of a vacuum. Since the Persian Gulf War, the stirrings of political discontent, particularly Islamist critiques of the Al Sa'ud, have been more open and public than at any time in recent Saudi history. Cassette tapes by Islamic activists criticizing the regime's decision to invite foreign forces to the kingdom circulated during the 1990–91 Gulf crisis. Immediately after the war, a brief petition signed by more than 400 scholars and religious activists, including a number of very senior clerics, was addressed to King Fahd ibn Abdul Aziz; while reaffirming their loyalty to the regime, the signatories called for "reform" in a number of areas and for more stringent application of Islamic law. The muted reaction from the government to this unusually public critique emboldened some Islamists to ratchet-up their campaign despite warnings from both King Fahd and Shaykh Abd al-Aziz bin Baz, the highest ranking cleric in the country, that criticism had already exceeded tolerable levels.

In summer 1992, more than 100 Islamic activists signed a 46-page "Memorandum of Advice" to the government, a document unprecedented in the bluntness of its tone, the specificity of its criticisms and suggestions, and the public nature of its dissemination in the kingdom. The signers asserted that the Saudi government displayed a "lack of seriousness" in abiding by shari'a (Islamic law) and that the 'ulama (religious scholars and officials) were being marginalized in the policy-making process. The memorandum chided Saudi policy in two areas where, in the past, the 'ulama's influence has been very limited—economic and security policy. It called for the establishment of a religious "supreme court" with the power to invalidate any law or treaty found to be opposed to shari'a—a step that, in effect, would make the 'ulama a separate and co-equal branch of government in Saudi Arabia. In May 1993, six Saudi Islamic activists announced the formation in the kingdom of the Committee to Defend Legitimate Rights (CDLR), calling on citizens to contact them with complaints about injustices.

THE ATTACK ON ISLAMIST CRITICS

The establishment of the CDLR moved the Saudi regime to a sustained counterattack against its Islamist critics. The six founders of the group were either arrested or removed from their government jobs. The group's spokesperson, Muhammad al-Mas'ari, a physics professor from King Saud University in Riyadh, escaped the country and set up shop in London. His faxes, e-mails, and press releases circulate in the kingdom and have attracted quite a bit of Western media attention. He has so angered the Saudis that they pressured London to deport him, but media pressure and legal proceedings have prevented the British government from taking that step. Riyadh also took the rare step in April 1994 of revoking the Saudi citizenship of 'Usama bin Laden, a scion of one of the kingdom's leading merchant families. Bin Laden was an active member of the Saudi- and U.S.-supported mujahidin who fought the Soviet Union in Afghanistan in the 1980s. He has continued from headquarters in Afghanistan and Sudan to call for the overthrow of the Saudi government. Meanwhile, the crackdown on Islamists in the kingdom continued in autumn 1994, when the regime took the unusual step of acknowledging the arrest of 157 Islamic activists.

The irony of the rise of Islamic opposition in Saudi Arabia is that its leaders, intellectually and organizationally, are products of official Saudi religious institutions and, frequently, employees of the Saudi state. The Saudis have, since the 1970s, built an extensive religious educational system and a vast religious bureaucracy to employ its graduates. In 1990, more than one-fourth of all Saudi university students were in religious schools. The 'ulama and graduates of the religious colleges staff their own educational institutions, much of the judiciary, the country's mosques, and international Islamic institutions (like the Organization of the Islamic Conference and the World Muslim League) headquartered in the kingdom. The Saudis built this system as a means to legitimate their rule and to control the men of religion by tying their interests materially and institutionally to the state. But it is clear that those institutions have also provided the intellectual and organizational infrastructure for the emergence of a home-grown Islamic opposition movement.

Given the importance of these religious institutions in producing Islamic activists, the Saudis worked to reassert their control over them. In December 1992, seven members of the Committee of Higher 'Ulama resigned their positions "for health reasons," and were replaced by ten younger 'ulama selected by the government. Western news sources reported that the seven were removed for their failure to condemn Islamist critics of the government. In July 1993, King Fahd appointed Shaykh bin Baz, who had provided the religious justifications for inviting the foreign forces to the kingdom during the Gulf crisis, Grand Mufti of the kingdom. The Grand Mufti is the country's highest religious official—the one who issues fatwas, or religious opinions—yet the position had been vacant for more than 20 years. At the same time, the king established a new Ministry of Islamic Affairs to manage the religious establishment. In October 1994, King Fahd appointed two new committees to oversee Islamic activities in the kingdom, staffing them with senior members of the ruling family, the government, and the 'ulama.

A CONTINUING CONFLICT

The Saudi hard line against Islamic activists continued into 1995. In August 1995, the government announced the execution of Abdallah al-Hudhayf, who had been convicted of attacking an officer of the state security services. The official account of his crimes included a contention that he had received instructions from the Committee for the Defense of Legitimate Rights in London; the CDLR responded by calling al-Hudhayf the first martyr of the struggle against the Al Sa'ud. In November 1995, a U.S. training mission attached to the Saudi National Guard in Riyadh was bombed, killing five Americans and two Indians. Four Saudis were arrested for the bombing and confessed on television to being members of the Islamic opposition, citing the influence on their thinking of both Muhammad al-Mas'ari and 'Usama bin Laden. They were executed in May 1996. Less than one month later, the Dhahran bombing occurred, killing 19 Americans and wounding nearly 400 others. One of the groups claiming responsibility for the blast was the "Legion of the Martyr Abdallah al-Hudhayf."

The violent Islamic opposition in Saudi Arabia remains relatively limited in numbers and in public profile. It has not been able to mobilize Saudis into the streets to confront the security forces. The regime retains control of substantial coercive, financial, and ideological resources with which to combat it. But the opposition has become the locus of the first serious challenge to the Saudi regime in more than 20 years, and U.S. officials, fearing its ability to mount new attacks, are moving U.S. military personnel in the kingdom away from populated areas and sending home military dependents. The confrontation between the Saudi regime and its home-grown Islamic opponents is not yet over.

CALLS FOR REPRESENTATIVE INSTITUTIONS

In Saudi Arabia, Islamic political opposition has taken a particularly violent and extremist path, but that is not the only manifestation of political agitation either in that country or in the region as a whole. In the wake of the Gulf war, petitions circulating in Saudi Arabia, Bahrain, and Qatar called for the establishment (or restoration, in the Bahraini case) of representative institutions, for more accountability in government and for greater freedom of expression. Kuwaitis organized to press the Al Sabah—the ruling family—to fulfill its promise, made in exile during the Iraqi occupation, to restore the elected parliament, which had been suspended in 1986.

Responding in part to this upsurge in popular political activity and in part to increased international attention, many GCC states took steps to provide new avenues for public participation—or the appearance of participation—in decision-making. . . .

Kuwait went the furthest of the Gulf monarchies to respond to popular demands for representative institutions. Shortly after liberation, the Al Sabah restored the Kuwaiti constitution, which had been suspended in 1986. In October 1992, elections were held for the Kuwaiti parliament, the only elected legislative body among the GCC states. A number of organized political factions, parties in everything but name (parties remain illegal), participated in a vigorous and open campaign. Thirty-three of the 50 seats were filled by candidates identified with the groups that had pushed the government to restore constitutional life. The largest ideological bloc were the Islamists, but they were divided among one Shi'i and two Sunni factions. A liberal group, the Democratic Forum, won two seats. The parliament has played an important role in Kuwaiti politics since 1993, conducting public investigations into official corruption, the events leading up to the Iraqi invasion in 1990, and Kuwaiti defense policy. Its term having expired, elections were held in October 1996 for a new parliament.

POLITICAL REFORM IN THE PERSIAN GULF

Some scholars have argued that the dawn of democracy in the Gulf is visible, noting that there is evidence of its presence in nearly every country in the region. Once one gets past the rhetoric about fundamentalism in Iran, democratizing trends can be detected in the ability of a few social groups to resist the state. In Iraq, following the spectacular defeat of the Iraqi army in the Gulf War, major segments of the population expressed violent dissatisfaction with their political regime in the form of the Shi'i and Kurdish revolts. In response to the pro-democracy movements of the 1980s and early 1990s, Kuwait bravely revived parliamentary life, resulting in a resurgence of public criticism directed at powerful individuals, the government and the character of public life. Meanwhile, a more conservative Saudi Arabia took bold steps toward institutionalizing consultative government, while tolerating a freewheeling expansion of the Saudi Arabian Chambers of Commerce.

Andrew C. Hess, *Journal of International Affairs*, Summer 1995.

It is no coincidence that Kuwait, with the most open political system in the GCC, has been spared the political disruptions and violence that have plagued some of its neighbors since the Gulf war. The Kuwaiti field is open for adherents of various political views—Islamist and otherwise—to organize in society, express their views in the mostly free press, and contest for positions of real influence in parliament. Violent underground movements, active in Kuwait in the 1980s, seem to have lost their *raison d'etre*, or at least their constituencies. The same cannot be said of Saudi Arabia or even of Oman. In August 1994, the Omani government revealed that it had arrested more than 200 people implicated in a plot organized by the Muslim Brotherhood to overthrow the government. Among those arrested were a former Omani ambassador to the United States, a former commander of the Omani air force, and two undersecretaries of government ministries.

THE SITUATION IN BAHRAIN

If political activity in Kuwait and in Saudi Arabia represents two ends of the spectrum—the first open and nonviolent and the second underground and tending toward violence—Bahrain falls somewhere in between. Demonstrations and acts of violence began in Bahrain in December 1994, with the arrest of the preacher of one of the large Shi'i mosques in the capital, Manama. At least one person died in clashes between demonstrators and security forces at that time, and hundreds were arrested. Sporadic outbreaks of violence occurred during spring and summer 1995, characterized mostly by street demonstrations in villages outside Manama and arson attacks on shops and public utilities like electric substations. The regime sought to contain the unrest through a mix of security measures and political gestures aimed at the dissidents, including releasing some of those arrested and entering into talks with opposition leaders, particularly Shi'i community leaders.

Yet, violence flared again in December 1995–January 1996. Arsonists attacked two hotels in downtown Manama in winter 1996, and in March 1996 a Molotov cocktail, thrown into a restaurant frequented by foreign laborers, killed seven Bangladeshi guest workers. The government responded by arresting eight prominent leaders of the Bahraini Shi'i community and forming a special security court to try those accused of violent political acts; as of July 1996, the court had passed a number of death sentences and had convicted 128 Bahrainis of various crimes. In June 1996, the government arrested 56 Bahrainis accused of plotting with the support of Iran to overthrow the regime and establish an Islamic Republic. Bahraini opposition leaders denied any Iranian involvement in their movement and reiterated their commitment to peaceful political change, accusing the government of concocting the plot to divert attention from their legitimate grievances.

The events in Bahrain are substantially different from those in Saudi Arabia. In Bahrain, opposition groups act publicly and call not for the downfall of the regime but for the restoration of the constitution and the reconvening of the elected parliament. They reject in their statements violent means of opposition and have been able to mobilize Bahrainis into the streets to protest government actions. No attacks have been made on U.S. facilities in Bahrain during nearly two years of tensions, even though the U.S. Fifth Fleet is headquartered on the island.

THE CAUSES OF DISCONTENT

The disturbances in Bahrain have a number of causes. Unemployment is a serious problem, more so than in other Gulf states: Outside analysts put the unemployment rate as high as 15 percent, though the government contends that it is in the single-digits. Sectarian tensions also play a role. The most serious disturbances have been concentrated in Shi'i neighborhoods and villages. The Shi'i majority on the island has historically chafed under the rule of the Sunni Al Khalifas, who have been very skillful in framing political dissent in sectarian terms to divide potential opposition movements. Some Bahraini Sunnis sympathetic to the cause of political reform have been put off by the violence in Shi'i communities. But economic distress and sectarian tensions do not tell the whole story. Since the Gulf crisis there has been an active movement, cutting across sectarian lines, to push the government to restore the Bahraini constitution and re-establish the elected legislature. The 1992 petition in this regard was followed by a similar document two years later, and opposition sources report it has received thousands of signatures. Further reports have emerged of another petition addressed to the amir making the same demands in October 1995, and of an April 1995 petition signed by 300 prominent Bahraini women calling on the authorities to seek a political solution to the unrest.

This mix of economic, political and sectarian grievances has kept discontent alive in Bahrain for nearly two years. The continuing inability of the government either to snuff out the violence or to appease the opposition means that tensions will continue. The nature of that discontent, and the forms it has taken, differ from the more violent opposition activity in Saudi Arabia, which in turn differs from the parliamentary maneuverings and political campaigning of Kuwaiti groups. The forms are different, but the phenomenon is regionwide: More people are making more political demands in the Gulf states than ever before. This upsurge in political activity may stem from increased educational levels, economic troubles, a global Islamic resurgence, or a reaction to the pressures generated during the Gulf war. But whatever its causes, the phenomenon is very real, and the regimes themselves have recognized its reality with the establishment (and, in Kuwait, re-establishment) of participatory institutions. They have been forced to do so in part because their previously most effective tool for damping down participatory desires—money—is no longer as abundantly available as it had been.

"*All camps—Christian, Muslim, Palestinian—splintered within and against each other.*"

ETHNIC AND RELIGIOUS HOSTILITIES CAUSE CONFLICT

Hazim Saghieyeh

In the following viewpoint, Hazim Saghieyeh argues that various religious and ethnic hostilities, coupled with nationalist fanaticism and a lack of democracy, foment conflict in the Middle East. In several nations, violent battles have occurred among several Muslim sects, Christians, and Jews. Many Muslim leaders who espouse Arab nationalism repress ethnic minorities and religious opposition within their domains—such is the case in Iraq, where Saddam Hussein, a Sunni Muslim, has waged war against ethnic Kurds and Shi'ite Muslims. Moreover, Saghieyeh contends, the uprooting of Palestinian Arabs by Israeli Jews has wounded Arab pride and has encouraged reactionary behavior, such as the mistreatment of minorities, in the Arab world. Saghieyeh is a columnist for *al-Hayat*, an Arabic newspaper based in London, England.

As you read, consider the following questions:
1. According to Saghieyeh, in what way did the Arab-Israeli conflict destabilize Lebanon?
2. What caused the feud between Sunni Muslims and Shiite Muslims, according to the author?
3. In Saghieyeh's opinion, why is the future bleak for Egyptian Copts?

Reprinted from Hazim Saghieyeh, "Minorities in the Arab Heartland," *Dissent*, Summer 1996, with permission.

The story of minorities in the contemporary Arab world is not an especially happy one. It is useful to begin a survey of them with Lebanon, if only because this small country was once perceived both as a refuge for minorities and as an alternative model for inter-communal relations in the region. Some seventeen sects, comprising a population of 3.5 million, lived here together in relative though sometimes precarious accord until civil war devastated the "Lebanese way of life" in the mid-1970s. An array of regional factors intruded then, exacerbating Lebanon's weaknesses and upsetting a delicate religious and ethnic balance. Thus ended a singular form of Mideast democracy, one that had lasted some three decades and contrasted sharply to the other Arab states, which were governed by either monarchical dynasties or dictatorships.

Lebanese politics was based on an unwritten "National Pact" fashioned when independence from France was achieved in 1943. It rested on a confessional system in which it was understood that each major group had certain prerogatives. For example, the president was to be a Maronite Christian, the prime minister a Sunni Muslim, the foreign minister a Greek Orthodox, the Defense Minister a Druze, the speaker of the assembly a Shiite, and so on. The Assembly had a six-to-five ratio of Christians to non-Christians (based on a 1932 census—the only one available).

This might seem a shaky way to govern, but the aim was to accommodate a plethora of minorities in a land where no single group composed a majority. One reason it worked as long as it did was that the middle classes were broader than in much of the Arab world. The country enjoyed relative stability and a coupling of political democracy with an active, prosperous private sector while nationalist radicalism, turmoil, and military coups engulfed Arabs elsewhere. As a consequence, there was an immense flow of capital into Beirut, Lebanon, which became the Arab world's banking and investment center; economic well-being bolstered political compromise, although capitalism thrived concurrently with the entrenched power of a powerful landlord class.

Lebanon's Collapse

Finally the country could not be isolated from regional developments. There was a brief but severe disruption in 1958. Pan-Arabism (especially Nasserism, the nationalism inspired by Egypt's former king, Gamal Nasser) was then stirring the Arab world; agitation, armaments, and money were supplied by Cairo, Egypt, and Damascus, Syria, to their allies in Lebanon, and Christian-Muslim tensions in Lebanon exploded in civil strife that brought foreign intervention (U.S. troops) in its wake. Things stabilized, only to unravel a decade later. The Arab-Israeli conflict, and especially the reemergence of Palestinian nationalism after 1967, put Lebanon—which contains a sizable population of refugees from the 1948 Arab-Israeli war—under great pressure. Palestinian incursions from Lebanon into Israel resulted in Israeli retaliations. This pressure increased after 1970–1971 when, following the Palestine Liberation Organization's defeat in the Jordanian civil war, the principal concentration of Palestinian armed forces moved into the miserable refugee camps in Lebanon. Although the country had avoided extensive entanglements in Arab-Israeli confrontations, now it could not escape them, and Palestinian groups also aligned with various Lebanese communal factions. This was complicated by Damascus's policy of supporting Palestinian attacks from Lebanon into Israel while preventing them from Syria, which thereby escaped counter-strikes.

THE PLIGHT OF MIDDLE EASTERN MINORITIES

The Muslim denial of collective minority rights is rooted in the historical rejection of non-Muslim peoplehood. *Dhimmitude*, a term coined by the historian Bat Ye'or, describes the Islamic practice of denying equality to Jews and Christians who live within the political realm of Muslim power. Islam offers them religious autonomy, not national freedom. The Palestine Liberation Organization, for example, long denied Israel's existence but offered to let Jews, after Israel's demise, live in a "secular and democratic" Palestinian state.

At times, minorities encounter the guarded tolerance of pan-Arabists. However, the ideological evaporation of pan-Arab nationalism has denied Arabic-speaking Christians access into the larger matrix of Middle Eastern political affairs. Between a weakened pan-Arabism and an exclusivist Islam, minorities cannot easily succeed in public life but are more and more relegated to nonpolitical roles; the Copts of Egypt are a case in point.

Mordechai Nisan, *Middle East Quarterly*, September 1996.

A collective hysteria increasingly possessed the Lebanese, and none of the country's communities was immune. A breach opened between Lebanese society and its past constitutional and political norms. All the Christian sects (Maronite, Greek Orthodox, and so on) may have together composed a majority, but they are part of a minority in the Arab world. Hence they emphasized Lebanonism rather than Arabism, and pressed for the protections democracy afforded them. In addition, the Christians (especially the Maronites), who dominated the army, advocated strong measures against the Palestinians. They also showed little understanding of the Shia Muslim population, which was now beginning to assert itself. Since the early 1970s a new breed of educated and well-to-do Shia leaders had emerged, calling for reforms that would increase the power of their community, which is poor and concentrated in the south and the Bekaa Valley.

Lebanese Muslims, especially Sunnis, allied with the Palestinians, whose fighters became an "alternative army" to the government's "Christian army." Even though Muslims and Christians enjoyed roughly equal social, economic, and political opportunities, at least theoretically, the Muslims grew fiercely antagonistic to the Lebanese state. They borrowed a majoritarian "Arabist" consciousness from the region around them and thought little of distinguishing what was "inside" (Lebanon itself) from what was "outside" (the Arab world as a whole); there was, moreover, little recognition that this would frighten non-Muslims. The Lebanese left, in the meantime, contributed to the undoing of the state by advocating a "Unity of Struggle"—the linkage of internal Lebanese problems to the Palestinian revolution. What came, finally, was not "unity" but a war of fragmentation in which all camps—Christian, Muslim, Palestinian—splintered within and against each other.

And in the end, Damascus, which never really accepted Lebanon's amputation from Syria during the French mandate, asserted its hegemony in Lebanon through "peace-keepers."

SYRIA AND IRAQ

Syria itself is dominated by a minority. Since 1963, the Alawi Muslims, who make up about 11 percent of the population but are entrenched in the military elite, have, through the Ba'ath party dictatorship, ruled over a vast Sunni majority. Ba'ath ideology is Pan-Arabist, so an interesting contrast emerges: whereas Maronites in Lebanon used "Lebanonism" to respond to their minority status in the Arab world, the Alawi turned to radical Arab nationalism and militancy toward Israel as responses to their minority status in Syria.

The Alawi are a dissident offshoot from Shiite Islam, which is itself a dissident offshoot from Islam's Sunni mainstream. They were long an oppressed, poverty-stricken rural community. Many of their ablest sons found a way out through military careers, which were shunned by well-to-do urban Sunnis. Alawi officers became the voice of their community and the backbone of the Ba'ath; and as Ba'ath Pan-Arabism was a vehicle of radical lower-middle-class revolt against older elites in the Arab world, so in Syria it served those dissatisfied with bourgeois (and, not incidentally, Sunni) hegemony. But whereas the Christian role in Lebanon was long fortified by that community's economic and cultural success, this was not so with the Alawi in Syria; hence the need for military dictatorship.

To Syria's east, Iraq has, since 1968, been governed also by a Ba'ath party. Thus a common Pan-Arabist ideology reigned in Baghdad, Iraq, and Damascus. The consequence, however, was competition for leadership rather than unity, and this intensified after Egypt was ostracized in the Arab world for its peace with Israel in 1978. While Syria's Sunnis are a majority dominated by a minority, Iraqi Sunnis are a dominating minority. Arab Sunnis, with about 20 percent of Iraq's population, have also used the Iraqi Ba'ath to rule their country, repressing Shiites (who make up about 60 percent and are ethnic Arabs, unlike their Iranian co-religionists next door) and brutally subjugating the Kurds. The latter, though mostly Sunni Muslim in religion, are a distinct ethnic/national community with their own language who compose about 20 percent of Iraq's inhabitants.

The Kurds

Historic Kurdistan comprises parts of Iraq, Iran, and Turkey, all three of which have sought to stifle any efforts aimed at Kurdish independence or autonomy. Iranian and Turkish Kurds have suffered considerable oppression—principally, though not entirely, cultural—yet it is hardly comparable to the violence perpetrated by Baghdad. The problem goes back at least to the 1920s, when Britain was given a League of Nations Mandate that stitched together three very different Ottoman provinces into contemporary Iraq. The Kurds were in the north, the Arab Sunnis in the center, and the Arab Shiites in the south; in addition there was an array of other groups such as Turkomans, Yazidis, Christians, and Jews (the latter were mostly gone after 1950). The common denominator was the absence of a common denominator. Baghdad sought, forcefully, to impose unity throughout the state. Needless to say, the Kurds viewed the whole arrangement with suspicion. Ensuing decades were marked by Kurdish revolts, often with foreign help.

The Ba'ath responded with an "iron fist." Expression of particularity by any community became a symptom of conspiracy and dissidence. For Baghdad's Pan-Arabism—whose early ideologists were, in the late 1920s, deeply influenced by German nationalism and romanticism—Kurds were an "anomaly." Even though Baghdad acquiesced to Kurdish "autonomy" in 1970, it almost immediately violated it. The onslaught against the Kurds became increasingly appalling, especially during the Iraq-Iran war of 1980–1988. Perhaps the worst moment was the March 1988 assault with chemical weapons on the Kurdish village of Halabja, resulting in a massive slaughter (in "retaliation" for Kurdish "collaboration" with Teheran).

After the Gulf War of 1991, Iraqi Kurdistan received international protection, preventing a return of Saddam Hussein's forces. This was coupled with the establishment of a Kurdish parliament and local government. Initial optimism was dashed quickly, as Kurds were soon ensnared in their own internecine rivalries, undermining prospects for stability and their own safety from within. There have been bloody clashes between the two leading Kurdish factions.

THE SUNNI-SHIA FEUD

Arab-Kurdish friction finds a parallel in the Sunni-Shia feud in Iraq, although here the problem is religious rather than ethnic, and the sources are ancient. The traditional Iraqi elite is Sunni, and when political misunderstandings or class tensions arise, fanatics in its ranks still look back in anger to Shia's origins in a rebellion against Islam's mainstream in the seventh century. The Shia, in turn, recall that it was then that their great leader the Imam Ali bin abi Taleb and his son al-Hussein were assassinated, leading to the Sunni-Shia split (whose cultural and political dimensions—and animosities—have reproduced over the centuries).

Since Iraq's birth, Baghdad has tried to keep the Arab Shia majority at bay. The Shia tribal organization (which is similar to that of the Kurds), together with their "dissident faith," was seen by Sunnis as obstacles to the consolidation of a modern, centralized state. And while the Sunni-dominated Ba'ath spoke ambiguously of "secularism," Shia were still barred from the officer corps. Not surprisingly the Shia struggled (with considerable success) to retain independence for their educational institutions and were also skeptical of Pan-Arabism. The latter, they feared, ultimately implied union with Syria and the consequent creation of a Sunni majority. Whatever Shia sympathy there was for the Ba'ath, it was gone by the 1970s, especially because Iraqi leader Saddam Hussein, dependent on the army and preparing to attack Iran, liquidated most Shia in the party leadership and then deported two hundred thousand Iraqi Shia as "Iranian fifth columnists."

The Shia and the Kurds face the same dilemma: how to build an opposition against a totalitarian regime that tolerates only one notion of what Iraq should be. Moreover, enemies of Baghdad have been happy to use Iraqi dissidents for their own purposes; al-Da'awa ("The Call"), the Shia fundamentalist political organization, is financed by Teheran, Iran; Ankara, Turkey, extends friendship to Iraqi Kurds partly to exploit them against Turkey's Kurds; and Syria seeks defecting Iraqi Ba'athists to use against Saddam. At the same time Saddam's atrocities against Kurds and the Shia intensify loyalties among these two groups to everything except an Iraqi state. Add to this unhappy picture the disintegration of liberated Kurdistan in northern Iraq and the fear of Sunni Arabs that they will be victimized in a post-Ba'ath Iraq (thus they see Saddam as protector), and it doesn't bode well for those few brave souls who would like to see their country united but democratic and tolerant. If ever a country was at a historical impasse, it is Iraq.

EGYPT'S CHRISTIANS

Cairo was traditionally Baghdad's rival for leadership of the Arab world. In Egypt we find an interesting, and strikingly different, story when it comes to minorities. Islam is Egypt's state religion and some 90 percent of the population is Sunni, although precise statistics are hard to come by. Coptic Christians, Egypt's chief minority, number three to four million according to official estimates, but the church estimates eight million and others speak of twelve million (out of a total Egyptian population of approximately sixty million).

Tensions between Copts and Muslims today are intense, but this should not obscure the fact that Copts once played a major role in Egyptian politics, beginning with the struggle for independence. Indeed, Copts were overrepresented in the Wafd which, from its 1919 challenge to British rule until Nasser's 1952 revolution, was the country's major political party. A Copt was number two in its hierarchy for years. But Nasser turned Egypt upside down. He nationalized foreign interests and this especially affected the Copts, whose urban middle classes played prominent middleman roles. The Copt educational system was integrated into the (generally more backward) state system and the church itself, with its proud traditions dating to the early Christian era, was subordinated to a narrow bureaucracy. Leading figures of Nasser's Egypt were mostly staunch Muslims, although an unknown and generally disdained Copt, Kamal Ramzi Stino, was given decorative cabinet portfolios.

It is not surprising that Copts felt marginalized, all the more so given the regime's often xenophobic rhetoric on behalf of Arab and Islamic unity. Urban Copts tended more toward cosmopolitanism and a loyalty to Egypt per se; they are at home with an Egyptianism that includes the land's pre-Islamic and Pharonic components, not Pan-Arabism. Nasser's Jacobin state sought uniformity and abolished the Christian quota in parliament on the grounds of the "oneness" of the "Arab people of Egypt."

ISLAMIC FUNDAMENTALISM IN EGYPT

The rise of Islamic fundamentalism in the 1970s raised new, important questions about this "oneness." When Anwar Sadat became president in 1970, following Nasser's death, he sought to counterbalance Nasserist and leftist challengers by encouraging Islamic movements. To curry favor with fundamentalists, he frustrated Coptic efforts to build new churches. Sadat defeated his foes, but only by initiating a process that would eventually lead to murderous attacks by fundamentalists on Copts—and then on tourists, police, army recruits, and on Sadat himself. In the meantime, Coptic religious authorities sought to enhance their standing in the country by taking a radical position against the Egypt-Israel peace process (even though Boutrous Boutrous Ghali, a Copt, was then minister of state for foreign affairs, and played a central role in the negotiations). This seems to have had little impact.

Egypt's political world has become increasingly Islamicized, with quotes from the Quran serving to proclaim what is good and what is bad. This leaves little room for the Copts, indeed for any non-Islamic minority. In the November 1995 elections only a few Copts ran and all lost. These pressures—from Nasserism to the growth of Islamic fundamentalism—led Copts to look to their church as their sole shelter. Now, however, there are additional, perilous trends within: a rise of Copt migration to the United States, Canada, and Western Europe, and a move by some Copts in Egypt from their "national" church into "alien" (Catholic or Protestant) churches. This represents a search for new lives and identities that may, in the long run, augur poorly for this minority's future.

THE ARAB-ISRAELI CONFLICT

The Arab-Israeli conflict exacerbated the problems of minorities in several Arab lands. At first glance, it might seem that Israel, a state built by a long-time minority, might serve as a democratic example for the region. The opposite was the case. The uprooting of the Palestinians wounded the Arab sense of self. Israel's accent on its Jewishness and its reduction to second-class status of the Palestinians who remained within its borders added insult to injury. Finally, Israel's successive military victories and the post-1967 occupation turned it into an absolute evil in humiliated Arab eyes.

All this provided easy pretexts for reactionary ideas and behavior among the Arabs. One might even say it encouraged powerful false equations to take subconscious hold in much of the Arab world. Democracy, the West, and "minoritarianism"— these meant Israel, something that exists at Arab expense. So, in turn, Arab masses deeply mistrusted democracy and mistreated their own minorities, some of whom didn't conceal their sympathy for Israel (for example, Iraqi Kurds and Lebanese Christians worked with Israel on various occasions; most Jews in the Arab world were gone by the mid-1950s). After each military defeat, fanatics among the Arabs imposed more restrictions on their own minorities. The "wisdom" behind this was simple: if you cannot avenge yourself on Israel, strike a weaker substitute.

Looking across the Arab world, it is evident that many of its minorities are eroding, either physically or politically. Minority elites are scattering to Western capitals where some become integrated and others feel lost. One lesson from the last half century may well be that Arab-Israeli peace is a necessary condition for the well-being of Mideast minorities, but it isn't enough. After all, the situation of the Copts has deteriorated since the 1978 Camp David accords. The complicated stories of Israel and Lebanon reveal that calls for democracy, however important, are also insufficient. Israel shows how fanaticism can materialize within democracy and Lebanon shows that democracy in one country cannot bring salvation to the Mideast—or thrive in isolation.

Still, what's needed is the spread of a democratic virus throughout the Mideast; this is the antidote to intolerant majoritarianism, to viewing any self-expression by a minority as a form of dissidence. A vast transformation is required, as much in the consciousness of the region's inhabitants as in its institutions. For it to take hold, there needs to be a metamorphosis in political culture as well. A democratic virus, a transformation, a metamorphosis— it is this combination that will allow Mideast minorities to flourish. And also the majorities.

"The danger to Israeli society from
Jewish fanatics is far more real than
the much-proclaimed threat posed
by its Arab neighbors."

RIGHT-WING ISRAELI EXTREMISM
PROMOTES CONFLICT

Rachelle Marshall

Right-wing Jewish extremism endangers Israel and the peace
negotiations between Israelis and Palestinian Arabs, argues
Rachelle Marshall in the following viewpoint. Orthodox Jewish
militants are to blame for the 1995 assassination of Israel's
prime minister, Yitzhak Rabin, and for the deaths of hundreds of
Palestinians, the author maintains. She contends that the Israeli
and U.S. Jewish community should rededicate itself to tolerance,
civility, and compassion to ensure justice for the Palestinians and
to honor essential Jewish values. Marshall is a freelance writer
living in Stanford, California.

As you read, consider the following questions:

1. According to the author, how many Palestinians were killed
   by Israelis between 1993 and 1995?
2. According to Alexander Cockburn, cited by Marshall, what
   did Benjamin Netanyahu believe Israel should have done
   during China's Tiananmen Square massacre?
3. How did the nineteenth-century Enlightenment influence
   European Jews, according to Marshall?

Excerpted from Rachelle Marshall, "Right-Wing Extremists Endanger Israel and the
Jews," *Washington Report on Middle East Affairs*, December 1995. Reprinted with permission.

Just when Israel has achieved its greatest triumph by concluding an agreement with the Palestinians that legitimizes its continued occupation of the West Bank and part of Gaza, the increasing militancy of Jewish extremists in both Israel and the United States is causing a widening split in Israeli society and threatens to undermine the very nature of Judaism. The assassination of Prime Minister Yitzhak Rabin by a right-wing Israeli on Nov. 4, 1995, was an event unprecedented in Israel's history. Although verbal abuse is an accepted mode of political discourse in the Jewish state, Israeli leaders rarely have been physically attacked. The murderous act by 27-year-old Yigal Amir is a frightening signal that the danger to Israeli society from Jewish fanatics is far more real than the much-proclaimed threat posed by its Arab neighbors.

WHO ARE THE REAL EXTREMISTS?

Israeli spin-doctors until now have succeeded in linking the word "extremist" exclusively with Arabs who protest Israel's takeover of their land, rather than with the ultra-orthodox Jews who claim God gave them title to the land 3,000 years ago. The day after Prime Minister Yitzhak Rabin and Palestine Liberation Organization (PLO) Chairman Yasser Arafat signed an agreement in Washington, DC (Sept. 28, 1995), Professor Nasir Aruri of the University of Massachusetts commented on a San Francisco radio station that because Israel will continue to control the land, water, and roads in the West Bank and Gaza, and can close the borders at will, Palestinians will enjoy no more freedom under the new arrangement than did Native Americans confined to their reservations or South Africans forced to live in bantustans. Israeli Consul Nimrod Barkan responded by calling Aruri's views "extremist."

But who are the extremists today? On the Palestinian side, the Muslim Hamas organization opposes the PLO's deal with Israel, just as do many Israelis. However, according to its spokesman, Mahmoud Zahar, Hamas intends to press its case through political means if given the opportunity. Only tiny groups such as Islamic Jihad have pledged to continue armed struggle.

Such Arab militants have plenty of counterparts among Israelis. In Hebron, where 65 Palestinians were killed between 1993 and 1995, hundreds of Jewish settlers stormed the streets after the signing, shouting "Slaughter the Arabs!" and stoning Palestinian homes. Other settlers blocked traffic from moving across the Allenby Bridge that links the West Bank and Jordan. As usual, and despite the new agreement, the Israeli army put

Palestinians, and not the Israeli protesters, under curfew and sealed the borders of Gaza and the West Bank. In the weeks following the signing, Jewish protesters physically attacked Rabin and several other cabinet ministers.

PALESTINIANS ARE TARGETED

But so far Palestinians have been the chief targets of right-wing Jewish violence. Between 1987 and 1995, Palestinians killed 297 Israelis, and Israelis killed 1,418 Palestinians, including 260 children. Most of the Palestinians were victims of the Israeli police and army, but several hundred were murdered by Jewish extremists. Rabin's assassin reportedly belonged to a group called "Eyal," composed of members of the late Meir Kahane's Kach party, which claimed responsibility for killing at least four Palestinians. Israeli militants have threatened more violence against Palestinians if terms of the new agreement are implemented. "They [the Palestinians] are the enemy," said Yisrael Harel, head of the Council of Jewish Communities in Judea and Samaria. Another settler leader, Pinchas Wallerstein, told reporters that settlers would shoot Palestinian policemen on sight.

The extremists are spurred on by Orthodox rabbis and members of the Likud party who regarded Rabin as a traitor for agreeing to remove troops from the center of West Bank towns. The Israeli Rabbinical Association ruled in July 1994 that the Torah prohibits any withdrawal from the "land of Israel," and therefore soldiers must disobey orders to leave. A coalition of settlers and right-wing groups is calling for a boycott of the national census in order to deny the legitimacy of the government. Likud leader Benyamin Netanyahu, who stands a good chance of becoming prime minister in 1996, did not exaggerate when he warned that Rabin's policies "have led to a split in the nation, and this is just the beginning." [Netanyahu was elected Prime Minister in 1996.]

PREDICTION OR THREAT?

Although Netanyahu says he disapproves of violence, his statement may have been as much a threat as a prediction, given his opposition to any compromise with the Palestinians. Professor Avishal Margalit of Hebrew University wrote in the *New York Review* of Oct. 5, 1995, that Netanyahu "is ferociously committed to a Greater Israel," which means all of the West Bank. In the *Nation* of Jan. 8–15, 1990, Alexander Cockburn revealed that after Chinese troops killed scores of students at Tiananmen Square in Beijing, an Israeli newspaper quoted Netanyahu as saying, "Israel should have taken advantage of the suppression of the demonstrations in China, while the world's attention was focused on these events, and should have carried out mass deportations of Arabs from the territories. This plan did not gain support, yet I still suggest to put it into action."

Today, according to Margalit, Netanyahu's policy is to grant the Palestinians "not one inch of territory." He would close off Gaza permanently behind a security fence and retain full military control over both the West Bank and Gaza. In his broader Middle East policy he has conjured up a new Cold War—this time the enemy is "international Islam," masterminded by Iran.

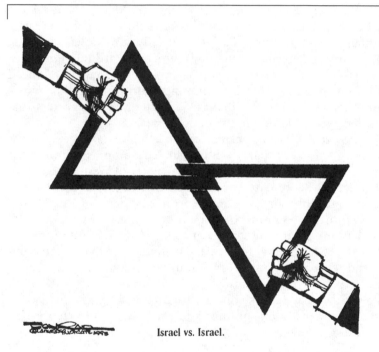

Israel vs. Israel.

Paul Conrad, ©1993, Los Angeles Times Syndicate. Reprinted with permission.

As a former Israeli ambassador to the U.N. and a frequent talk-show guest, Netanyahu has considerable appeal in the U.S., far more than the blunter Yitzhak Shamir, whose views he shares. As a master of public relations, Netanyahu not only provides ammunition to fiercely pro-Israel American Jews, but promotes hostility toward those he calls "Arab-loving, self-hating Jews" who are dangerous to Israel.

Extremist Jews in Israel and the U.S. could do lasting damage to Jewish communities in both countries. Most Jews in Israel and the West today are products of the Enlightenment, the liberal reform movement that began in the 19th century among Russian Jews who broke from the confines of rigid Orthodoxy and encouraged the dissemination of European culture and science. Influenced by the Enlightenment, many European Jews adopted more liberal theories of government and brought these new attitudes to America and Palestine. As a result, Israel for most of its existence has been a welfare state (for Jews), and American Jews have been identified with liberal politics and support for civil liberties and human rights in the United States.

In Israel today, growing military strength and prosperity, along with the immigration of Jews from Arab countries and more recently from Russia, have changed the old political configurations. Religious parties and ultra-conservative secular groups together are a powerful force against giving up any part of the occupied territories. At the same time, those enjoying the benefits of free-wheeling private enterprise are pressuring to rid the economy of any remaining vestiges of socialism. The Jewish community in the U.S. is undergoing parallel shifts. Although a majority of Jews remain liberal Democrats, a substantial minority is now forming close ties not only with the Republican leadership but with fundamentalist Christians whose social views they share. Many Orthodox Jews who fervently support Israel also favor prayer in the schools, oppose abortion, and consider homosexuality a sin. . . .

A Turn to the Right

As yet liberal and moderate Jews outnumber the ultraconservatives, but the balance could shift. The percentage of American Jews supporting Israeli-PLO peace talks dropped from 77 percent in September 1994 to 68 percent in 1995. A year before that, 84 percent were in favor. Although many fewer Israelis than Palestinians are victims of violence each year, every attack by Palestinians against Israelis reduces the number of Jews in Israel and the U.S. who support peace. In Israel, political observers say that a terrorist act just before the 1996 elections could swing a majority of votes to Netanyahu. In America, Orthodox Jews who agree with the conservative social agenda and respond to Republican leaders who have suddenly become ultra-Zionists, are combining with secular Jews whose affluence and hawkish Middle East views make them natural allies of the political right.

If the result of this turn to the right means that the Jewish community in America is no longer distinguished by its support for the disadvantaged and its dedication to tolerance and freedom, then a vital quality of Jewishness will have been lost. The essence of Judaism is not loyalty to a Jewish state, as so many Jews have come to believe, but loyalty to the values that have enabled the Jewish people to survive—justice, compassion, righteousness, and civility. The government of Israel has violated every one of these precepts in dealing with the Palestinians, and too many American Jews (as well as Christians) have excused those violations or remained silent. The Jewish peace activists in Israel and the U.S. who continue to speak out for justice and independence for the Palestinians are not only defending the Palestinians' cause but also honoring the precepts that give meaning to Judaism.

"The fact is that many Palestinians
continue to use terror and violence
as a political tool against Israel."

PALESTINIAN TERRORISM INTENSIFIES CONFLICT

Mortimer B. Zuckerman

Palestinian terrorism exacerbates tensions in the Middle East, argues Mortimer B. Zuckerman in the following viewpoint. The mid-1990s Oslo peace accords between Israel and the Palestine Liberation Organization (PLO) broke down after Palestinian extremists launched hundreds of terrorist attacks against Israelis in 1996 and 1997, Zuckerman contends. Furthermore, he asserts, Palestinian leader Yasser Arafat has betrayed the peace process by refusing to crack down on known Palestinian terrorist groups. When Israel gives in to Western pressure to grant more land to the Palestinians, Israelis face more terrorism from Palestinian extremists and Islamic fundamentalists, Zuckerman maintains. Zuckerman is editor-in-chief of the weekly magazine *U.S. News & World Report*.

As you read, consider the following questions:

1. According to Zuckerman, what precaution did Yitzhak Rabin take during the Oslo peace negotiations with Yasser Arafat?
2. How many terrorist attacks occurred in Israel in 1997, according to the author?
3. In Zuckerman's opinion, why should Israel not give up its territory on the mountain ridges of the West Bank?

Israel's peacekeeping Prime Minister Yitzhak Rabin died in 1995 with the bitter knowledge that he had been betrayed. At Oslo [the mid-1990s peace negotiations between Israelis and Palestinians], Yasser Arafat had given him a commitment: "You give us territory, and we'll fight terrorism from that territory." Rabin took the historic chance. He also took the precaution of asking two outstanding professionals to report on Arafat's fulfillment of the promise: Gen. Amnon Shahak, as chief of the Israeli Defense Forces (IDF); and Gen. Moshe Ya'alon, head of military intelligence.

Knowing what happened is essential to knowing where we are today. In September 1995, Ya'alon reported that instead of fighting the armed fundamentalist terrorists—Hamas and Islamic Jihad—Arafat was permitting their military strength to grow in the territories turned over by Israel. Other Arab leaders, from Egypt to Algeria, were fighting the fundamentalists because they recognized their menace. But Arafat, Ya'alon concluded, was using proxy terror to push Israel for more concessions. When Ya'alon advised Rabin that Arafat was dealing with Mohamed Def, one of the most radical terrorists, Rabin confronted Arafat with the allegation. Arafat's response was to say, "Mohamed esh?" ("Mohamed who?"). It was, Rabin judged, a brazen deception. Soon afterward, with more damning intelligence in his hands, Rabin decided on a showdown with Arafat—but planned to wait until the Palestinian election on Jan. 20, 1996, in hope that a political endorsement would strengthen Arafat's hand against the terrorists.

THE PARALYSIS OF OSLO

Rabin died before he could carry out his plan. Four days after the Palestinian election, the new [Israeli] prime minister, Shimon Peres, visited Arafat. Israeli intelligence had learned that a terrorist group was planning five major bombings. Arafat was given that information—and did nothing. In February and March, 1996, four bombs exploded in buses, cafes, and shopping areas, killing dozens of Israelis and wounding hundreds. The impact on Israeli politics was devastating, leading to the election of Prime Minister Binyamin Netanyahu as the expression of Israel's security concerns. The rise of Netanyahu did not bring about the paralysis of Oslo. It was the paralysis of Oslo that brought about the rise of Netanyahu.

Arafat mourned Rabin's death, but he continues his double game. In 1997, some 463 terrorist attacks were mounted; an additional 100 were foiled. Recently, Israel discovered a Hamas cell that planned the takeover of a major building; the planting of mines; a suicide bombing in a major residential area; car bombings in Haifa, Beit El, and Ariel; and infiltration of explosives into videotapes. Only intense Israeli pressure induced the Palestinian Authority (PA) to raid this group: 1,500 pounds of explosives were found. Meanwhile evidence of Arafat's betrayal multiplies. He has twice as many police under arms as agreed at Oslo but will not use them against terrorist havens minutes from major Israeli cities. He has freed Islamic Jihad terrorists responsible for the January 1995 Beit Lid bombing that killed a score of Israelis, as well as those who attacked the Jerusalem mall in September 1997. He retains the chief of the 12,000-strong police force in Gaza and the West Bank, Gen. Ghazi Jabali, who is known to be involved in terrorism. He allows Palestine Liberation Organization (PLO) leaders to exhort their people to violence against Israelis. He has recruited 150 police officers from known terrorist groups, including at least 25 wanted for terrorist attacks on Israelis. A cartoon sums up Arafat's definition of cracking down on terrorism: "No kiss. All you get is a hug."

THE INJUSTICE OF PRESSURING ISRAEL

Does Arafat get criticized in the Western media for this appalling record? Of course not. All kinds of rationalizations are devised to excuse his abrogation of security commitments, which were underwritten in the Oslo "Note for the Record" by the United States itself. All sorts of pressures are brought on Israel to reward Arafat's campaign by making further concessions. Israel knows full well that this would not buy peace. Withdrawal from Hebron has been followed by suicide bombings, more violent intifada— and demands for more withdrawals, more retreat from Oslo.

That is the bad news. The good news is that, despite the one-eyed vision of the media, an impressive body of U.S. senators has finally broken the spell. Eighty-one senators—who cannot be dismissed as partisan—have sent a letter to President Bill Clinton containing the following truths: "The fact is that many Palestinians continue to use terror and violence as a political tool against Israel. Chairman Arafat, himself, repeatedly threatens renewals of widespread violence and continues to withhold full security cooperation with Israel." The senators point out the injustice of pressuring Israel. It would be "particularly unfair and counterproductive since Israel has kept the promises it made at Oslo, and today is prepared to withdraw from even more territory of the West Bank before final status negotiations." Then they assert: "On the other hand, the Palestinians have not provided

Mike Shelton/*Orange County Register* 1997. Reprinted with permission.

Israel with adequate security." They conclude: "Presenting an American plan—especially one that includes a specific redeployment figure beyond what Israel believes to be in its national-security interest before final status arrangements—runs counter to [former Secretary of State Warren] Christopher's commitment and can only undermine Israel's confidence."

UNDERMINING ISRAEL'S SECURITY

Unfortunately, the State Department has become Arafat's de facto advocate, pressuring Israel to pull out from more of the West Bank. This is unwise as well as unfair. In the light of the broken promises, and the need to retain some bargaining chips for the final negotiations, Israel has been remarkably forthcoming, especially since those same Rabin-appointed, nonpolitical military advisers still make the same assessment of Arafat's failure on security policy that they did in 1995. Israel has offered more land, but the Clinton administration seems to miss the point, as it tries to increase the percentage yielded. The argument should not be about how much extra land Israel yields but how every bit of land given up undermines Israel's fundamental security. Israel is constrained by the imperative of survival—survival against not just the treacherous Arafat but also the radical Islamic government that might well succeed him. Every 1 percent in this argument is an area the size of Tel Aviv; every decimal point is a multiplier of risk. For instance: Israel cannot give up mountain ridges on the West Bank without losing early-warning sites of Iraqi or Syrian attack. It cannot give up the vital underground aquifers that provide a huge share of Israel's fresh water. It cannot do without a buffer zone against Arab infiltration along the so-called Green Line, Israel's pre-1967 border. It must have a means of swiftly deploying into the Jordan Valley by means of four east-west roads that enable the IDF to bypass Palestinian communities and local traffic. It must have a Jerusalem defense zone to protect its capital, and it must have a security zone to protect passenger planes landing in the Ben Gurion Airport: The Palestinians have been trying to acquire shoulder-to-air missiles.

The backdrop of the chill between Washington and Jerusalem is antipathy toward Israeli Prime Minister Netanyahu. Beyond the gap of perception between what Israel knows it needs for its security and what America thinks it needs to appease Arafat, there is an ominous breakdown of trust. Given his remarkable early political success in Israel, Netanyahu has demonstrated an amazing tin ear for the politics of the situation. He seems not to realize the importance of inspiring trust in the people he must work with. His political foul-ups have diverted attention from Palestinian failures on security. This has allowed the United States to convince itself it needs to beat up only on the awkward partner—on Netanyahu—when it should be leaning on Arafat to tighten security, the key to the whole confrontation. While Netanyahu is politically inept, he is strategically dead right— and right to reject American pressure. The record shows the Israelis right in their judgment that a progressive turnover of territory to the PA would be no more than a series of unilateral concessions. They would whet the appetites of the Palestinians and raise their expectations without bringing about any genuine PLO acceptance of the Jewish state, any elimination of terrorism.

"*As long as [Iraq] is ruled by Saddam or a Saddam-like dictator, Israelis are bound to view Iraq as a formidable enemy.*"

TYRANNICAL AGGRESSION CAUSES CONFLICT

Ehud Ya'ari

The ambitions of Iraq's despotic president, Saddam Hussein, are causing conflict in the Middle East, Ehud Ya'ari maintains in the following viewpoint. He contends that Israel will consider Iraq an enemy as long as its leader aggressively pursues territory and attempts to amass chemical, biological, and atomic weapons. The international community must continue imposing sanctions against Iraq to help contain Saddam and to allow the Arab-Israeli peace process to continue, he concludes. Ya'ari is a journalist for Israeli television.

As you read, consider the following questions:

1. According to Ya'ari, what alternative course of action could Iraq have taken during the Gulf War of 1991?
2. In what way have Saddam Hussein's ambitions proved to be beneficial to the Arab-Israeli peace process, in the author's opinion?
3. In Ya'ari's opinion, what measures should the United States take to help remove Hussein from power?

From Ehud Ya'ari, "Still a Formidable Enemy." This article appeared in the September 1998 issue of, and is reprinted with permission from, *The World & I*, a publication of the Washington Times Corporation, ©1998.

Americans—as well as Arabs and indeed everybody else—remember the Gulf War of 1991 as it actually occurred. Their perception of the threat posed by Saddam Hussein is consequently affected by his defeat at the time. Israelis still retain a different recollection: Rather than the memory of the war as it did take place, we are still very much aware of the way it could have developed. Namely, instead of moving into Kuwait before his nuclear device was ready for use, Saddam could have deferred action until a little later and then sent the heavy armored divisions of the Republican Guards into Jordan within easy strike of Israel.

There is ample evidence to indicate that Baghdad, Iraq, was considering this alternative course of action, and from an Israeli point of view it was a matter of sheer luck—some would say a miracle—that Saddam could not resist the temptation to grab the oil-rich tiny sheikhdom next door before he was ready.

Had Saddam opted for the other script, Israel would likely have had to face Iraq's might on its own. No coalition would have formed, no U.S. troops would have been rushed to the region, and General Norman Schwarzkopf would have remained an anonymous general. An Israeli-Iraqi confrontation would have been a bloody, costly, devastating clash in which the winner—had there been one—would have paid much more than it could afford for a "victory."

THE MENACE OF SADDAM

In brief, Israel to this day considers Saddam a potential menace to its soft belly—the long border with Jordan. Even after the destruction of much of the Iraqi army and after the embargo, imposed since 1990, military analysts estimate that Iraq is capable of invading Jordan with four to six divisions in the course of 36 hours.

It is this recollection of the Gulf War as it could have happened and a sound respect for Iraqi power that will dictate Israel's attitude toward Saddam (and whoever may someday replace him). Iraq despite its present predicament is considered potentially the single most powerful Arab state, the only one that combines enormous oil wealth, freshwater and land sufficient for cultivation with skillful manpower, an almost uninterrupted track record of military endeavors, and a fierce ambition to achieve regional hegemony.

As long as the country is ruled by Saddam or a Saddam-type dictator, Israelis are bound to view Iraq as a formidable enemy. The emphasis that all Israeli governments have placed on forging a close alliance with Jordan emanates from a wish to maintain the Hashemite Kingdom as a solid buffer between Israel and Iraq. A buffer that, hopefully, may be converted down the road into a bridge for cooperation, once a new regime in Baghdad chooses to join the peace process. Indeed, it should be noted that the scope for economic relations between Israel and Iraq is greater than with any other Arab country.

Bob Gorrell/*Richmond Times-Dispatch*. Reprinted with permission.

In many ways, Saddam's ill-calculated adventures—attacking Iran, then Kuwait while intermittently fighting with the Kurds in the north and the Shiites in the south—proved a blessing for the peace process. The isolation of Iraq, and its preoccupation with its domestic front following attrition in unsuccessful wars, have effectively removed Saddam from the Middle Eastern diplomatic game.

THE NEED TO CONTAIN IRAQ

The prevailing assumption is that a few more years—under the best of circumstances—are still needed to achieve a final settlement between Israel and the Palestinians, as well as with Syria and Lebanon. Reemergence of Saddam as a regional player as a result of lifting the UN sanctions, and/or a collapse of the

United Nations Special Commission (UNSCOM) effort to contain his weapons of mass destruction, will undoubtedly jeopardize the prospects for a peaceful resolution to the Arab-Israeli conflict.

Saddam has frequently indicated that under his whip Iraq will remain opposed to the very notion of a compromise with Israel, and it goes without saying that given the opportunity he will resume as fast as he can his pursuit of long-range missiles equipped with chemical, biological, and even atomic or perhaps "only" radioactive devices. Thus, the continuing containment of Saddam has become a prerequisite for the peace process and not just a condition for maintaining stability in the Persian Gulf.

The bottom line, therefore, from an Israeli perspective, is that the most effective policy available would be to try to maintain the present blockade of Saddam's Iraq in the face of growing pressure from Russia, France, China, and some Arab states to relax sanctions.

Simultaneously, the United States should initiate a combination of measures to demonstrate to the Iraqi public—primarily the officer corps—the tangible benefits of removing Saddam. As often outlined by several Republican critics of the Clinton administration's policy toward Iraq, such measures can include unfreezing Iraqi assets for the use of anti-Saddam groups, expanding the no-fly zone, withdrawal of recognition of Saddam's government, and other moves aimed at sharpening the message that as long as Saddam stays in power Iraq is destined to remain a pariah state.

PLAY FOR TIME

As much as many Israelis would eagerly support military pressure on Saddam's regime or a new effort to launch an armed rebellion from within Iraq, it is obvious to them that such ambitious ventures would carry a high risk of failure, which might leave Saddam in a stronger position.

Realizing President Bill Clinton's lack of enthusiasm to strike Iraq even when it was deemed almost inevitable, taking into account Arab and European reluctance to participate in a military operation, and aware of the inherent weakness of local opposition, I think the best bet is to play for time in the hope that over the long run something has to give. Such persistent pressure has already been shown to crack the inner circle of Saddam's confidants—both his own family as well as the top echelons of his intelligence and security apparatus.

"Water is returning as the likeliest
cause of conflict in the Middle
East."

SCARCE WATER COULD CAUSE CONFLICT

Adel Darwish

In the following viewpoint, Adel Darwish maintains that future water shortages are likely to create conflicts among the nations of the Middle East. The aridity of the region—as well as the area's growing population, contradictory laws on shared natural resources, and political instability—will cause strife unless the various nations agree to work together on water projects, the author contends. Darwish, a journalist, is coauthor of *Water Wars: Coming Conflicts in the Middle East.*

As you read, consider the following questions:

1. According to Darwish, what percentage of renewable water supplies does the Middle East use annually?
2. According to the author, which world leaders have suggested that water will be a likely cause of war in the Middle East?
3. How has the High Dam on the Nile affected the environment of the Nile Valley, according to Darwish?

Reprinted from "Arid Waters," by Adel Darwish; *Our Planet*, vol. 17, no. 3, 1995, by permission of the United Nations Environment Programme.

A lone figure dressed all in black materializes out of the mirage where the dry sky glare meets the desert. As he moves closer, his attitude becomes tense. His eyes blaze as he reaches the well where a man is drinking, and with a single stroke of his sword, he strikes off the stranger's head.

That opening scene from the film *Lawrence of Arabia*—based on a story told by Lawrence himself—provides a stark warning that water in the arid environment of the Middle East is a matter of life and death.

Since the first oil well—discovered during drilling for water—gushed in Bahrain in 1932, countries have argued over borders in the hope of getting access to new riches. Now that most borders have been set, oil fields mapped and reserves accurately estimated, history is coming full circle. Water is returning as the likeliest cause of conflict in the Middle East. Whoever controls water or its distribution can dominate the region.

From Turkey, the southern bastion of the North Atlantic Treaty Organization (NATO), down to Oman on the Indian Ocean, from the snow-helmeted Atlas Mountains in Morocco, to the depths of the Jordan valley, governments are searching for more water.

The population of the region will rise by 34 million within 30 years, and will then need 470 billion cubic metres of water annually—132 billion more than the total available supplies based on current levels of consumption (even assuming that there will be a 2 per cent improvement in conservation each year.

A Dwindling Resource

Water is being used faster than nature can replace it. On average the region uses 155 per cent of its renewable water supplies each year. Individual countries' consumption ranges from the Libyan Arab Jamahiriya at 374 per cent to Bahrain at 102 per cent.

In 1994, the World Bank estimated that renewable per capita water supplies would fall fivefold in the space of one lifetime—1960–2025—to 667 cubic metres per year (well below the official level of water scarcity). In several countries this will barely cover basic human needs into the twenty-first century.

When President Anwar Sadat signed the peace treaty with Israel, he said that Egypt will never go to war again, except to protect its water resources. King Hussein of Jordan has said he will never again go to war with Israel, except over water. [Former] United Nations Secretary-General Boutros Boutros-Ghali has warned bluntly that water will cause the next war in the area.

In 1989 Israel withdrew hydrologists and surveyors who were investigating building a dam in Ethiopia on the Blue Nile, which provides 85 per cent of Egypt's water, amid threats of war in the People's Assembly in Cairo. In 1990 Turkey stopped the flow of the Euphrates altogether to fill its Ataturk Dam. The media of the two downstream nations, the Syrian Arab Republic and Iraq, united in denouncing the stoppage and there were threats of armed retaliation. The CIA gave its opinion in 1992 that trouble between Turkey and the Syrian Arab Republic over water was the likeliest prospect for a full-scale war in the region.

Few agreements have been reached about sharing such cross-border water resources as international aquifers or the rivers of the region. Two of the three main aquifers lie for the most part under the West Bank of the Jordan. Muslim fundamentalists have recently made it Jihad—a sacred mission—to recover water used by Israeli settlers, for the use of Muslims.

CONTRADICTORY LAWS

International law on shared water courses, rivers or cross-border aquifers is unclear. Governments and organizations negotiate agreements using a mixture of customary use and local and traditional laws, and the established right of use over an unspecified period of time. Such mixtures are often contradictory and in themselves a cause of conflict. There are few, if any, precedents that the United Nations International Law Commission or the International Court of Justice could cite to establish rules to arbitrate on water sharing.

Since the late 1940s, the World Bank has insisted that agreements are concluded between riparian nations on sharing the benefits of the water projects that it helps to finance. It also commissions independent studies to modify plans and alter designs to minimize the harm that the project might inflict on neighbouring peoples.

But when governments finance their own water schemes, there is no provision in international law to stop them imposing their will on neighbours, uprooting ethnic minorities or inflicting far reaching and lasting effects on the environment.

THE HIGH DAM ON THE NILE

To taunt the late Egyptian leader Colonel Gamal Abdel Nasser in the 1950s, Britain unwisely induced the World Bank to turn down Egypt's request to finance the building of the High Dam on the Nile near Aswan. The Soviet Union was only too happy to finance and construct instead, winning a foothold in the region. The dam was built away from international supervision and Colonel Nasser turned down alternative projects, which would have been environmentally and economically more sound. 'Here are joined the political, national and military battles of the Egyptian people, welded together like the gigantic mass of rock that has blocked the course of the ancient Nile,' he told the crowds in May 1964 when the first phase of the project was complete.

COMPETITION OVER WATER

In arid and semi-arid countries, competition over water is natural. It occurs not only among user sectors within a specific country but also among riparian countries sharing the use of international river waters, shared ground water aquifers, or both. The strategic importance of water triggers competition among riparians that could escalate into a hot conflict if not properly controlled. In such an environment, the careful management of sovereignty over water resources is critical to the equitable and peaceful resolution of disputes and to the development of durable cooperative arrangements.

Munther J. Haddadin, *Harvard International Review*, Summer 1995.

The dam is providing multiple benefits to farmers and generating about twice the national requirement for electricity. But it has also had less benign effects. It has damaged valuable ecosystems and fishing grounds (the sardines that once bred in the Nile have almost disappeared from the Mediterranean), eroded beaches by changing the hydrology of the area (the coastal defences built on the Mediterranean coast in the 1940s have been overwhelmed since the dam was built) and deprived the Nile Valley and delta of the silt and natural fertilizers which had nourished its agriculture for thousands of years.

The ultimate solution to the water problems of the region is to shift production and economic patterns away from agriculture, the major user of water, and import food supplies instead—which would be cheaper than building unrealistic water projects—or to grow crops that consume less water for exports. But political insecurity and distrust of neighbours make this difficult for governments to do.

A DOUBTFUL FUTURE

Similar problems dog plans for a joint Jordanian-Israeli Canal from the Red Sea to the Dead Sea, which would use the 100 metre drop between the seas to generate electricity for desalination: it can only work when all neighbours agree to cooperate on peaceful terms. Even if it happens, demand will soon outstrip supply if the nations in the region continue to abuse its water resources.

It remains likely that water conflict will add to the troubles of the region. 'A time may well come,' one leading politician of the area said privately, 'when we have to calculate whether a small swift war might be economically more rewarding than putting up with a drop in our water supplies'.

"Fear-mongering about an Islamic bomb could become a self-fulfilling prophecy."

THE POTENTIAL FOR NUCLEAR PROLIFERATION CREATES TENSION

Ahmed S. Hashim

The potential for a nuclear-weapons buildup increases tensions in the Middle East, argues Ahmed S. Hashim in the following viewpoint. Israel is thus far the only Middle Eastern nation that has nuclear weapons capability, he maintains, and for various reasons, Iran and the Arab nations have largely not been able to develop their own nuclear power. But in the 1980s and 1990s, Iraq, a professed enemy of Israel, came very close to building its own atomic bomb, Hashim reports. Intervention from Israel and the international community has slowed Iraq's weapons development. However, Hashim points out, in May 1998, when India (an Israeli ally) and Pakistan (a Muslim nation) both emerged as nuclear powers, many analysts expressed concerns about the possibility of a future "Islamic bomb." Hashim is a defense analyst at the Center for Naval Analyses.

As you read, consider the following questions:

1. According to Hashim, why did Egypt fail to harness nuclear power?
2. How did Israel sabotage Iraq's nuclear efforts in 1981, according to the author?
3. Why do analysts view Iran as a nuclear-proliferation concern, according to Hashim?

Reprinted from Ahmed S. Hashim, "Nuclear Fears and Phantoms," *Middle East Insight*, September/October 1998, with permission. *Endnotes in the original have been omitted in this reprint.*

The emergence of an openly nuclear India and Pakistan in May 1998 highlighted what U.S. intelligence has often called the most dangerous nuclear flashpoint in the world: the Indian subcontinent. It also drew considerable attention to what has been termed the next most logical arena for the proliferation of nuclear weapons, namely the Middle East. However, contrary to gloomy prognostications of the past, the Middle East still only boasts one nuclear weapons state (NWS), Israel—which has not openly declared itself a nuclear power. In the past decade, however, its longstanding nuclear ambiguity has been eroded by events such as the revelations by Mordechai Vanunu of the extent of Israeli separation of plutonium at its Dimona facility; the regional focus on the Israeli nuclear monopoly in the 1990s; and significant Israeli statements that have come close to admitting that Israel is a nuclear weapons state.

ISRAELI CAPABILITY AND ARAB REACTION

Surprising, considering the general belief that the Middle East is a dangerous proliferation zone, is how little nuclear proliferation has actually occurred. States in the region have yet to succumb to the many possible motivations that can propel a country along the road towards nuclear capability—enhancing one's prestige, relieving genuine security concerns, supporting grandiose plans for regional hegemony, offsetting a rival's nuclear capability, and dealing with existential threats. Since Israel was the first Middle Eastern state to initiate a nuclear weapons program in the 1950s, it is especially instructive to evaluate the regional response or—more accurately—*non-response* to Israeli nuclearization. . . .

While the Israeli nuclear force is suspected of being considerably larger and more sophisticated than some defense analysts predicted 30 years ago, the Arabs today have no nuclear weapons capability, and two of these powers—Egypt and Syria—never seriously attempted to build the necessary infrastructure to manufacture nuclear weapons. Only Iraq came close to having an "Arab bomb". Its strategic shortsightedness and the miscalculations of its leadership ended that quest in the early 1990s. Given the strategic ambitions of Iraq's leadership, the sudden enforced end of the Iraqi nuclear program probably benefited the security and stability of the entire region. . . . Nonetheless, in every decade for the past 30 years, the Middle East has given considerable cause for concern in the nuclear proliferation arena:

• In the 1960s and '70s, Israel was the focus of attention. It was suspected of having a nuclear weapons capability, and the region was gripped by stories about Israel's nuclear program;

• In the late 1970s and early '80s, Iraq was the focus of proliferation concern;

• In the early 1990s, the revelations about Iraq's massive nuclear program by the United Nations Special Commission (UNSCOM) showed how close the Middle East had come to having a second nuclear power;

• Following the successful dismantling of Iraq's nuclear capabilities by UNSCOM and the International Atomic Energy Agency (IAEA), the world focused its attention on Iraq's next-door neighbor and erstwhile adversary—the Islamic Republic of Iran;

• The nuclear tests by India and Pakistan in May 1998 did much to refocus attention on the prospects for nuclear proliferation in the Middle East, and once again raised primordial fears of the "Islamic bomb".

Israel began its nuclear weapons program in the 1950s under the stewardship of Prime Minister David Ben-Gurion. Ben-Gurion saw an Israeli nuclear capability as an implicit response to Arab demographic superiority, as a symbol of Israel's technological edge over the Arabs, and as an assertion to the Arabs that Israel was here to stay and that their agenda for Israel's 'politicide' would never prevail. Israel has succeeded in these objectives without being an open nuclear power.

The Arab reaction to Israel's nuclear weapons program was essentially unfocused in the 1960s and '70s when stories of the Israeli nuclear weapons capability first emerged. The fact that Israel refused to acknowledge that it was seeking a nuclear capability contributed considerably to Arab disarray in the formulation of an effective response to Israel's nuclear ambiguity. It fell to Egypt, the leading Arab military power and the major Arab 'confrontation state', to be the first Arab country to develop some form of response to the threat of Israeli nuclearization in the region.

EGYPT

Initially, Egypt threatened to launch a preemptive strike against the Israeli nuclear infrastructure. It was highly unlikely that Egypt would have succeeded in such an endeavor; its air force did not have the capability or training to undertake such an attack. Egypt reportedly sought to buy nuclear weapons from the Soviet Union and the People's Republic of China (PRC). However, the USSR was not in the habit of arbitrarily proliferating nuclear capabilities, and the PRC—despite its rampant radicalism in the 1960s and early early '70s—probably told Egypt what it was to tell Libya's Muammar Ghadaffi when he came seeking to buy an atomic bomb: that self-reliance (i.e., building one's own bomb) was the only way to go. Indeed, Egypt was the first Arab country to establish an atomic energy infrastructure and the first to acquire a research reactor. Its universities were the best in the Arab world and they did produce world-class scientists and engineers. Yet Egypt never succeeded in harnessing nuclear power either for peaceful purposes or for the development of a nuclear weapons capability.

IRAN'S NUCLEAR EFFORTS

Iran's decision to revive its nuclear program is clearly tied to post–Gulf War revelations regarding Iraq's pre-war nuclear efforts. Like others in the region, Iran seems to have been completely surprised to discover how close Iraq had come to obtaining nuclear weapons. The construction of the power reactors at Bushehr contributes to Iran's science and engineering infrastructure, and thus could later ease its efforts to build nuclear weapons. Indeed, at a propitious time, Iran may terminate its membership in the Non-Proliferation Treaty (NPT), thus ending the safeguards currently applied to its nuclear facilities by the International Atomic Energy Agency (IAEA). This would allow Iran to extract whatever amounts of plutonium accumulate at Bushehr for separation into weapons-grade material.

Shai Feldman, *Journal of International Affairs*, Summer 1995.

There are a host of reasons for this failure. First, the Egyptian political elite never extended its support to the nuclear program, nor were scientists and engineers able to gain the confidence of the political elite, as they did in Israel, Pakistan, and India.

Second, largely following from the first problem, was the fact that Egypt's nuclear infrastructure was always poorly funded from its earliest days. Other major problems included the emigration of a significant number of Egyptian scientists and engineers and the almost complete lack of inter-Arab cooperation in the nuclear field. Third, in the Nasserist era, Egypt squandered its meager resources on unrealistic plans to build long-range ballistic missiles and jet fighters.

Fourth, the catastrophic Arab defeat in the June 1967 war—in which Egypt suffered the most severe losses—actually contributed considerably to lessening the significance of nuclear weapons in the conflict from the Egyptian perspective. The Arab states needed to reassess their irrational and unattainable quest to exterminate Israel and drive the Jews into the sea. Egypt's

conventional military had been wiped out by Israel's smaller—
but better-trained and more motivated—conventional forces; no
weapons of mass destruction had been used. Egypt's focus after
1967 was to expunge the shame of defeat; and the only way to
do this was via the complete rebuilding of Egypt's conventional
forces. Nuclear weapons were not relevant to a limited war designed to expunge the defeat of 1967 and ultimately designed
to get Israel to return its territorial gains.

Fifth, the 1973 war restored Egyptian honor and ultimately
led to the separate Egyptian-Israeli peace agreement at Camp
David in 1979. Under President Anwar Sadat, Egypt moved further and further away from considering a nuclear capability. After Sadat broke off Egypt's longstanding alliance with the Soviet
Union, Egypt looked to the United States to refurbish and modernize its Soviet-equipped conventional forces. Washington
would have balked at any Egyptian attempts to acquire a nuclear
weapons capability. Following Sadat's peace agreement with Israel—even as the Egyptians sought to build their chemical and
biological weapons and ballistic missile capabilities—they maintained a very low profile in these areas so as to avoid irritating
the Americans and alarming the Israelis.

The Arab world's reluctance to endorse the permanent renewal of the Nuclear Non-Proliferation Treaty (NPT) in 1995—
unless Israel did so, along with moving to dismantle its nuclear
arsenal—fed Arab and Iranian accusations of a nuclear double-
standard. Egypt led the campaign to draw attention to the Israeli
nuclear capability on the eve of, and during, the NPT Review
and Extension Conference in spring 1995. The strategy of the
Egyptian government over the past several years has been one of
calling for a nuclear weapons–free zone in the Middle East, and
of raising the profile of Israel's "opaque" nuclear capability with
the ultimate intention of forcing Israel to give up that capability.
Of the other Arab countries, only two—Syria and Iraq—were
ever capable of a concerted response or strategy to counter Israel's monopoly on nuclear weapons.

SYRIA

Syria was the other traditional Arab confrontation state along-
side Egypt. It has fought the same wars and suffered the same
devastation as Egypt. But Syria itself has never had a well-funded
or well-staffed nuclear infrastructure that could have been the
foundation for a nuclear weapons capability.

After the 1967 debacle, in which Syria lost the Golan Heights
to Israel, the focus of the Syrian leadership was the rebuilding of

the Syrian conventional forces in order to regain the lost territories. As in Egypt's case, this was not a task that could be accomplished through nuclear weapons. Syria proceeded to build a formidable armored and mechanized force that came close to defeating the Israelis in the 1973 war.

After 1973, Syria sought to rebuild its shattered conventional forces and began to focus its attention on developing a chemical weapons program and acquisition of ballistic missiles to counter the long arm of the Israeli Air Force. As early as 1974, when Egypt began its disengagement from the Arab-Israeli conflict, Syrian President Hafez al-Assad enunciated the goal of "strategic parity". The need for parity with Israel became even more pressing after Syria's embarrassing losses in the 1982 Lebanon war that dramatically highlighted the technological gap between Israel and Syria.

Syria today is generally credited with one of the most advanced chemical and biological weapons (CBW) and missile capabilities in the Middle East. Several years ago, President Assad made it clear that Syria would never capitulate to Israeli nuclear coercion and that it would not be without cost for Israel to use its nuclear weapons militarily. The Syrians seem convinced that their CBW and ballistic missiles, some of which are armed with chemical weapons, represent a sufficient deterrent against a belligerent Israel.

With neither Egypt nor Syria prepared to institute a nuclear weapons program, the Arab world's quest for a nuclear balance with Israel had to come from another quarter.

IRAQ

In 1968, civilian and military Arab nationalists of the Ba'th party—which was led by Hasan al-Bakr and his relative, Saddam Hussein—seized power in Iraq. Once the civilian Ba'thists consolidated domestic control in 1975—a situation paralleled by a dramatic rise in oil revenues—Iraq was poised to become a major regional actor.

Unlike the other two major Arab military powers, Egypt and Syria, Iraq enjoyed the luxury of rising oil wealth. More importantly, the emergence of Saddam Hussein as sole leader in 1979 saw the rise of a political elite determined to transform Iraq from a marginal strategic player in the region into the foremost Arab military power. For Iraqi Ba'thists, mastery of nuclear technology was a critical step towards diminishing the gap between the industrialized states and the developing nations. The Iraqis cleverly spoke in generalities about mastery of nuclear "technology" with the implication that they sought it for exclusively peaceful purposes.

In this context, Iraq proceeded aggressively to seek nuclear technology between 1974 and 1981. In 1974, Iraq signed a nuclear cooperation agreement with France to acquire a large reactor and to establish a university for training nuclear scientists and technicians. The Franco-Iraqi accord called upon France to supply a 40-megawatt research reactor—christened "Osirak" by the French—capable of irradiating uranium in order to produce weapons-grade plutonium. France was under heavy economic pressure to please the Iraqis, especially since Iraq was France's second largest supplier of oil after Saudi Arabia.

A FOCUS OF PROLIFERATION CONCERN

Iraq's high-profile activities in the nuclear field fueled international alarm. It was in this context that the Israelis decided to sabotage the Iraqi nuclear effort over the course of 1979–1981, culminating in the successful destruction of the Osirak reactor by the Israeli Air Force in June 1981. Following the strike, Israel announced that it would never allow any (potential) enemy to develop or acquire a nuclear capability. But no Middle Eastern country would ever repeat the mistake of centralizing its entire nuclear program in such a vulnerable way, so this Begin Doctrine (after Israeli Prime Minister Menachem Begin) was effectively obsolete as soon as it was enunciated.

As the Middle East entered the 1990s, Iraq once again became a focus of proliferation concern. There was considerable unease over Iraq's powerful conventional force, its growing defense-industrial infrastructure, a huge arsenal of chemical weapons and ballistic missiles, and suspected biological and nuclear programs. By 1989, most American analysts had believed that the Iraqis were five-to-ten years away from having a nuclear capability. It was only after Iraq's defeat in the 1991 Gulf War that the world learned how far Iraq had come in its quest for a nuclear capability.

The Desert Storm coalition's aerial bombardment barely made a dent in Iraq's nuclear infrastructure. It took UNSCOM and the IAEA working in Iraq after the war to reveal the enormous size of Iraq's covert and widespread nuclear effort. Iraq's own "Manhattan Project" involved 10–20,000 civilian and military experts spread in 16 major installations at a cost of $10 billion. Iraq was driven by its determination to become a major player in the Arab-Israeli conflict as the Arab deterrent to Israeli nuclear coercion, and by its abiding fear of Iranian revanchism and that country's crushing demographic and territorial weight vis-à-vis Iraq.

IRAN

By the mid-1990s, UNSCOM had dismantled Iraq's fearsome missile, chemical, biological, and nuclear programs. Not surprisingly, the spotlight shifted to Iraq's neighbor, Iran, which—in the eyes of the United States and Israel—had re-emerged as a "rogue" power only marginally less threatening than Saddam's Iraq. Every aspect of an alleged massive Iranian military buildup was subjected to careful scrutiny from the early 1990s on.

One reason why Iran is viewed as a proliferation concern is that the Islamic Republic inherited a large technical nuclear infrastructure from the Shah's regime. Imperial Iran had extensive plans in the civilian nuclear field, having argued that it needed civilian nuclear power because its oil reserves were limited. In 1974, the Shah established the Atomic Energy Organization of Iran (AEOI) and launched the most ambitious commercial nuclear energy program in the Middle East, which would have provided Iran with 23 nuclear power stations by the mid-1990s. At the same time the Shah cosponsored—along with Egypt—a call to make the Middle East a nuclear weapons–free zone. Though the Shah insisted that Iran had no intention of acquiring nuclear weapons, he made clear that Iran's non-acquisition of such weapons depended on the extent of non-proliferation in the region. Even with the rise of the Islamic Republic of Iran, any Iranian decision to seek nuclear weapons over the past several years has been motivated primarily by what has gone on in Iraq.

Between 1979 and 1984, Iran's civilian nuclear program collapsed due to several factors:

• post-revolutionary chaos;
• flight of thousands of skilled Iranian technical experts to the West;
• disorganization of Iran's higher education for a number of years;
• preoccupation with the 1980–88 war with Iraq;
• overt lack of interest in nuclear energy on the part of the clerical leadership.

Officials of the Islamic Republic have conceded that the early 1980s constituted a low-point in the development of the AEOI, which lost much of its financing and over half its personnel, either through transfer to other jobs or through emigration. It was in the mid-1980s that Iran began reversing its position on nuclear energy and may even have considered developing a nuclear weapons capability as a counterweight to its bitter enemy Iraq. Despite considerable help from several countries for revitalizing its 'civilian' nuclear infrastructure over the past six years—most notably from Russia and the People's Republic of China—Iranian nuclearization remains a distant prospect.

AN "ISLAMIC BOMB"?

Most of the recent studies of Iran's nuclear prospects have not fully addressed two questions: 1) Will Iranian nuclearization introduce a nuclear element to Arab-Iranian relations or rivalries? 2) Will the Iranian bomb become an "Islamic bomb" at the service of the Islamic Umma (community) against Israel and other enemies?

At the end of the 1970s, there were fears that Pakistan would give the Islamic world its first bomb. Prime Minister Zulfiqar Ali Bhutto, the father of the Pakistani bomb, had encouraged this expectation by noting that all civilizations—save the Islamic—had produced nuclear powers. There was related concern in the late 1970s and early '80s over the suspected financial aid that Saudi Arabia and Libya had provided the Pakistani nuclear program. Concern over the prospect of a Pakistani-born Islamic bomb died down in the 1980s as Islamabad became the frontline in the crusade against 'godless communism' in Afghanistan.

In the early 1990s, it was feared that Iran would give the Islamic world its nuclear capability. However, despite calls by Iranian officials that the Islamic world should have a nuclear capability, no Iranian official has explicitly proposed that Iran shoulder the burden. Furthermore, the sorry state of Iran's nuclear infrastructure meant that Iran could not be in the forefront of developing an Islamic bomb.

The hoary specter of the Islamic bomb has again reared its head with the nuclear tests by Pakistan in May 1998. Naturally, the Pakistanis were jubilant, and there was considerable satisfaction and glee in the Arab Middle East that Pakistan—a Muslim country—had come out of the nuclear closet. But in the Middle East, and in Pakistan itself, there was resistance to seeing the Pakistani nuclear capability as an *Islamic* bomb. In fact, in many Middle Eastern countries, the Pakistani tests merely inspired pro-nuclearists to suggest that the Arabs could do the same as Pakistan if they showed more determination and cooperation with one another. Many pointed out that Pakistan is poorer than many Arab countries. As for Pakistan, its attitude has been one of 'the Pakistani bomb is no more Islamic than the Indian bomb is a vegetarian one'.

For Pakistan's senior politicians and military officers, the Pakistani bomb is a *national* bomb meant to safeguard the country's national existence against the Indian behemoth. In the final analysis, Indian and Israeli fear-mongering about an Islamic bomb could become a self-fulfilling prophecy, if the Pakistanis see continued Indo-Israeli military cooperation as being directed against Pakistani nuclear capabilities.

PERIODICAL BIBLIOGRAPHY

The following articles have been selected to supplement the diverse views presented in this chapter. Addresses are provided for periodicals not indexed in the *Readers' Guide to Periodical Literature*, the *Alternative Press Index*, the *Social Sciences Index*, or the *Index to Legal Periodicals and Books*.

Jonathan I.Z. Agronsky	"The Secret War Against Hamas," *World & I*, January 1996. Available from 3600 New York Ave. NE, Washington, DC 20002.
Naseer Hasan Aruri	"Oslo's Muddled Peace," *Current History*, January 1998.
Gabriel Ben-Dor, ed.	"Israel in Transition," *Annals of the American Academy of Political and Social Science*, January 1998.
William J. Broad and Judith Miller	"Iraq's Deadliest Arms: Puzzles Breed Fears," *New York Times*, February 26, 1998.
Richard N. Cooper	"The Gulf Bottleneck," *Harvard International Review*, Summer 1997. Available from University Microfilms, Inc., 300 N. Zeeb Rd., PO Box 1346, Ann Arbor, MI 48106-1346.
Steven Emerson	"The Terrorist Infrastructure," *Wall Street Journal*, August 4, 1997.
Alain Gresh	"End of an Era," *Index on Censorship*, July/August 1996.
Jeff Halper	"Israel's War on Palestinians," *Tikkun*, May/June 1998.
Nubar Hovsepian	"Competing Identities in the Arab World," *Journal of International Affairs*, Summer 1995.
Fawzy Mansour	"The Arab World Today," *Social Justice*, Spring/Summer 1996.
Aliza Marcus	"Turkey, the Kurds, and Human Rights," *Dissent*, Summer 1996.
Nation	"The 'War of the Future,'" September 21, 1998.
Danny Rubinstein	"Israel at Fifty," *Nation*, May 4, 1998.
Edward Said	"Fifty Years of Dispossession," *Index on Censorship*, May/June 1998.

CHAPTER 2

HOW DOES RELIGION AFFECT THE MIDDLE EAST?

Chapter Preface

Islamic fundamentalists are often perceived as militants bent on overthrowing governments and terrorizing the non-Islamic world. However, most experts on the Middle East agree that the myriad Islamic revivalist groups described as fundamentalist differ in their approaches to political activism. Perhaps the one factor that unites them all is a conviction that Islam is the ultimate truth and that today's Muslims must return to the early foundations of their faith.

Islamic fundamentalists believe that Islamic culture went into decline in the late seventeenth century, when various European powers colonized parts of North Africa and the Middle East. Secular laws and customs replaced much of the Islamic *shari'a* (religious laws), and encouraged values considered immoral in Islam, such as an emphasis on self-gratification, materialism, and nationalism. Most damaging of all, in the fundamentalist view, were school systems that did not offer Muslims the opportunity to learn the tenets of their faith. Fundamentalists maintain that this ignorance of Islam, coupled with decadent Western influences, damaged the social structures and economies of several Muslim societies and eventually allowed corrupt and tyrannical leaders to prevail.

To revitalize Islamic civilization, fundamentalists believe that Muslim society must return to the "straight path" outlined in the Qur'an, the Muslim holy book. There is disagreement, however, over how this is to be accomplished. Some fundamentalists argue that after the Muslim people are "re-Islamized," a successful Islamic state should be established. In the 1940s, the Society of Muslim Brothers attempted to re-Islamize Egypt through grassroots political and educational activities; however, they were perceived as a threat by Egypt's secular rulers and were violently repressed. Other fundamentalists, such as the Shi'ites in Iran, believe that Muslims must achieve government power before societal re-Islamization can succeed. In 1979, a Shi'ite Islamic revolution confronted and gained state power in Iran.

Many fundamentalists reside in nations ruled by powerful secular elites with political and economic ties to the West. Protecting their positions, these elites often use violence to quell the spread of Islamic revivalism. On the other hand, maintains history scholar Lawrence Davidson, "Islamic fundamentalists are increasingly willing either to initiate violence in their own pursuit of change, or to respond to state violence in kind." This cycle of violence and terror is one of the topics explored by the authors in the following chapter.

"Resort to political violence . . .
became the preferred option after
Iran's revolution emboldened
[Islamic] fundamentalists
everywhere."

ISLAMIC FUNDAMENTALISM FOSTERS VIOLENCE

Martin Kramer

Martin Kramer is the director of the Moshe Dayan Center for Middle Eastern and African Studies at Tel Aviv University in Israel. In the following viewpoint, Kramer argues that Islamic fundamentalism—the conviction that Islam is the one true religion—leads to political violence in the Middle East. Islamic fundamentalists believe that the tenets of Islam should govern all facets of life, from private conduct to state and political affairs. Although they often claim that their beliefs do not justify violence, Kramer contends, fundamentalists have resorted to war, assassination, and terrorism in an attempt to spread the influence of Islam throughout the Middle East and the world.

As you read, consider the following questions:

1. According to Kramer, what evidence led an Arab critic to compare Sayyid al-Afghani's thinking to fascism?
2. What is the "double identity" of the Muslim Brethren, according to the author?
3. What doctrine of Ruhollah Khomeini's led to the success of an Islamic revolution in Iran, according to Kramer?

Excerpted from Martin Kramer, "The Drive for Power," Middle East Quarterly, June 1996. Reprinted by permission of Transaction Publishers. Copyright ©1996 by Transaction Publishers; all rights reserved. Footnotes in the original have been omitted in this reprint.

A s the twentieth century closes, two words, Islam and fundamentalism, have become intimately linked in English usage.
The *Concise Oxford Dictionary of Current English* now defines *fundamentalism* as the "strict maintenance of ancient or fundamental doctrines of any religion, especially Islam." However problematic
this formula, it does acknowledge that fundamentalism in Islam
is today the most visible and influential of all fundamentalisms.

The nature of fundamentalist Islam, and even the use of the
term, is hotly debated. But this debate is largely a self-indulgent
exercise of analysts. Within Islam, there are Muslims who have
created an "-ism" out of Islam—a coherent ideology, a broad
strategy, and a set of political preferences. They do not defy definition. They defy the world.

What Is Fundamentalist Islam?

What is fundamentalist Islam? Its contradictions seem to abound.
On the one hand, it manifests itself as a new religiosity, reaffirming faith in a transcendent God. On the other hand, it appears as
a militant ideology, demanding political action now. Here it takes
the form of a populist party, asking for ballots. There it surges
forth as an armed phalanx, spraying bullets. One day its spokes-
men call for a *jihad* (sacred war) against the West, evoking the
deepest historic resentments. Another day, its leaders appeal for
reconciliation with the West, emphasizing shared values. Its economic theorists reject capitalist materialism in the name of social
justice, yet they rise to the defense of private property. Its moral-
ists pour scorn on Western consumer culture as debilitating to Islam, yet its strategists avidly seek to buy the West's latest tech-
nologies in order to strengthen Islam.

Faced with these apparent contradictions, many analysts in
the West have decided that fundamentalism defies all generaliza-
tion. Instead they have tried to center discussion on its supposed
"diversity." For this purpose, they seek to establish systems of
classification by which to sort out fundamentalist movements
and leaders. The basic classification appears in many different
terminological guises, in gradations of subtlety.

> We need to be careful of that emotive label, 'fundamentalism',
> and distinguish, as Muslims do, between revivalists, who choose
> to take the practice of their religion most devoutly, and fanatics
> or extremists, who use this devotion for political ends.

So spoke the Prince of Wales in a 1993 address, summarizing
the conventional wisdom in a conventional way. The belief that
these categories really exist, and that experts can sort fundamen-

talists neatly into them, is the sand on which weighty policies are now being built.

Fundamentalist Islam remains an enigma precisely because it has confounded all attempts to divide it into tidy categories. "Revivalist" becomes "extremist" (and vice versa) with such rapidity and frequency that the actual classification of any movement or leader has little predictive power. They will not stay put. This is because fundamentalist Muslims, for all their "diversity," orbit around one dense idea. From any outside vantage point, each orbit will have its apogee and perigee. The West thus sees movements and individuals swing within reach, only to swing out again and cycle right through every classification. Movements and individuals arise in varied social and political circumstances, and have their own distinctive orbits. But they will not defy the gravity of their idea.

The idea is simple: Islam must have power in this world. It is the true religion—the religion of God—and its truth is manifest in its power. When Muslims believed, they were powerful. Their power has been lost in modern times because Islam has been abandoned by many Muslims, who have reverted to the condition that preceded God's revelation to the Prophet Muhammad. But if Muslims now return to the original Islam, they can preserve and even restore their power.

By Any Means Necessary

The most pressing question that has faced Islamists has been how to pursue rulership. The rule of thumb here is that Islamist movements usually follow what looks to their leaders like the path of least resistance. They are not committed to any one strategy in the pursuit of their ends, and any means are legitimate as long as they are in accordance with Islamic law, the shari'a. This law is not pacifist. It sanctions violence for the legitimate purposes of defending Muslims and establishing the rule of Islam. This explains why Islamist movements have slipped so readily into violence whenever it has seemed like a shortcut to power. In such circumstances, the use of force is not deemed a deviation, but an obligation.

Martin Kramer, *Harvard International Review*, Spring 1997.

That return, to be effective, must be comprehensive; Islam provides the one and only solution to all questions in this world, from public policy to private conduct. It is not merely a religion, in the Western sense of a system of belief in God. It possesses an immutable law, revealed by God, that deals with every aspect of life, and it is an ideology, a complete system of belief about the organization of the state and the world. This law and ideology can only be implemented through the establishment of a truly Islamic state, under the sovereignty of God. The empowerment of Islam, which is God's plan for mankind, is a sacred end. It may be pursued by any means that can be rationalized in terms of Islam's own code. At various times, these have included persuasion, guile, and force.

What is remarkable about fundamentalist Islam is not its diversity. It is the fact that this idea of power for Islam appeals so effectively across such a wide range of humanity, creating a world of thought that crosses all frontiers. Fundamentalists everywhere must act in narrow circumstances of time and place. But they are who they are precisely because their idea exists above all circumstances. Over nearly a century, this idea has evolved into a coherent ideology, which demonstrates a striking consistency in content and form across a wide expanse of the Muslim world.

FUNDAMENTALIST FORERUNNERS

The pursuit of power for Islam first gained some intellectual coherence in the mind and career of Sayyid Jamal al-Din "al-Afghani" (1838–97), a thinker and activist who worked to transform Islam into a lever against Western imperialism. His was an age of European expansion into the heartlands of Islam, and of a frenzied search by Muslims for ways to ward off foreign conquest. . . .

A contemporary English admirer described Afghani as the leader of Islam's "Liberal religious reform movement." But Afghani—not an Afghan at all, but a Persian who concealed his true identity even from English admirers—was never what he appeared to be. While he called for the removal of some authoritarian Muslim rulers, he ingratiated himself with others. While he had great persuasive power, he did not shrink from conspiracy and violence. A disciple once found him pacing back and forth, shouting: "There is no deliverance except in killing, there is no safety except in killing." These were not idle words. On one occasion, Afghani proposed to a follower that the ruler of Egypt be assassinated, and he did inspire a supple disciple to assassinate a ruling shah of Iran in 1896. Afghani was tempted by power, and believed that "power is never manifested and concrete unless it weakens and subjugates others." Quoting this and other evidence, one Arab critic has argued that there is a striking correspondence between Afghani's thought and European fascism. . . .

Between Afghani and the emergence of full-blown fundamentalism, liberal and secular nationalism would enjoy a long run in the lands of Islam. Europe had irradiated these lands with the idea that language, not religion, defined nations. In the generation that followed Afghani, Muslims with an eye toward Europe preferred to be called Arabs, Turks, and Persians. "If you looked in the right places," wrote the British historian Arnold Toynbee in 1929, "you could doubtless find some old fashioned Islamic Fundamentalists still lingering on. You would also find that their influence was negligible." Yet that same year, an Egyptian schoolteacher named Hasan al-Banna (1906–49) founded a movement he called the Society of the Muslim Brethren. It would grow into the first modern fundamentalist movement in Islam.

THE MUSLIM BRETHREN

The Muslim Brethren emerged against the background of growing resentment against foreign domination. The Brethren had a double identity. On one level, they operated openly, as a membership organization of social and political awakening. Banna preached moral revival, and the Muslim Brethren engaged in good works. On another level, however, the Muslim Brethren created a "secret apparatus" that acquired weapons and trained adepts in their use. Some of its guns were deployed against the Zionists in Palestine in 1948, but the Muslim Brethren also resorted to violence in Egypt. They began to enforce their own moral teachings by intimidation, and they initiated attacks against Egypt's Jews. They assassinated judges and struck down a prime minister in 1949. Banna himself was assassinated two months later, probably in revenge. The Muslim Brethren then hovered on the fringes of legality, until Gamal Abdel Nasser, who had survived one of their assassination attempts in 1954, put them down ruthlessly. Yet the Muslim Brethren continued to plan underground and in prison, and they flourished in other Arab countries to which they were dispersed.

At the same time, a smaller and more secretive movement, known as the Devotees of Islam, appeared in Iran, under the leadership of a charismatic theology student, Navvab Safavi (1923–56). Like the Muslim Brethren, the Devotees emerged at a time of growing nationalist mobilization against foreign domination. The group was soon implicated in the assassinations of a prime minister and leading secular intellectuals. The Devotees, who never became a mass party, overplayed their hand and were eventually suppressed. Navvab himself was executed, after inspiring a failed assassination attempt against another prime minister. But the seed was planted. One of those who protested Navvab's execution was an obscure, middle-aged cleric named Ruhollah Khomeini, who would continue the work of forging Islam and resentment into an ideology of power. . . .

Islamic fundamentalists sought to replace weak rulers and states with strong rulers and states. Such a state would have to be based on Islam, and while its precise form remained uncertain, the early fundamentalists knew it should not be a constitutional government or multiparty democracy. . . . This preference for a strong, authoritarian Islamic state, often rationalized by the claim that Islam and democracy are incompatible, would become a trademark of fundamentalist thought and practice.

The pursuit of this strong utopian state often overflowed into violence against weak existing states. These "reformers" were quick to disclaim any link to the violence of their followers, denying that their adepts could read their teachings as instructions or justifications for killing. Afghani set the tone, following the assassination of Iran's shah by his disciple. "Surely it was a good deed to kill this bloodthirsty tyrant," he opined. "As far as I am personally concerned, however, I have no part in this deed." Banna, commenting on the assassinations and bombings done by the Muslim Brethren, claimed that "the only ones responsible for these acts are those who commit them." Navvab, who failed in his one attempt at assassination, sent young disciples in his stead. For years he enjoyed the protection of leading religious figures while actually putting weapons in the hands of assassins. (Only when abroad did he actually boast. "I killed Razmara," he announced on a visit to Egypt in 1954, referring to the prime minister assassinated by a disciple three years earlier.) But despite the denials, violence became the inescapable shadow of fundamentalist Islam from the outset—and the attempt to separate figure from shadow, a problematic enterprise at best.

A PAN-ISLAMIC BENT

The fundamentalist forerunners also determined that fundamentalist Islam would have a pan-Islamic bent. The peripatetic Afghani took advantage of steamship and train, crossing political borders and sectarian divides to spread his message of Islamic solidarity. His Paris newspaper circulated far and wide in Islam, through the modern post. Egypt's Muslim Brethren also looked beyond the horizon. In 1948, they sent their own volunteers to fight the Jews in Palestine. Over the next decade, branches of the Muslim Brethren appeared across the Middle East and North Africa, linked by publications and conferences. Egyptian Brethren fleeing arrest set up more branches in Europe, where they mastered the technique of the bank transfer.

The fundamentalist forerunners even laid bridges over the historic moat of Sunni prejudice that surrounded Shi'i Iran. Iran's Devotees of Islam mounted massive demonstrations for Palestine, and recruited 5,000 volunteers to fight Israel. They were not allowed to leave for the front, but Navvab himself flew to Egypt and Jordan in 1953, to solidify his ties with the Muslim Brethren. Visiting the Jordanian-Israeli armistice line, he had to be physically restrained from throwing himself upon the Zionist enemy. Navvab presaged those Iranian volunteers who arrived in Lebanon thirty years later to wage Islamic jihad against Israel.

From the outset, then, fundamentalists scorned the arbitrary boundaries of states, and demonstrated their resolve to think and act across the frontiers that divide Islam. The jet, the cassette, the fax, and the computer network would later help fundamentalists create a global village of ideas and action—not a hierarchical "Islamintern" but a flat "Islaminform"—countering the effects of geographic distance and sectarian loyalty. Not only has the supposed line between "revivalist" and "extremist" been difficult to draw. National and sectarian lines have been erased or smudged, and fundamentalists draw increasingly on a common reservoir for ideas, strategies, and support.

A resolute anti-Westernism, a vision of an authoritarian Islamic state, a propensity to violence, and a pan-Islamic urge: these were the biases of the forerunners of fundamentalist Islam. No subsequent fundamentalist movement could quite shake them. Indeed, several thinkers subsequently turned these biases into a full-fledged ideology. . . .

THE AYATOLLAH KHOMEINI

It was Ruhollah Khomeini (1902–89) who wrote the ideological formula for the first successful fundamentalist revolution in Islam. Khomeini added nothing to fundamentalist ideology by his insistence on the need for an Islamic state, created if necessary by an Islamic revolution, but he made a breakthrough with his claim that only the persons most learned in Islamic law could rule: "Since Islamic government is a government of law, knowledge of the law is necessary for the ruler, as has been laid down in tradition." The ruler "must surpass all others in knowledge," and be "more learned than everyone else." Since no existing state had such a ruler, Khomeini's doctrine constituted an appeal for region-wide revolution, to overturn every extant form of authority and replace it with rule by Islamic jurists. In Iran, where such jurists had maintained their independence from the state all along, this doctrine transformed them into a revolutionary class, bent on the seizure and exercise of power. Much to the astonishment of the world—fundamentalists included—the formula worked, carrying Khomeini and his followers to power on a tidal wave of revolution in 1979. . . .

Khomeini's delegitimation of rule by nominal Muslim kings and presidents found a powerful echo, and he demonstrated how a revolution might succeed in practice. Khomeini also showed how cultural alienation could be translated into a fervid antiforeign sentiment, an essential cement for a broad revolutionary coalition. Later it would be assumed that only "extremists" beyond Iran were thrilled by Iran's revolution. In fact, the enthusiasm among fundamentalists was almost unanimous. As a close reading of the press of the Egyptian Muslim Brethren has demonstrated, even this supposedly sober movement approached the Iranian revolution with "unqualified enthusiasm and unconditional euphoria," coupled with an "uncritical acceptance of both its means and goals." Sunni doubts would arise about implementation of the Islamic state in Iran, but for the next decade, much of the effort of fundamentalists would be invested in attempts to replicate Khomeini's success and bring about a second Islamic revolution.

ATTEMPTS AT A SECOND REVOLUTION

The attempts to make a second revolution demonstrated that fundamentalists of all kinds would employ revolutionary violence if they thought it would bring them to power. Frustrated by the drudgery of winning mass support, full of the heady ideas of Mawlana Mawdudi and Sayyid Qutb [early twentieth-century fundamentalist revolutionaries], and inspired by Khomeini's success, they lunged forward. From the wild-eyed to the wily, Sunni fundamentalists of all stripes began to conspire. A messianic sect seized the Great Mosque in Mecca in 1979. A group moved by Qutb's teachings assassinated Egyptian President Anwar Sadat in 1981. The Muslim Brethren declared a rebellion against the Syrian regime in 1982. Another path of violence paralleled this one—the work of the half-dozen Shi'i movements in Arab lands that had emerged around the hub of Islamic revolution in Iran. They targeted their rage against the existing order in Iraq, Saudi Arabia, Kuwait, Lebanon, and the smaller Gulf states. In Iraq, they answered Khomeini's appeal by seeking to raise the country's Shi'is in revolt in 1979. In Lebanon, they welcomed Iran's Revolutionary Guards in 1982, first to help drive out the Israelis, then to send suicide bombers to blow up the barracks of U.S. and French peacekeepers there in 1983. Another Shi'i bomber nearly killed the ruler of Kuwait in 1985. Some of Khomeini's adepts went to Mecca as demonstrators, to preach revolution to the assembled pilgrims. Others hijacked airliners and abducted foreigners. Khomeini put a final touch on the decade when he incited his worldwide following to an act of assassination, issuing a religious edict demanding the death of the novelist Salman Rushdie in 1989.

This violence was not an aberration. It was a culmination. From the time of Afghani, fundamentalists had contemplated the possibility of denying power through assassination, and taking power through revolution. Because resort to political violence carried many risks, it had been employed judiciously and almost always surreptitiously, but it remained a legitimate option rooted firmly in the tradition, and it became the preferred option after Iran's revolution emboldened fundamentalists everywhere. For the first time, the ideology of Islam had been empowered, and it had happened through revolution. Power for Islam seemed within reach, if only the fundamentalists were bold enough to run the risk. Many of them were. They included not just the avowed revolutionaries of the Jihad Organization in Egypt, but the cautious and calculating readerships of the Muslim Brethren in Syria and the Shi'i Da'wa Party in Iraq.

Violent Upheaval

It was a seesaw battle throughout the 1980s. Nowhere was Iran's experience repeated. The masses did not ignite in revolution, the rulers did not board jumbo jets for exile. Regimes often employed ruthless force to isolate and stamp out the nests of fundamentalist "sedition." Fundamentalists faced the gaol and the gallows in Egypt. Their blood flowed in the gutters of Hama in Syria, Mecca in Saudi Arabia, and Najaf in Iraq. Yet fundamentalists also struck blows in return, against government officials, intellectuals, minorities, and foreigners. While they did not take power anywhere, they created many semiautonomous pockets of resistance. Some of these pockets were distant from political centers, such as the Bekaa Valley in Lebanon and several governates of Upper Egypt, but fundamentalists also took root in urban quarters and on university campuses, where Islamic dress for women became compulsory and short-cropped beards for men became customary. From time to time, impatient pundits would proclaim that the tide of fundamentalist Islam had gone out, but its appeal obviously ran much deeper. Its straightforward solution to the complex crisis of state and society spoke directly to the poor and the young, the overqualified and the underemployed, whose numbers were always increasing faster than their opportunities.

After Iran's revolution and the subsequent revolts, it was impossible to dismiss the ideological coherence fundamentalist Islam had achieved. It had succeeded in resurrecting in many minds an absolute division between Islam and unbelief. Its adherents, filled with visions of power, had struck at the existing order, turned against foreign culture, and rejected not only apologetics but politics—the pursuit of the possible through compromise. Fundamentalism mobilized its adherents for conflict, for it assumed that the power sought for Islam existed only in a finite quantity. It could only be taken at the expense of others: rulers, foreigners, minorities. Fundamentalists did not admit the sharing of this power, anymore than they admitted the sharing of religious truth, and although fundamentalists differed on the means of taking power, they were unanimous on what should be done with it. One observer has written that even in Egypt, where the fundamentalist scene seemed highly fragmented, the political and social program of the violent fringe groups "did not seem to differ much from that of the mainstream Muslim Brethren," and was shared by "almost the whole spectrum of political Islam." This was true, by and large, for fundamentalist Islam as a whole.

> "The Muslim Brotherhood dissociates itself and denounces, without any hesitation, all forms of violence and terrorism."

ISLAMIC FUNDAMENTALISM DOES NOT FOSTER VIOLENCE

Muhammad M. El-Hodaiby

Muhammad M. El-Hodaiby is Deputy General Guide of the Muslim Brotherhood in Egypt, an Islamic liberation movement. In the following viewpoint, El-Hodaiby maintains that the tenets of Islam uphold justice, human dignity, pluralism, and nonviolence. Misleading Western interpretations of Islamic fundamentalism, he contends, have led many to conclude that Islamic renewal movements are narrow-minded and inherently violent. Islamic teachings, however, eschew violence. Those Muslims who do participate in violence are reacting, in a misguided way, to governmental attempts to suppress Islamic resurgence. In actuality, El-Hodaiby argues, most Islamic revival movements simply wish to help Muslims—many of whom have lived under imperialist domination—return to the principles of true Islam.

As you read, consider the following questions:

1. How did Western imperialism affect Muslim societies, in El-Hodaiby's opinion?
2. According to the author, why is "Political Islam" a misleading term?
3. According to the texts of the Qur'an, cited by El-Hodaiby, what rights do non-Muslims have in Muslim states?

Excerpted from Muhammad M. El-Hodaiby, "Upholding Islam: The Goals of Egypt's Muslim Brotherhood," *Harvard International Review*, Spring 1997. Reprinted with permission.

Ever since the Egyptian people, along with other African and Asian peoples, embraced Islam in the deep-seated conviction that it is a true religion revealed to a true prophet, Islam has fully characterized the life and activities of those peoples. The two basic sources of Islam—the Holy Qur'an and the *sunna* (authentic traditions of the Prophet)—became the sole reference point for the life of the Muslim individual, family, and community as well as the Muslim state and all economic, social, political, cultural, educational, and legislative and judiciary activities. The Islamic creed and *shari'a* (law) ruled over the individual and society, the ruler and the ruled; neither a ruler nor a ruled people could change anything they prescribed.

Since the Islamic shari'a was revealed by God, judges applied its teachings and fulfilled its rules with no intervention from the rulers. A massive wealth of jurisprudence developed (*fiqh*) from the work of scores of scholars who devoted their lives to the interpretation of the Qur'an and sunna through the use of *ijtihad*, the exercise of independent judgment. Various schools of thought emerged, differing mainly on secondary matters, as well as on some points of application. Believers in religions other than Islam, meanwhile, lived in the Islamic homeland secure in their persons, honor, and property as well as everything they held dear. Except for isolated cases, history does not show Muslim persecution of non-Muslims.

The comprehensive Islamic system remained dominant in the Islamic states. This does not mean that the application was perfectly sound or that the rulers perpetrated no wrongs. In fact, many of the texts were abandoned or incorrectly interpreted. After the first three caliphs who succeeded the Prophet as leader of the Muslim community, disputes arose over the selection of head of state. Internal wars broke out, and the leadership of the state soon changed from a caliphate chosen through *shura*, a process of consultation, to a hereditary and tyrannical monarchy. This deviation from the tenets of Islam occurred even though the relevant text remained clear and unchanged in the Qur'an. Still, the rulers' tyranny was restricted by the jurisprudence of scholars based on the Qur'an and sunna, which left little room for the rulers to promulgate public laws out of character with the shari'a.

IMPERIALISM AND ISLAMIC RESPONSE

In the period of colonial Christian invasion, the Islamic shari'a was excluded from serving as the constitution and law of the state. Egypt was occupied by the British in September 1882; less than a year later, in July 1883, Islamic religious courts were replaced by "national courts." Most of the new judges were non-Egyptians, and the law they applied were translated French laws, which became the dominant laws in civil, commercial, and criminal cases. The jurisdiction of Islamic religious courts was restricted to areas of personal status, marriage, divorce, and the related issues of establishing lineage, dowries, and alimonies. The Islamic economic system was replaced by a system of banks, despite the prohibition of the interest rate under Islamic shari'a. In the educational realm, new schools offered few opportunities for the young to learn the creed and tenets of their religion. The social system permitted alcohol, prostitution, gambling, and other activities forbidden in Islam.

The countries and peoples subjected to the armies, creed, and social, economic, and ethical systems of the West struggled for independence. After many years, they managed to regain some of their freedom, but they emerged from the age of imperialism with a weak social structure and a ruined economic system in which poverty, ignorance, disease, and backwardness prevailed. Consequently, the system of government became corrupt and weak. Tyrants emerged that were supported by the forces of imperialism, which withdrew their armies but retained much of their influence.

Since the overwhelming majority of these peoples in Muslim societies believed in Islam and embraced it as a full system of life, forces soon appeared among them that strove to awaken the spirit of faith and remove ideas that had emerged during the decadent era of imperialism. Movements of Islamic revival became active to spread correct Islamic thought and demand the application of the rulings of the Islamic shari'a, particularly the basic principles which ensure shura, freedom, justice, and socioeconomic balance. Among the strongest of these movements is the Muslim Brotherhood, which originated in Egypt in 1928, during the waning years of military colonialism, and has continued its struggle to the present.

THE PRINCIPLES OF THE BROTHERHOOD

The call of the Muslim Brotherhood was based on two key pillars. First, the Muslim Brotherhood aimed to institute Islamic shari'a as the controlling basis of state and society. About 97 percent of the Egyptian people are Muslims, the majority of whom perform the rites of worship and the ethics enjoined by Islam. But in Egypt, legislation, the judiciary, and economic and social systems are founded on non-Islamic bases. The disjunction between government legislation and policy, on the one hand, and the Islamic shari'a on the other, led to the emergence of many social, economic, and political practices that are invalid under Islamic shari'a. Realizing that a government that is committed to Islam cannot be established without a popular base that believes in its teachings, the Muslim Brotherhood strove to provide a mechanism for the education of society in Islamic principles and ethics.

Second, the Muslim Brotherhood worked to help liberate Muslim countries from foreign imperialism and achieve unity among them, contributing to the struggle against the occupying British armies in Egypt while continuously backing liberation movements in many Arab and Islamic countries. The ruling powers in many of these countries are totalitarian, tyrannical, and personalist, denying popular will and elections, despite the extensive propaganda they finance to convince people otherwise. Because these governments rely on foreign influence, and in view of their special formation and military nature, there have been repeated clashes between them and the Muslim Brotherhood. In Egypt, three years after the assassination in 1949 of Hasan Al-Banna, the founder of the Brotherhood, clashes broke out between the Brotherhood and the military regime. In the era of Gamal Abdel-Nasser, thousands of group leaders and members were arrested, jailed, and tortured; six of the Brotherhood's top leaders were executed by Nasser in 1954 and many others killed in prisons and detention camps. Twelve years later, the famous intellectual Sayyid Qutb and two other leaders were also killed.

After a period of relative calm, the authorities in Egypt resumed their campaign against the Brotherhood. Shortly before the parliamentary elections of 1995, they arrested 62 of the most prominent Brotherhood leaders and brought them before military courts on the pretext of their political activity and preparations for running in elections. Despite these obstacles, the Muslim Brotherhood remains the largest and most effective political and doctrinal movement in Egypt.

WESTERN MISINTERPRETATIONS

In the West the rise of Islamic movements led to attempts, especially in the media, to characterize the nature of Islamic resurgence. The Western media usually tries to relate events in other parts of the world to historical experiences in the West, but their efforts to draw analogies often result in a mixing of fact and fantasy. Among the catch words in the Western media are the misnomer "Islamic fundamentalism" and the misleading term "political Islam."

In the Western experience, religious groups called "fundamentalists" have been characterized by narrow-minded and artificial interpretations of some of their holy books, interpretations which would petrify life and isolate society from thought and culture and even the natural sciences. When Western propaganda and media call some movements of Islamic renewal "fundamentalist," they aim to create a link in the mind of the public between those Islamic movements and the negative connotations of fundamentalism in the West.

As a result, the image of Islamic movements is distorted and their call made repulsive. The fact of the matter is that there is no similarity between the western notion of fundamentalism and Islamic liberation and renewal movements. The majority of Islamic movements today accept all the exigencies of the modern age, and the natural sciences and technology, unlike the fundamentalisms of the Western experience.

The Western media also speaks of "Political Islam," a misleading term because it gives the false impression that there is a distinction between Islam as a religion, with its creed, rites, and ethics, and Islam as a political system. Groups reflective of political Islam are then seen as falsely attributing to themselves religious sanction in order to gain backing for their political views. But Islam is inherently political: there are categorical texts in the Qur'an making it mandatory to apply the shari'a and act in accordance with it. One verse declares: "O you who believe! Obey God, and obey the Apostle, and those charged with authority among you. If you differ in anything among yourselves, refer it to God and His Apostle, if you do believe in God and the Last Day: that is best, and most suitable for final determination" (Qur'an 4:59). Another one states: "But no, by the Lord, they can have no (real) faith, until they make you judge in all disputes between them, and find in their souls no resistance against your decisions, but accept them with the fullest conviction" (Qur'an 4:65). And there are others.

The Islamic Shari'a

The teachings of the Islamic shari'a have introduced and regulated the principles of justice, fairness, equality, human dignity, and inviolability of person and property. The shari'a includes texts relating to systems which are now considered to be an integral part of politics. The Muslim Brotherhood demands that these particular shari'a injunctions be implemented. Their enforcement cannot be ignored. Scholars of Al-Azhar University in Cairo, the most important institution specializing in the study of Islam, and the scholars and jurisprudents of all Islamic institutions throughout the world are unanimous in upholding this view.

Muslim scholars are also agreed, however, that no one other than prophets of God are infallible: indeed, the first ruler to come after the Prophet, Abu Bakr Al-Siddiq, came to power saying: "I have become your ruler though I am not the best among you. Obey me as long as I obey God's injunctions regarding you. If I disobey, correct me." Rulers are no more than human beings. Therefore, while the government in Islam is required to abide by the principles of the Islamic shari'a, it is still a civil government that is subject to accountability.

The fixed and unchangeable tenets of the Islamic shari'a are very few, consisting of basic principles designed to achieve justice and social and economic equality, as well as protect human rights, dignity, soul, and property; and preserve and protect the teachings of religion and the system of state. There can always be access to ijtihad to deduce views that are appropriate to global, economic, and social changes. Islam knows no infallible religious government that speaks in the name of God. . . .

A COMMITMENT TO NONVIOLENCE

In past years, the Muslim Brotherhood has repeatedly stated that it is involved in political life and has committed itself to legal and nonviolent methods of bringing about change. Its only weapons are honest and truthful words and selfless dedication to social work. In following this course, it is confident that the conscience and awareness of the people are the rightful judges of all intellectual and political trends which compete honestly with one another. Thus, the Muslim Brotherhood reiterates its rejection of any form of violence and coercion as well as all types of coups which destroy the unity of the ummah [nation] because such plots would never give the masses the opportunity to exercise their free will. Furthermore, these methods would create a great crack in the wall of political stability and form an unacceptable assault on the true legitimacy in the society.

Indeed, the present atmosphere of suppression, instability, and anxiety has forced many young men of this nation to commit acts of terrorism which have intimidated innocent citizens and threatened the country's security, as well as its economic and political future. The Muslim Brotherhood dissociates itself and denounces, without any hesitation, all forms of violence and terrorism. In addition, it considers those who shed the

91

blood of others or aid such bloodshed as complicit in sin. Hence, the Brotherhood requests all Muslims to abandon such actions and return to the right way, because "a Muslim is one who refrains from attacking others either physically or verbally." We invite all those who are involved in acts of violence to remember the advice of our Messenger (s.a.w.), in the farewell pilgrimage sermon when he commanded us to protect the sanctity of blood, honor, and property of every Muslim. (Muslims use "s.a.w.," meaning "peace and blessings of God be upon him," after the name of the Prophet).

MOST MUSLIMS ARE COMMITTED TO PEACE

In the mass media, Islam and Muslims are frequently depicted as the "other" in global politics and cultural warfare. The Iranian revolution under Ayatollah Khomeini in 1978–79, the tragic death of 241 marines near Beirut airport in 1983, and the bombing of the World Trade Center in New York in 1993 are among the violent images associated with Muslims. But those images resonate poorly with the majority of Muslims. Most Muslims, like other human beings, are engaged in their day-to-day life in this world, struggling to provide for their usually large extended families, working for peaceful resolution to the conflicts that face them, and committed to honor universal human values of freedom and peace with justice.

Abdulaziz Sachedina, *World & I*, September 1997.

The Muslim Brotherhood's continuous policy has been one of urging the government not to counter violence with violence, and to abide, instead, by the rules of law and jurisdiction. Some people deliberately and unfairly accuse the Muslim Brotherhood of being involved in terrorist acts. These accusations, stemming from the Brotherhood's unwillingness to support wholeheartedly the confrontational policies of the government, cannot be taken seriously in the light of the clear long-term record of the Muslim Brotherhood's contribution to political life, including its participation in general elections and representative bodies.

The Brotherhood has declared fifteen democratic principles, included in my political program for the November 1995 elections, which we invite all political parties and powers in Egypt to support as a National Charter. These principles declare that "it is not permissible for any one individual, party, group, or institution to claim the right to authority, or to continue in power except with the consent of the people." We upheld the principle "power exchange through free and fair general elections." We confirmed our complete commitment to freedom of religion, opinion, assembly, parliamentary representation and participation (for men and women), an independent judiciary, and an army free from political involvement.

THE RIGHTS OF NON-MUSLIMS

The texts of the Qur'an and sunna obligate Muslims to ensure the safety and security of non-Muslims with revealed books preceding Islam (particularly Jews and Christians) as citizens in the Muslim state. These texts ensure for non-Muslims the freedom of belief and the freedom to abide by the laws in which they believe, not the Islamic shari'a. For example, non-Muslims marry under their own laws, and their marriages are recognized by the Muslim state. Nor are they bound by the dietary laws of Muslims. The Islamic texts allow Muslims to deal with those non-Muslims as long as the Muslims observe the shari'a in such dealings.

The non-Muslims also have the right to own property, real estate, and all kinds of assets. They can engage in various professions like medicine, engineering, agriculture, and trade. They have the right to assume all offices of state that are not related to enforcing the Islamic shari'a in which they do not believe. In addition, they are free to take their disputes and litigation to competent and knowledgeable persons of their own law. A Muslim judge cannot examine or pass verdicts in these cases unless non-Muslims themselves refer these cases to him.

The stand of the Muslim Brotherhood is based on the clear Qur'anic edict of no compulsion in religion: we do not wish to compel people to act against their faith or ideology. Our stance regarding our Christian compatriots in Egypt and the Arab world is not new and it is clear and well-known. The Christians are our partners in the country; they were our brothers in the long struggle to liberate the nation. They enjoy all rights of citizenship, financial, psychological, civil, or political. To care for and cooperate with them in every good cause is an Islamic obligation which no Muslim would dare to take lightly.

ISLAM AND PLURALISM

Today, politicians and thinkers worldwide are raising the banner of pluralism, exhorting recognition of diversity in ideas and actions. However, when the Qur'an was revealed to Prophet Muhammad (s.a.w.) more than 1400 years ago, Islam accepted these differences as universal, and based its political, social, and cultural systems on such variation: "And we made you into nations and tribes, that you may know each other—not that you may depose each other . . ." (Qur'an 49:13). Pluralism according to Islam obliges the recognition of the "other" and requires the psychological and intellectual readiness to accept what truth and good others may possess: as Muslims believe, "wisdom is what a believer should be looking for; wherever he finds it, he should utilize it in the best possible way." Muslims do not hide behind an iron curtain, isolated from relationships with other nations.

The Muslim Brotherhood reaffirms its commitment to this enlightened and wise Islamic viewpoint and reminds all those who follow or quote the Muslim Brotherhood to be sincere in their words and actions. Every Muslim should befriend others and open his heart and mind to everyone, never look down on any person nor remind him of past favors, nor lose patience with him. Brothers' hands should always be extended to others in kindness and love. Their approach to the whole world is one of peace in words and actions, following the example of our Messenger (s.a.w.), a mercy sent to all the worlds. . . .

It is worthwhile to remind ourselves and others that Islam is the only ideological and political system that has honored man and humanity to the utmost degree. Islam is absolutely free from all forms of discrimination, whether based on race, color, or culture. From the beginning Islam has protected the lives, privacy, dignity, and property of all individuals and considered any violation of these sanctities a sin. It has also made their protection a religious duty and an Islamic act of devotion, even if non-Muslims do not follow such standards.

The Qur'an explains this as follows: ". . . And let not the hatred of others make you swerve to wrong and depart from justice. Be just: that is nearer to piety." (Qur'an 5:8). If some Muslims, now or in the past, have not committed themselves to this obligation, their misdeeds should not be attributed to Islam. It has been commonly accepted in writings on the philosophy of Islamic jurisprudence that "you can identify true men by seeing them stick to truth, but truth cannot be identified by seeing those who follow it."

HUMAN RIGHTS

The Muslim Brotherhood would like to proclaim to everyone that we are at the forefront of those who respect and work for human rights. We call for providing all safeguards for these rights, securing them for every human being and facilitating the practice of all liberties within the framework of ethical values and legal limits. We believe that human freedom is the starting point for every good cause, for progress and creativity. The violation of human freedom and rights under any banner, even Islam, is a degradation of man and a demotion from the high position in which God has placed him, and it prevents man from utilizing his initiative and powers to prosper and develop.

At the same time, we present to the world's conscience tragic acts of injustice afflicting those Muslims who have never hurt anyone. It is the duty of all wise men to protest loudly, calling for the universality of human rights and the enjoyment of human freedom on an equal footing. Such equality is the true way toward international and social peace and toward a new world order. This is our faithful testimony, and this is our call in all truth and sincerity. We invite everyone to turn over a new leaf in human and international relations, so that we may enjoy justice, liberty, and peace: "Our Lord! Decide between us and our people in truth for You are the best to decide." Praise be to Allah and His blessings upon Prophet Muhammad.

> "The Jewish state is the only democracy in the world where Jews do not have full religious freedom."

ORTHODOX JUDAISM IS A THREAT TO ISRAEL

Uri Regev

Democracy in Israel is threatened because the Orthodox Jewish establishment is allowed too much control over governmental, legal, and private affairs, argues Uri Regev in the following viewpoint. Non-Orthodox and secular Israelis are subject to discriminatory Orthodox laws concerning marriage, divorce, adoption, conversion, and Sabbath activities, Regev points out. Israelis must continue to fight for democracy, pluralism, and civil rights to prevent the formation of a theocratic state, he concludes. Regev is the executive director of the Israel Religious Action Center (IRAC). As an advocate for the liberal Reform movement in Israel, IRAC promotes religious pluralism and social justice.

As you read, consider the following questions:

1. How did religion and state become linked in Israel, according to Regev?
2. According to the author, what are the restrictions on marriage in Israel?
3. In what ways has Israel's Supreme Court fought to defend civil liberties, in Regev's opinion?

Excerpted from Uri Regev, "Background: Religion and State in Israel," online report of the Israel Religious Action Center (IRAC), 1997, at www.irac.org/message/back.html. Reprinted by permission of the author, who wishes to state that this material is not updated and gives only a general background of the issue.

In the United States, human and civil rights are better protected than in most places around the world. Everyone is allowed to practice his/her religion freely, and religious freedom
is entrenched in the Constitution.

This is not the case for Jews in Israel. Despite assurances in its
Declaration of Independence, the Jewish state is the only democracy in the world where Jews do not have full religious freedom.
For Israeli Jews, all lifecycle events and other religious matters
that require State sanction—e.g. marriage, divorce, conversion
and kashrut (code of dietary regulations)—come under the authority of the Orthodox religious establishment. This establishment consists of the Chief Rabbinate, local religious councils,
Rabbinical courts, the Ministry of Religious Affairs (historically
and currently controlled by one of the Orthodox parties) and
various interlocking Orthodox institutions.

Israel does not have a written constitution or bill of rights
and all legislative power is vested in the Knesset [the Israeli par-
liament]. Unlike the United States Supreme Court which can re-
scind laws that violate or restrict religious freedom, the Israeli
High Court does not have that authority.

RELIGION AND STATE IN ISRAEL

The linkage of Religion and State in Israel dates back to the Ottoman Period (the Turkish rule over Palestine until 1917) which
granted autonomy in religious matters to the different communities and subjected the members of these communities to their
respective clergy. The British Mandate over Palestine (1917–
1948) essentially left this system in place.

After the establishment of the State of Israel in 1948, legislation passed by the Knesset reiterated the monopoly of the Orthodox religious establishment and law. The Rabbinical Courts
Jurisdiction (Marriage and Divorce) Law (1953) provides that
"matters of marriage and divorce of Jews in Israel, being nation-
als or residents of the State, shall be under the exclusive jurisdiction of [Orthodox] rabbinical courts" and that "marriages and
divorces of Jews shall be performed in Israel in accordance with
Jewish religious law [interpreted by the courts to mean Orthodox halacha]."

This state of affairs, which is commonly referred to as the status quo, recently received substantial exposure on account of
the struggle to close down a major thoroughfare in Jerusalem
on the Sabbath and ensuing attacks on the Supreme Court and
its Chief Justice, Professor Aaron Barak. The status quo refers to
the precedents established during one of two points in time—at

the founding of the State of Israel in 1948, or until the Orthodox were no longer a part of the ruling coalition in 1992. Under the status quo, for instance, public transportation exists on the Sabbath in Haifa but not in any other Israeli city.

The most striking expression of the Orthodox monopoly in religious matters concerning the Jewish community is in the area of personal status, marriage and divorce. This violates not only freedom of religion in the narrow sense of the term but also freedom from religion and the basic human right of founding a family. In Israel there is no civil marriage and the only way to marry and start a family is through the religious Orthodox authority. As a result of this, Reform and Conservative rabbis are unable to perform legally recognized marriages in Israel, and members of their congregations or other Jewish couples who seek their services do not have access to a liberal marriage ceremony. Secular Israeli couples have no civil marriage options. The ability to marry is denied altogether in Israel on account of ritual restrictions required by the Orthodox rabbinate. . . .

THE INTOLERANCE OF ORTHODOX PARTIES

Disturbingly, some Jews are given less religious freedom in their own homeland than in most Western democracies. Israel has become a sad example of what happens when religion and government merge. . . .

One wonders if the Zionist ideal, an ideal that cherishes self-determination and dignity for all Jews, still drives the soul of the Jewish state. The Orthodox religious parties have a history of being anti-Zionist. Their self-serving desire to declare Conservative and Reform Jews, their rabbis, cantors, educators and lay leaders anti-Jewish is a modern application of their doleful history.

Michael Gotlieb, *San Diego Union-Tribune*, November 23, 1997.

The Orthodox control remains inviolate concerning matters of person status, and extends to all aspects of Israeli life. In 1992 the Knesset passed a constitutional bill entitled Basic Law: Freedom of Occupation. In part, based on this law, the Supreme Court has declared illegal the established governmental policies of not allowing the import of non-kosher meat into Israel. Following pressure by the religious political parties, the basic law has been amended to facilitate the passing of an explicit bill which outlaws import of non-kosher meat. A meat importer is currently challenging the legality of the amendment and the new bill in the Supreme Court. On October 15, 1996, the Knesset passed the first reading of a bill which will extend by two years the time needed to change the basic law.

In a sectarian environment, as we have in Israel, both central and local government fund religious services for the public. Religious councils supervise these services and distribute public funding for their maintenance. Over the years these religious councils have refused funding for non-Orthodox Jewish religious institutions and excluded non-Orthodox Jews from membership on those very councils. This discriminatory policy has been successfully challenged by the Israel Religious Action Center (IRAC) and the Association for Civil Rights in Israel (ACRI). The Supreme Court declared the disqualification of Reform and Conservative Jews illegal and voided city council votes where non-Orthodox candidates have been turned down on the basis of their religious beliefs and practices. In spite of such unanimous Supreme Court rulings, which have for instance, twice voided such votes of the Jerusalem City Council, the city still refuses to abide by the ruling. IRAC was scheduled to return to the Court for the third time on October 8, 1996. Because IRAC was given insufficient time to plead its case, the Court scheduled another hearing in the ensuing weeks. This example highlights the religious coercion and sectarian pressures in Israel which deny equality and religious pluralism and undermine the rule of law and the authority of the judiciary.

RELIGIOUS VERSUS CIVIL COURTS

There is a tension in Israel between two separate court systems, the religious courts on the one hand (for the Jewish community, rabbinical courts) and the civil courts on the other hand, which have parallel jurisdiction in some matters of personal status. According to civil law in Israel, a married woman enjoys joint property rights. That concept is alien to Jewish religious law. A few years ago, the Supreme Court voided a ruling by a rabbinical court which denied the joint property rights of a wife, and held that in property matters, it is inconceivable that a woman would be stripped of her rights merely because of a change of judicial forum. It further held that although the rabbinical courts were empowered to apply religious law on matters of marriage and divorce for all Jews in Israel, this application was limited only to the actual status of marriage and divorce and could not be expanded to cover property rights. The Supreme Court further held that the religious courts were bound by civil law regarding property rights and were required to apply it. This ruling was met with vehement criticism from Orthodox circles and their political allies and fueled an attempt to curtail the authority of the Supreme Court and bar it from interfering with issues of religion and state.

Adoption law in Israel is limited only to instances where both the child and the adoptive parents share the same religion. This results in the impossibility of an intermarried couple adopting a child in Israel. IRAC is currently representing a couple where the wife is an Israeli born Jew who is married to a man of Swiss Christian origin. Both spouses consider themselves to be secular but are unable to adopt under Israeli law because of their religious affiliation.

A 1995 ruling of the majority of the Supreme Court (representing six of the seven Justices) upheld IRAC's legal argument and declared illegal the basis on which the State justified its distinction between conversions performed overseas and those performed in Israel. In doing so, the Supreme Court rejected the only legal grounds that the State proposed for discriminating against non-Orthodox conversions performed in Israel. The majority opinion further ruled that the question of defining Jewish status for the purpose of the Law of Return [which grants every Jew the right to immigrate to Israel] and the Population Registry is not subject to the approval of the Chief Rabbinate and should not be decided according to halacha [Jewish law], but rather according to secular liberal concepts.

In the meantime, and to the extent that the Knesset does not enact further legislation on the matter, Chief Justice Barak stated that the governing principle in interpreting the law should be the definition of a Jew used in the Law of Return. Orthodox Knesset members immediately submitted a draft bill proposing that the Chief Rabbinate be the only arbiter of the validity of conversions in Israel. The Likud party has consented to the Orthodox religious parties' demands to include this rule in the Guidelines of the New Government. This represents a clear attempt to circumvent and contradict the Supreme Court ruling. According to the Guidelines, the Chief Rabbinate would be the only authority to decide the validity of conversion in Israel.

As a result of their political power, Israeli Orthodox institutions are heavily funded by the state. Reform and Conservative Judaism have only recently begun to receive some small allocations for their programs and institutions, and this occurred only after hard-won court battles initiated by the Israel Religious Action Center.

Archaeological research in Israel is constantly met with strong opposition from religious circles in instances where excavations are viewed as desecrating the dead. Following religious

Orthodox political pressure, the Antiquities Law in Israel has been molded so as to exclude anthropological research from the scope of archaeology and there is mounting pressure to further amend the law so as to make archaeological research in areas where ancient grave sites existed conditional upon approval by the rabbinical authorities.

Because of religious opposition and the maintenance of the so called status quo on religious affairs, public transportation is almost thoroughly prohibited in Israel. The result is that mobility on the weekend is dependent upon economic means and is denied of people who cannot afford private automobiles.

The status quo continues to be maintained because the Orthodox political parties play a key role in the current government coalition and have held a "swing vote" in the Knesset in most previous governments. In recent elections, the Orthodox religious parties received less than 20 percent of the votes. However, since they are essential to Prime Minister Benjamin Netanyahu's coalition, they were able to dictate provisions in the Coalition Agreements and Guidelines of the New Government specifically delineating religious bills.

FEW PROTECTIONS FOR CIVIL LIBERTIES

It should be noted that the majority of the Jewish public in Israel objects to the status quo and resents the Orthodox monopoly. However, public opinion does not find expression in the political arena because of the nature of the current political and electoral system in Israel.

In Israel, no political party has ever been able to obtain an overall majority in the elections, with the result that it has always been necessary to form a coalition government. The religious parties have served as an integral partner in these coalition governments, both left and right wing. Even in governments where they did not serve, such as the previous government headed by Yitzhak Rabin, the ruling party sought to include them in the coalition and to expand its power base when the coalition did not depend on the religious parties (such as the unity government that existed following the 1988 elections). The ruling party attempted to keep on good terms with the religious parties in anticipation of the need for a future coalition. The same often applies to local government as well. As a result, neither the Knesset nor the government has provided much protection to civil liberties and personal freedoms in areas of religion and state. . . .

A fierce debate has recently arisen regarding the role of the

Supreme Court and the function of judicial review. Attacks have been mounted orally and in writing by ultra-Orthodox political and media circles against the Supreme Court and its Chief Justice, Professor Aaron Barak. These attacks have been clearly motivated by the realization that the Supreme Court has emerged as a defender of civil liberties and are intended to maintain Orthodox control and emasculate the Supreme Court.

The Supreme Court has emerged as the major defender of democracy and civil liberties, even while being handicapped by the lack of a written constitution. In recent years, the Supreme Court has (often at the initiative of IRAC) overturned long-practiced discriminatory policies. Examples include equitable entitlement to state funding to non-Orthodox religious institutions, entitlement of non-Orthodox Jews to sit on religious councils, recognition of non-Orthodox conversions in Israel, instituting non-Orthodox burials, etc. The Orthodox political and rabbinical establishment has identified the fact that the Supreme Court is the main challenge to their monopolistic powers and prerogatives. Given their ambivalent, if not outright, hostility to democracy, the rule of law and due process, they have targeted the Supreme Court and specifically Chief Justice Barak as the arch-enemies of Judaism and have been attempting to curtail the review powers.

It is too early to foresee what the future dynamics will be between the Supreme Court and the Knesset. There is overwhelming public support for the Court and for judicial review. A public opinion poll IRAC conducted recently shows a clear majority supporting Supreme Court intervention in matters of Religion and State. At the same time, it is clear that the governing coalition is driven by strong pressures to undermine the Court. Prime Minister Netanyahu has expressed himself, in a meeting which IRAC organized prior to his election, in the clearest terms against judicial review and a constitution for Israel. Clearly, support for IRAC and other similar organizations that work in the field of strengthening democracy, religious freedom and civil rights in Israel is crucial.

All of this further highlights the vital role that our work plays in maintaining the democratic character of the State of Israel and stemming the tide of those wishing to push Israel in the direction of a theocratic society. The Israel Religious Action Center has labored with increasing impact and success for the advancement of both religious freedom and pluralism as well as democracy and civil rights. In the coming years we will find ourselves faced with yet greater challenges in the battle for the soul of Israel.

| "No one ever calls the progressive forces extremist, but that is what they are becoming."

SECULAR EXTREMISM IS A THREAT TO ISRAEL

Tom Bethell

In the following viewpoint, Tom Bethell maintains that Israel is embroiled in a cultural war between religious and secular forces. While many claim that the tenets of the Orthodox religious establishment are creating discord, it is really the actions of the secular constituency that have incited conflict, Bethell argues. Orthodox Jews are facing discrimination and scorn from increasingly extremist and fanatical secular forces, he contends. Bethell is a correspondent for the *American Spectator*, a monthly conservative journal.

As you read, consider the following questions:
1. According to Bethell, what group of people founded the state of Israel?
2. According to the author, how has the Israeli controversy over Jewish identity been misinterpreted in the United States?
3. What is fanatical about Yossi Beilin's opinions on Oslo, in Bethell's opinion?

Reprinted from Tom Bethell, "Whose Country Is It?" *The American Spectator*, January 1998, by permission of the author.

I spent a week in Jerusalem, and what an extraordinary city it is. My visit was arranged by the Institute for Advanced Strategic and Political Studies, a think tank that has mostly concentrated on Israel's excessively socialist economy, and now is paying attention to cultural considerations as well. Old photographs show that before the state of Israel was created, little more than barren waste and bare hills existed outside the tumbled walls of the Old City. Today Jerusalem covers a huge area and it is sobering to reflect how much was achieved despite the tireless obstruction of a socialist bureaucracy. What might have been done without it! Jerusalem today is much more than a city restored, of course. You sense that what happens there is of significance to the rest of the world.

When Mark Twain visited Jerusalem he portrayed it as a comic backwater, the ruined reality in sharp contrast to its illustrious name. Arab goatherds trod the barren terrain. It illustrated time's mockery of history; another Troy in the making. How improbable the more recent transformation. How unforeseen. And how impossible to see it as a mere coincidence that the three great religions of the world somehow meet at a physical point; with the Via Dolorosa and the site of the Crucifixion little more than a stone's throw from the mosque called the Dome of the Rock; itself perched atop the foundations of the Second Temple. Here, as nowhere else in the world, geography is destiny. Pascal in the mid–seventeenth century said how amazing it was that the Jews had survived as a separate entity for 4,000 years. How much more amazed would he have been to know that, 300 years later, they would return to the Holy Land. To me, at any rate, it is an astonishing thing. It gives a shape and meaning to history that it otherwise would not have.

ISRAEL'S CULTURAL WAR

I think that those who think about this subject at all are mostly made uncomfortable by it, perhaps the Jews in particular. The idea of "chosenness" is not only at odds with the egalitarian ethos, but is about as far removed from it as could possibly be. Among non-Jews the idea is also unpopular (outside some Christian fundamentalist circles) and it seems to form no part of the contemporary discussion of national or international politics. It seems so outlandish an idea, so alien to the modern world, that it is usually dismissed out of hand. Others who may suspect its truth fear its political ramifications. But no particular "ought" follows logically from this "is." The belief that Israel demonstrates the hand of God in history can on the one hand lead to passivity and quiescence (if God is in charge, why not wait patiently on the sidelines?); on the other, to intense activism (demonstrated by those who start settlements in places like Hebron, hoping to hasten the Messiah's return).

This by way of background—as I see it, the only illuminating one—to the growing cultural war in Israel. At its most elemental, it is a conflict between the secular and religious worldviews. As may be imagined, within the precincts of the Holy Land, it is heated and will no doubt become more so. Little has been written about it in the U.S., where the press, unlike its Israeli counterpart, is dedicated to the proposition that the Jews are united. No such proposition can be sustained in Israel itself. As the Israeli journalist Ze'ev Chafetz told me in Jerusalem: "Nations boast of what they have least of. Arabs talk about honor; we talk about Jewish unity."

The balance of power is something like this. The ultra-orthodox religious community is about 20 percent of the population, and they hold 23 of the 120 seats in the Knesset, or parliament. The secular may be about 25 percent. This leaves a large middle ground who neither deny God nor eat Kosher food nor observe the Sabbath. Deputy housing minister Meir Porush of the Torah Judaism Party told me that if the criteria for observance are fasting on the day of Atonement, marriage according to Jewish law, and lighting candles on Passover, then "more than 70 percent" are observant.

But these figures give little idea of the intensity of the conflict. When the British controlled Palestine after World War I, Chaim Weizmann and the Zionist Executive collaborated with quotas that prevented most religious or oriental Jews from immigrating. The state of Israel was founded by secular socialists who dominated the country for decades. "I am in favor of Bolshevism," said the first prime minister, David Ben Gurion. In 1948 the Soviet Union cast its crucial United Nations vote in favor of the new state. The idea was that it would become a beacon of progressive humanism, a secular light unto the nations. But that god failed, and even as the Berlin Wall fell and the Soviet Union collapsed, a new wave of immigrants, almost a million strong, arrived in Israel from Russia. It was time for a new faith, which is to say the old faith; the God of Abraham and Isaac and Jacob.

In the minds of many secular Israelis, this old superstition was supposed to have . . . well, withered away by now. But increasingly Jerusalem was populated by these bearded, frock-coated, black suited gents with hats and skull-caps, nodding and bowing and praying and strapping on their phylacteries before the Western Wall, avoiding birth control and filling up neighborhoods with their numerous children, throwing stones at cars, cordoning off streets, disrupting archeological digs. Moreover they believed (for it said so in the Bible) that God had given this land to the Jews in perpetuity and for that reason weren't too enthusiastic about surrendering it for the promise of peace. Obviously they were fanatics, or extremists, or both.

Israel's Religious War

It was the frogs that Yossi Werzansky wanted to hear. In the evenings, they would start up, calling to one another in the swampy field just beyond Werzansky's new home in suburban Pardess Hannah, Israel. Then one day came a different cacophony. Werzansky's new, ultra-Orthodox neighbors had set up a loudspeaker and were broadcasting sermons from a rented house they had turned into a synagogue. Infuriated, the community's secular majority retaliated, organizing a weekly Sabbath-night disco in the next house to outblast the worshippers. A fire bombing and a melee soon followed.

Such is the state of relations, generally, between religious and secular Israelis these days. As Israel celebrates its 50th anniversary, its citizens identify the rift over religion as their No. 1 problem. With the country well established and peace in the region a growing reality, Israelis are fighting among themselves as never before. "For 50 years, we had an external enemy who obliged us to lower the tenor of our internal tensions," says author A.B. Yehoshua. "But the external enemy doesn't unite us anymore."

Lisa Beyer, *Time*, May 11, 1998.

Here is a recent comment from Yosef Lapid, an editorial writer for *Ma'ariv*, a left-wing newspaper. His column was headlined: "It Just Isn't My Country Anymore":

Jerusalem used to have an eccentric minority, a vestige of the ghettoes of Lodz and Casablanca, sanctifying superstitions, fasting on strange days, locking its women up in the delivery room, keeping its men in yeshivas [divinity schools], far away from reality, from the 20th century. It was a curiosity. Today this curiosity has become a vast, ever expanding army. And it is taking over our lives.

Then again, a frequently heard comment is that, while the influence of the ultra-orthodox is increasing, so is the Americanization of the culture. Dedi Zucker, one of nine Knesset members in the left-wing party called Meretz, told me that Israel is actually becoming more secular.

"The number of places open on the Sabbath has increased eight times in the last ten years," he said. "Television didn't operate at all on Friday evening and Saturday," whereas now it does. The orthodox rabbinical court has a monopoly on marriage and divorce. Yet between 1974 and 1995, while the population doubled, the number of marriages performed by the rabbinate remained unchanged. "That tells you that people found non-religious alternatives," such as marriage in Cyprus, or by mail-order from Mexico and Uruguay.

"Both sides are right," I was told by Yair Sheleg, a reporter with the newspaper *Ha'aretz,* also on the left. "Today, members of the religious parties have 23 seats in the Knesset, up from 16 in 1948. And they are increasing in numbers. Meanwhile, the secular side is getting stronger in the life of the street. In the eyes of the religious, the posters are more immodest, the legitimacy of homosexuality and lesbianism is growing, many cinemas and clubs are open on the Sabbath, even in Jerusalem. So you can see that both sides have facts for their fears. This is the main reason for the new tension."

The secular forces have also discovered, again showing American influence, that the judiciary can be a handy weapon for the progressives. Lawsuits have been used to by-pass the Knesset, and this is the origin of the controversy over Jewish identity. It has been (mis)represented in the U.S. as the claim that the non-orthodox are not recognized as Jews in Israel; Prime Minister Benjamin Netanyahu himself has called up U.S. newspapers to correct the error, which, as it stands, helps the Reform and Conservative congregations raise funds and is intended to do just that. Above all, the erroneous interpretation disguises the cultural aggression of the secular—the use of courts they dominate to overturn the status quo—as aggression by the orthodox.

Secular Cultural Aggression

The ill-starred "peace process" has also made a major contribution to the cultural war. The Oslo Accord [the mid-1990s peace negotiations between Israelis and Palestinians] was no doubt the most divisive event in the history of modern Israel. A pure surrender of territory was camouflaged as a *quid pro quo*: "peace" would be offered in return. But everyone understood that Yasser Arafat didn't have to do anything—certainly not amend the Palestine Liberation Organization (PLO) Charter as promised. In return for shaking Yitzhak Rabin's hand he would receive land, and then money from the "international community." Israel's participation delegitimized its earlier capture and tenure of the land, and above all (by entering into the agreement) Israel implicitly accepted that the absence of peace had all along been its fault.

The orthodox took the view that the land was not Rabin's to give and strongly opposed its surrender. In turn, shortly before he was assassinated, Rabin dismissed the Bible as an "antiquated land registry." (More recently, Ezer Weizmann, the president of Israel, has questioned the good sense of the Book of Deuteronomy.) The minister of education in the 1992 Labor government insisted that all references to God be eliminated from armed forces memorial services and declared Jewish dietary laws to be unnecessary. The deputy minister ordered religious teachers purged from the state school system. Former foreign minister Shimon Peres (prime architect of "land for peace") has argued that Israel should join the Arab League, and his deputy, Yossi Beilin, called for Jewish aid to the PLO. A new code of ethics for the Israeli Defense Forces claimed that "democracy" is what they are defending and rejected all references to the land of Israel, and to the Jewish state and people.

According to Yoram Hazony of the Shalem Center in Jerusalem, the man appointed to head a committee to reform the history curriculum used media interviews "to compare orthodox Jewish children to Hitler Youth, the Bible to Mein Kampf, and the armed forces to the SS." I was told that in state-subsidized avant-garde theater in Israel these days, Jewish characters are beginning to appear on stage wearing Nazi uniforms.

No one ever calls the progressive forces extremist, but that is what they are becoming. Notice that the Ma'ariv writer contrasted the "reality"-based secular vision with the "superstitions" of the orthodox. Yet in their assessment of Arab intentions, which are not peace-loving, the orthodox are far more realistic. Consider this from Yossi Beilin, explaining Oslo to skeptics: "I want to live in a world where the solution to our existential problem is possible. I have no proof that this really is the case, [but] I am simply not prepared to live in a world where things are unsolvable." Here an influential politician frankly substitutes his preferred world for the real one and makes policy on that basis. That is fanaticism.

It occurred to me when I left Israel that the difference between that country and the U.S. is that it has a substantial community that is not intimidated by the cultural power of the secular forces. You might say that Israel really does have a "religious right." That's what makes their cultural war more interesting than ours. Theirs has two sides.

| "The most intractable and dangerous obstacle to peace [is] intolerance fueled by religious dogma and personalities."

MUSLIM LEADERS PROMOTE TERRORISM AGAINST ISRAEL

Abraham Cooper

In the following viewpoint, Abraham Cooper contends that Islamic spiritual leaders encourage terrorism by refusing to disclaim the belief that Muslims become martyred heroes by engaging in suicide attacks against Israel. Although many Muslim leaders seem eager to promote peaceful Islamic-Jewish relations, they have not spoken out in public to condemn the fundamentalist fanaticism that leads to terrorism, Cooper maintains. Cooper is a rabbi and the associate dean of the Simon Wiesenthal Center in Los Angeles, California.

As you read, consider the following questions:

1. According to Cooper, what is a *fatwa*?
2. How did Jewish religious leaders respond to Yigal Amir's assassination of Yitzhak Rabin, according to the author?
3. In Cooper's opinion, what should the secular world do in response to anti-Israeli terrorism?

Reprinted from Abraham Cooper, "No Heaven for These Martyrs," *Los Angeles Times*, March 5, 1996, by permission of the author.

As Israel reels from the latest terrorist outrages in Tel Aviv and Jerusalem, I recall my last conversation with the late Yitzhak Rabin. It took place at the prime minister's Jerusalem office on Aug. 21, 1995. Earlier that day, a Hamas suicide bomber had blown up a packed city bus virtually within earshot of Rabin's desk. [Hamas is an acronym for the Islamic Resistance Movement, a Palestinian group.]

The day before, dean of the Simon Wiesenthal Center Rabbi Marvin Hier and I met with the grand mufti of Egypt. We were the first Jewish leaders ever to talk with the spiritual leader of 60 million Sunni Muslims. We told Rabin that the grand mufti, who had questioned peace with Israel and derided the Jewish faith in some of his early writings, used our two-hour meeting to speak of tolerance and the need for dialogue.

Rabin, while encouraged by this news, nonetheless pointedly asked, "Do you think he is prepared to issue a public *fatwa* (a ruling by a religious leader) against suicide killings by Muslims?" Rabin said that Israel had desperately, but unsuccessfully searched for a respected Muslim religious scholar in the region to publicly rebuke the notion that a suicide attack against men, women and children earns the killer martyr status and automatic entrance to heaven.

THE NEED FOR PUBLIC DIALOGUE

The much publicized Arab-Israeli territorial negotiations have helped accelerate dialogue between Muslim and Jewish leaders. Rabbi Hier and I have met with the imam of Jericho and the Ayatollah Rouhani, who is the leading Shiite cleric in Europe. Religious leaders from Morocco, at the behest of King Hassan II, attended a Wiesenthal Center sponsored conference in Paris. All indicated a desire to help write a new chapter in Islamic-Jewish relations. Such substantive contacts would have been unheard of a few short years ago and their importance cannot be minimized.

Still, it is the question about the missing *fatwa* posed by Rabin, who himself would soon be assassinated by a Jewish extremist invoking God's name, that lies at the heart of the problem. His query speaks to the most intractable and dangerous obstacle to peace: intolerance fueled by religious dogma and personalities. The stakes go way beyond Hamas' attacks against innocent Israelis. Deadly terrorist attacks by fundamentalists have driven tourism from Egypt; car bombs and bloody attacks on journalists and foreigners in Algeria have helped bring that North African nation to the brink of utter chaos.

While the Jewish world is still reeling from the implications that the Rabin assassination was committed by a religious Jew, at least our religious scholars have openly discussed and publicly refuted Yigal Amir's attempt to invoke the *halacha* (Jewish law) to justify his murderous action. Rabbis and Talmudic scholars understood that their silence on this could lead to a breach in Judaism's firewall between zealotry and murder.

Lurie's World ©1992 Worldwide Copyright by Cartoonews International Syndicate, N.Y.C., USA. Reprinted with permission.

What has been lacking in the Muslim world is a parallel public debate and unequivocal pronouncements by their spiritual leaders. If the leaders would speak out, Islam's faithful would respond. Anyone doubting the impact of a *fatwa* should consult Salman Rushdie. [In 1989, Iran's Ayatollah Khomeini issued a *fatwa* demanding the assassination of Rushdie for blasphemy against Islam in his novel *The Satanic Verses*. Iran retracted this *fatwa* in 1998.]

DESTROYING TERRORISM

In the meantime, there is plenty that the secular world can do. World leaders should stop invoking the hollow mantra that terrorist attacks should not be allowed to derail peace. Instead, it is time to make the attackers and those who refuse to destroy terrorism's infrastructure pay a price high enough to change their behavior. Civilized nations would do well to revisit the Rushdie affair. They successfully stared down the radical Mullahs and the powerful regime standing behind their outrageous *fatwa*. In wake of the horrific scenes on the streets of Jerusalem and Tel Aviv, failure to do anything less could help bring the fanatic clerics closer to their most cherished dream: the destruction of Israel.

| "Hamas [the Islamic Resistance Movement] has used military operations to retaliate for what it feels are acts of terror by the Israeli government against the Palestinian people."

ISRAEL PROMOTES TERRORISM AGAINST MUSLIMS

Ahmad Yusuf, interviewed by *Middle East Quarterly*

In the following viewpoint, Ahmad Yusuf contends that Israelis procure land by committing terrorist acts against Palestinian Muslims. Islamic liberation movements, such as Hamas, are often accused of anti-Semitic terrorism; however, Hamas has used violence solely in retaliation for Israel's terrorism against Palestinians, Yusuf maintains. Yusuf is the executive director of the United Association for Studies and Research, an Islamist think tank based in Annandale, Virginia. He is also the editor of the *Middle East Affairs Journal*. Yusuf is interviewed by *Middle East Quarterly*, a periodical published by the Middle East Forum. The forum works to define and promote American interests in the Middle East.

As you read, consider the following questions:

1. What is Yusuf's reason for quoting the *hadith* that predicts the Muslim defeat of the Jews?
2. What are the goals of Hamas, according to the author?
3. According to Yusuf, how many Palestinian civilians were killed after Defense Minister Yitzhak Rabin issued an order of "force, might, and beatings" in January 1988?

Excerpted from Ahmad Yusuf, "Hamas Is a Charitable Organization," *Middle East Quarterly*, March 1998. Reprinted by permission of the *Middle East Quarterly*.

M iddle East Quarterly: *You have written that "God has promised that when the Muslims fight the Jews, the Muslims will vanquish them." This sounds like a call for Muslims to attack Jews in Israel, in the U.S., and everywhere else around the globe; is it?*

Ahmad Yusuf: The actual quote is, "God has promised that the Muslims will fight the Jews and defeat them." I took this from an authentic Islamic *hadith* (or tradition) that does not say when this defeat will happen or where. It only says that it will happen. My objective in using this quote is to assure the Palestinian people that one day justice will be realized and to encourage them to continue their struggles with the assurance of victory against the occupation. It is not a call to attack Jews in Israel or anywhere else. Palestinians as a rule are opposed to expansionist Zionism, not to the Jewish faith, or to Jews or any other race or religion.

HAMAS

Is Hamas a terrorist group?

No. Hamas was founded during the *intifada* [the Palestinian uprising of 1987–1990] and it operated within the confines of the Geneva Convention. It later became a charitable and social service organization in the West Bank and Gaza, helping Palestinians forced off of their land and into unimaginable suffering, humiliation and poverty.

What about the fact that one component of Hamas, namely the 'Izz ad-Din al-Qassam Brigades, claimed credit for several attacks on innocent civilians?

If this makes Hamas a terrorist group, then the Israeli government is a terrorist government and the Israeli military and security forces, as well as their agents, are also terrorist. The bombings of Israelis, according to an interview on 60 *Minutes* with Hamas member Hasan Salama, are at least sometimes in retaliation for Israeli terror against Palestinians.

As Ehud Sprinzak of the Hebrew University writes, "Hamas only resorted to this atrocious type of terrorism after February 1994, when Baruch Goldstein, an Israeli physician and army reserve captain massacred 29 praying Palestinians in a Hebron shrine." Since the massacre, the Israeli government has built a shrine to Goldstein in Kiryat Arba, where he is memorialized as a "martyr." Based on Dr. Sprinzak's observations, Hamas has used military operations to retaliate for what it feels are acts of terror by the Israeli government against the Palestinian people. . . .

On what basis do you claim the Israeli government is terrorist?

Terror can be defined as a state of intense fear or fright. So a terrorist is one who uses intense fear or fright to coerce others. In this sense of the word, every soldier is a terrorist and every government in the world sponsors terrorism to some extent. Leah Rabin, widow of the late Israeli prime minister Yitzak Rabin, said prior to a meeting with Secretary Madeleine Albright, "I have doubt about how much terrorism can be uprooted. We were also terrorist once, and they did not uproot us and we went on dealing in terrorist activities. Despite all the efforts of all the British army in the land, we went on with terrorism."

DISGUISED ACTS OF TERROR

Dictionary definitions and common understanding of what terrorism is involve the infliction of grave bodily harm, intense fright, prolonged horror or panic. It can mean the use of terrorizing methods of governing; in other words, "terrorism" requires the sanction of authorized government or its proxy. It is practiced also to resist a government. . . .

Throughout the Israeli occupation [of Palestine], newspapers in Israel have reported many acts of violence—I would call them terrorism—against the Palestinian communities of the West Bank and Gaza. But not only does the world media—especially in the U.S.—fail to report these acts of mayhem, they are disguised as actions for "law and order," not what they are—acts of terror.

Edna Homa Hunt, *Washington Report on Middle East Affairs*, August/September 1997.

Let's look at the record. Defense Minister Yitzak Rabin on January 21, 1988, issued an order of "force, might, and beatings" against Palestinian youth involved in the *intifada,* which led to 1,600 unarmed civilians—including women and children—being murdered for throwing rocks, plus 100,000 Palestinians wounded and 120,000 imprisoned. In February 1988, a hidden camera crew recorded the brutal bludgeoning to death of two Palestinian teenagers by Israeli soldiers on an isolated hillside. . . . The purpose of these murders is pure and simple: to terrorize the Palestinian people, forcing them to leave their homes and land so they can be taken over by Jewish settlers.

Well, I'd challenge you to produce tapes of the February 1988 event, for no such killings took place.

I am not in possession of the tapes, but as a journalist I viewed them, and I assumed that the severity and brutality of the beatings caused the young men to die either on the spot or soon after.

Do you consider the suicide bombings in Jerusalem in July and September 1997, carried out by Hamas, to have been terrorist attacks?

In my opinion, based on Dr. Sprinzak's observations, Hamas

uses military operations in retaliation for what it considers acts of terror against the Palestinian people by the Israeli government. *Are such attacks as those by Hamas legitimate "resistance"?*

I use the word "resistance" to define the Hamas movement because that is how Hamas has defined itself; "Hamas" is an acronym for the Islamic Resistance Movement. The organization has never claimed that its military attacks are strategic but that they are always retaliatory. Hamas reserves its right to resist occupation within a purely national context, as sanctioned by the Geneva Convention. The Hamas movement is much more than these attacks; it embodies the socio-political expressions of the Palestinian people. The Palestinian people and Muslims generally consider it a legitimate resistance movement. . . .

Noting that the Hamas covenant (Article 32) cites the Protocols of the Elders of Zion and in two places calls for the killing of Jews, do you consider Hamas to be an antisemitic organization?

Every paper we have published by experts analyzing the Hamas movement has said there is no evidence Hamas is antisemitic or that its activities are directed toward Jews by virtue of their race or religion. Hamas policies are directed toward the Israeli occupation and are limited to Palestine.

"Fundamentalists built their
theocracy on the premise that
women are physically, intellectually,
and morally inferior to men, which
eclipses the possibility of equal
participation in any area of social or
political activity."

ISLAMIC FUNDAMENTALISM
SUPPRESSES IRANIAN WOMEN

Donna M. Hughes

Women in Iran face repression under an Islamic fundamentalist
government, maintains Donna M. Hughes in the following viewpoint. Iranian women are denied equal participation in family
life, public activities, education, employment, and politics, she
reports. Although many women are demanding civil rights, they
are still subject to strict dress codes, gender segregation, and restrictions on freedom of expression. Iran's women should not
expect the fundamentalist leadership to ever entertain any no-
tions concerning female empowerment, Hughes concludes.
Hughes is the director of the women's studies program at the
University of Rhode Island in Kingston.

As you read, consider the following questions:
1. According to Hughes, what punishments are given to Iranian
   women who break the dress code?
2. What are Mohammed Khatami's views on the emancipation
   of women, in Hughes's opinion?
3. What is temporary marriage, according to the author?

Reprinted from Donna M. Hughes, "Women in Iran," Z Magazine, October 1998, by
permission of Z Magazine.

Women in Iran want equality, respect, and the right to participate in all social, political, and economic activities. They want to live their lives productively and with dignity. Throughout the 20th Century Iranian women have organized and fought for human and political rights, from the Constitutional Revolution at the turn of the century to the democratic movement that overthrew the Shah of Iran.

Iranian women were strong participants in the 1979 revolution, but fundamentalists, led by Ayatollah Ruhollah Khomeini, seized control after the revolution. Once in power, the fundamentalists betrayed the work of women by implementing a crushing system of gender apartheid. Fundamentalists built their theocracy on the premise that women are physically, intellectually, and morally inferior to men, which eclipses the possibility of equal participation in any area of social or political activity. Biological determinism prescribes women's roles and duties to be child bearing and care taking, and providing comfort and satisfaction to husbands.

RESTRICTIVE POLICIES

Men were granted the power to make all family decisions, including the movement of women and custody of the children. "Your wife, who is your possession, is in fact, your slave," is the mullah's legal view of women's status. The misogyny of the mullahs made women the embodiment of sexual seduction and vice. To protect the sexual morality of society, women had to be covered and banned from engaging in "immodest" activity.

Based on these woman-hating principles, Khomeini and his followers crafted laws and policies that are still in effect. The hejab, or dress code, is mandatory in all public places for all women. Women must cover their hair and body except for their face and hands and they must not use cosmetics. Punishments range from a verbal reprimand to 74 lashes with a whip to imprisonment for one month to a year. Stoning to death is a legal form of punishment for sexual misconduct. Women are banned from pursuing higher education in 91 of 169 fields of study and must be taught in segregated classrooms. A woman may work with her husband's permission, although many occupations are forbidden to women.

The legal age at which girls can be married is 9 years (formerly 18 years). Polygamy is legal, with men permitted to have four wives and an unlimited number of temporary wives. Women are not permitted to travel or acquire a passport without their husband's written permission. A woman is not permitted to be in the company of a man who is not her husband or a male relative. Public activities are segregated. Women are not allowed to engage in sports in which they may be seen by men; or permitted to watch men's sports in which men's legs are not fully covered.

Although these laws were implemented with great brutality, women have always resisted. Recently in Iran there have been signs that women are increasingly rejecting subordinate lives ruled by the mullahs. Women have campaigned for inheritance rights equal to men's and for more rights to custody of their children. Women keep modifying or enhancing their public dress in ways that press the limits of the hejab. More publications by or about women are appearing. Women are demanding they be allowed to participate in and view sports events.

DOES KHATAMI SUPPORT WOMEN'S RIGHTS?

Some analysts have said that the election of Mohammed Khatami as president was due to the votes of women. No doubt Khatami's upset election in 1997 gained him the label of "moderate," and raised expectations of people inside and outside of Iran.

There is a widely held view that Khatami supports the rights of women, but his statements and appointments don't validate that view. Prior to his election Khatami said, "One of the West's most serious mistakes was the emancipation of women, which led to the disintegration of families. Staying at home does not mean marginalization. Being a housewife does not prevent a woman from having a role in the destiny of her people. We should not think that social activity means working outside the home. Housekeeping is among one of the most important jobs."

Under Khatami's leadership the Supreme Council of the Cultural Revolution decided not to sign the United Nations Convention on the Elimination of All Forms of Discrimination Against Women (CEDAW), the most important international agreement on the rights of women. An international study comparing workforce conditions for women around the world ranked Iran 108 out of 110. In urban areas women make up only 9.5 percent of the workforce, and in rural areas the percent is 8.8 percent. Even Khatami's advisor on women's affairs acknowledged that there is discrimination in employment and promotion against women in government offices: "Some officials are of the opinion that men have more of a role in running the family, so they favor the men."

Khatami's advisor on women's affairs, Zahra Shoja'l, says she is an advocate of women's rights, but all within a fundamentalist defined Islamic context. She defends the restrictive and symbolically oppressive hejab, calling the chador "the superior national dress of the women of Iran."

Plantu/*Le Monde*. Reprinted by permission of the Cartoonists & Writers Syndicate.

Khatami's highly publicized woman appointment is Massoumeh Ebtekar, vice-president for Environmental Protection. She has a long association with the fundamentalists: after the Islamic Revolution in 1979 she was spokesperson for the hostage takers who captured the U.S. embassy in Tehran. She does not favor loosening restrictions on women that would give them more personal freedom or stop the most barbaric institutionalized violence against women. She supports the law that requires women to get their husband's permission to travel. She justifies this law by saying, "Man is responsible for the financial affairs and safety of the family. Thus, a woman needs her husband's permission to make a trip. Otherwise problems will arise and lead to quarrels between them." She also defends stoning women to death by saying, "One should take psychological and legal affairs of the society into consideration as well. If the regular rules of family are broken, it would result in many complicated and grave consequences for all of the society."

Since Khatami was not the hard-line mullahs' favored candidate for presidency, his election has created factions within the Iranian government. A power struggle has ensued, but this is not an ideological fight between those loyal to religious fundamentalists and proponents of secular democracy. All sides, including Khatami, are committed to a theocracy based on *velayat-e-fahiq*—the absolute supremacy of the mullahs.

CLOTHING AS CRIME

Women's public clothing continues to obsess the mullahs. In 1997, the Martyr Ghodusi Judicial Center, a main branch of the judiciary, issued a stricter hejab, or dress code. The new guidelines call for prison terms from 3 months to 1 year or fines and up to 74 lashes with a whip for wearing "modish outfits, such as suits and skirt without a long overcoat on top." The regulations ban any mini or short-sleeved overcoat, and the wearing of any "depraved, showy and glittery object on hats, necklaces, earring, belts, bracelets, glasses, headbands, rings, neckscarfs and ties."

Women continue to be arrested for improper veiling. In November 1997, an Agence France Presse correspondent in Tehran witnessed approximately ten young women being arrested and placed into a patrol car for improper veiling or wearing clothing that did not conform to Islamic regulations. The women were wearing colorful headscarves and light makeup. In late July 1998, the Tehran police arrested a number of young women who failed to conform to the strict dress code. They were boarded on minibuses and taken to a center for fighting "social corruption." Most of the women were wearing makeup or in the company of young males who were not related to them.

CONTINUING REPRESSION

Under fundamentalist's interpretation of Islamic texts, women are banned from being judges because they are not considered capable of making important decisions. One of the claims of moderation in Iran is the appointment of women as judges, but in reality no women are allowed this rank. Judiciary Chief Yazdi recently made the issue clear in his Friday prayers sermon: "The women judges I mentioned hold positions in the judiciary, they receive salaries, they attend trials, they provide counsel, but they do not preside over trials and/or issue verdicts."

In 1998, women's groups campaigned for a bill that would give women the same inheritance rights as men, but Parliament overwhelmingly rejected the bill saying the proposal was contrary to Islamic law, which stipulates that a woman's share may only be one half that of a man's.

Women made a small gain by getting Parliament to pass a law that granted women some custody rights to children after a divorce, but only if the father was determined to be a drug addict, an alcoholic, or "morally corrupt."

GENDER APARTHEID

New laws strengthening gender apartheid and repression of women are not a thing of the past. During 1997 Parliament and other religious leaders proposed a number of new laws and policies that will adversely affect the health, education, and well being of women and girl children in Iran.

Temporary marriage, in which a man can marry a woman for a limited period of time, even one hour, in exchange for money, is permitted in Iran. In 1998, Ayatollah Haeri Shirazi, a prominent religious leader called for a revival of this practice so clerical officials could have religious sanctioned sexual relationships with women. This practice is an approved form of sexual exploitation of women and allows the regime to have an official network of prostitution.

A new law approved by Parliament imposes more restrictions on the photographs of women that can be published in newspapers and magazines. The Iranian state television announced on August 1, 1998, a decision by the Justice Department in Tehran to shut down a newspaper and put its proprietor on trial. One of the charges leveled against the publication, *Khaneh*, was that it had published "obscene" photographs of women playing football.

Parliamentary deputies submitted a plan to make girls' schools a "no-male zone," which will require all teachers and staff to be women. This requirement will make education for girls even more inaccessible and difficult. Official statistics recently released reveal that 90 percent of girls in rural districts drop out of school.

More ominously, the Parliament also approved a law prohibiting the discussion of women's issues or rights outside the interpretation of Shari'a (Islamic law) established by the ruling mullahs.

In early July 1998, Mohsen Saidzadeh, a cleric, was arrested after writing articles that opposed these bills. He said that laws that deprive women of their rights are based on incorrect interpretations of the Koran. So freedom to criticize the government

121

position on the rights of women does not exist even for fellow mullahs.

In some Western writings Khatami is said to have given new freedoms to the press, but the experience of publishers is contrary to that claim. In February 1998, the newspaper *Jameah* started to publish articles critical of the government, color photographs of smiling women harvesting wheat, and an interview with a former prisoner. By June a court revoked their license. Also, police filed charges against *Zanan*, a monthly women's magazine, for "insulting" the police force by publishing an article on the problems women face with the authorities on Iranian beaches, which are segregated by sex.

No Moderation in Iran

Although Khatami is the president of Iran, he is not the supreme spiritual leader, the most powerful position in Iran. The supreme leader, Ayatollah Ali Khamenei, controls the armed forces, the police, the security and intelligence services, radio and television, and the judicial system. The *velayat-e-fahiq* is a serious impediment to any reforms that may benefit women or society at large. Ayatollah Khamenei's opinion of women and their place in society is the same as his predecessor Ayatollah Khomeini's: women should be wives and mothers. Supreme leader Ayatollah Ali Khamenei has publicly stated: "The real value of a woman is measured by how much she makes the family environment for her husband and children like a paradise." In July 1997, Ayatollah Khamenei said that the idea of women's equal participation in society was "negative, primitive and childish."

There is no moderation in Iran. Both the UN special rapporteur and the U.S. state department found that there was no improvement in human rights in Iran since Khatami took office. The Iranian government engaged in summary executions, extrajudicial killings, disappearances, and widespread use of torture. The hard-line mullahs will not lift the severe restrictions on women; in fact, they favor stronger gender apartheid. Khatami, although not aligned with the hard-liners, does not support the empowerment and emancipation of women from the *velayat-e-fahiq* or supreme rule of the mullahs. If the women in Iran want the rights and freedoms they deserve they will have to look elsewhere for change.

| "'By their *sheer* numbers, women are challenging the Islamic Republic to change,' says political scientist Farideh Farhi."

IRANIAN WOMEN ARE CHALLENGING ISLAMIC FUNDAMENTALISM

Part I: Scott MacLeod, Part II: Lindsey Hilsum

The authors of the following two-part viewpoint argue that a growing women's movement is challenging the restrictive policies of Iran's Islamic fundamentalist government. In Part I, freelance writer Scott MacLeod reports that Iranian women are contesting discriminatory laws and voting in large numbers for moderate political candidates. In Part II, broadcast journalist Lindsey Hilsum maintains that a growing population of literate, educated women are widening the rift in Iran between the conservative religious forces and a liberalized, urbane culture.

As you read, consider the following questions:

1. According to MacLeod, what percentage of Iranian women approved of moderate candidate Mohammed Khatami in Iran's 1997 presidential election?
2. What new legislation have Islamic clerics proposed to help curb Iranian feminism, according to MacLeod?
3. In Hilsum's opinion, what small signs of change reveal feminist defiance in Iran?

I

Ever since its 1979 revolution the image of Iran's women has been the long, black chador. To the outside world, Iranian women appear to live in medieval isolation, obedient to their husbands and to the mullahs who make the rules on what they can wear, where they can go and whom they can kiss.

So how to explain Faezeh Hashemi, a mother of two children who has become the most outspoken member of the Iranian parliament? She recently joined a political demonstration that was violently broken up by thugs after she criticized the policies of Islamic hard-liners. What about magazine editor Shahla Sherkat, whose monthly *Zanan* (*Women*) has won an enthusiastic readership by exposing the often tragic results of laws favoring men in child custody cases? Or Sherin Ebadi, an internationally recognized human rights lawyer who took on the defense of an Iranian writer accused of espionage?

During the past few years women of Iran have launched a struggle to moderate Iran's hard-line policies and ease the strict social guidelines put in place by the late Ayatullah [Ruhollah] Khomeini's Islamic Revolution. "By their sheer numbers, women are challenging the Islamic Republic to change," says political scientist Farideh Farhi, a former professor at the university of Hawaii. "Women have refused to play dead."

Such activism is striking, especially in comparison with such countries as Saudi Arabia, where the ruling royal family still forbids women to drive, or Afghanistan, where the new Taliban regime limited education for girls. In Iran, women are demanding and sometimes winning modification of discriminatory legislation. For example, a husband may no longer obtain a divorce automatically and without sizable alimony. This year [1998], for the first time, more women than men took university entrance exams, and women are moving up in sectors like banking and taking jobs once exclusively male, such as bus driving.

Moreover, women have achieved power in politics that no ayatullah can afford to ignore: opinion surveys show that more than 80% of women, often disregarding their husbands' preferences, favored President Mohammed Khatami in last year's [1997] presidential election. That propelled the moderate reformer to a surprise win and put political and social change on Iran's agenda. Since Khatami's inauguration a year ago women have taken advantage of the loosening climate to increase their visibility in everything from politics to sports. Khatami appointed the country's first female vice president, hosted an international women's sporting competition and has fostered the opening of a wide debate on women's rights. Iranian feminists optimistically held the "first annual" fair of women publishers, and women led a 10,000-strong protest demonstration against discriminatory child custody laws. About 5,000 defied public segregation regulations to attend a welcome home celebration for Iran's World Cup football squad.

The progress is relative, of course, and often literally cosmetic. More Iranian women are discarding the drab black chador in favor of tailored raincoats in bright colors. Young women can be seen holding hands with their boyfriends in public, behavior that can still get them into trouble. Hard-liners, including powerful figures like Supreme Leader Ayatullah Ali Khamenei, cannot give in to such change without abandoning the Islamic codes that stand behind their claim to theocratic rule. They have proposed new legislation aimed at blocking the incipient feminist revolution, including a law that would ban the voicing of opinions critical of what the mullahs deem to be the proper role of women.

IRANIAN WOMEN TAKE UP THE GAUNTLET

The women of Iran, . . . newly awakened to fresh possibilities, have taken up the gauntlet and, using the leadership's own rhetoric and logic, have held the government's feet to the fire in regard to implementing the "equality of men and women in Islam." They have seized the initiative to demand changes in education, in family laws, and in the workplace. . . . Out of the ashes of the revolution may rise a new female identity, one whose cultural and ideological authenticity give it the legitimacy to question and contest many of the traditionally oppressive institutions supposedly sanctified by Islam—whether polygyny, divorce, or seclusion. Grasping the moment, women have forged a vocal voice, a visible (if veiled) presence, and a viable women's movement through which to realize their aspirations.

Nesta Ramazani, *Middle East Journal*, Summer 1993.

And, despite their growing power, women are very much second-class citizens in the Islamic Republic. They technically remain the virtual property of men: girls can be married off age nine, wives may not go out after dark without their husbands' consent, and mothers have no rights to child custody following a divorce. Publisher Shahla Lahiji feels Khatami has done too little to pay his political debt to women, but concedes, "We know it is not easy."

What they do have is the right to vote, and they are using it. Besides their role in putting Khatami into the presidency, women voters made Faezeh Hashemi the second-biggest vote-getter nationwide in 1996 legislative elections. Hashemi's success lies partly in fact that she stands as a symbol of both past and future. She is the daughter of former President Ali Akbar Hashemi Rafsanjani, a shrewd politician who straddles the fence between hard-liners and moderates, favors bright colors but wears the chador out of respect for her tradition-minded supporters. But as Iran's husbands are fast discovering, there is a growing determination beneath those long, black garments.

II

In Tehran, Iran, change is in the air. It's not just that the US secretary of state, Madeleine Albright, made a speech suggesting the two enemy countries could begin to repair relations, nor even the prospect of European oil companies reinvesting. It's to do with the girls playing volleyball in the park, and the young clerics discussing a less authoritarian form of theocratic state. In the Islamic Republic, there is no dividing line between religion, culture, society and government: the outcome of the political struggle will determine not just who holds power but how people live.

Under Iran's constitution, committees of clerics hold most of the political and economic power, with Ayatollah Ali Khamenei, the Supreme Leader, at the head. The democratically elected president cannot therefore take on the old guard directly. Instead, President Muhammed Khatami, dedicated to reform, is trying to foster a new feeling on the streets.

Iran has the youngest electorate in the world. Fifteen year olds have the franchise. Young people and women voted for President Khatami in May 1997. The tens of thousands of teenagers who martyred themselves for the glory of the Islamic Republic during the eight-year war against Iraq are national heroes, and demand to be taken seriously. The youths now want a voice as well as a vote.

SIGNS OF CHANGE

The outer signs of change are small but significant, and women are in the forefront. They must still be cloaked from head to toe in hijab, the all-concealing cloak and headscarf which has come to symbolise to the world Islamic orthodoxy. But the once-dreaded neighbourhood komiteh thugs who used to beat women in the street for "bad hijab" have lost their zeal. In Tehran, young women are pushing their headscarves back to reveal a little more hair. Wearing make-up has become a feminist statement. Football victories have brought boys and girls out on to the streets to dance together—something unthinkable in the dreary days of revolutionary fervour.

"We have to recognise the fact that young people's understanding, their interpretation of the revolution, might be quite different from ours," says Massoumeh Ebtekar, one of Iran's seven vice-presidents and arguably the most powerful woman in the country.

Ebtekar is a political survivor. She speaks only reluctantly about her own youthful aspirations. Dubbed "Sister Mary" by the media because of her nunlike attire, in 1979 she acted as interpreter for the revolutionaries who seized the hostages at the American embassy. She appeared nightly on American television, threatening the hostages and restating the tenets of Islamic purity. She spoke perfect English—not surprisingly, as she was raised in Philadelphia.

Today she sits, clothed in strict grey and black hijab, not showing a wisp of hair or a trace of make-up, below a magnificent stuffed peacock secured to her office wall. Aged 44, the mother of two boys, she is a close political adviser to President Khatami. She looks back on the American embassy siege without regret. "I think that was . . . a necessity of the revolution that led to our national dignity," she said.

It is hard to cut through Ebtekar's Beijing UN women's conference jargon—"empowering women", "enhancing human development", having a "gender perspective"—but she is clear about change and how it affects women. "We now have an emerging elite of educated, expert women in different fields. Two decades ago the literacy rate was quite low. Now more than 70 per cent of Iranian women are literate. Forty per cent of university students are women. This means a genuine change has occurred in ... the condition and status of women."

IRAN'S NEW WOMEN

Twenty-two-year-old Mona Zaheed is one of Iran's new women. She studies film at Tehran University, and hopes to join the growing number of Iranian film directors achieving recognition at home and overseas. On a sunny Saturday morning she and fellow students gathered round an outside table next to a mural of Charlie Chaplin at Tehran's newly built Bahman Cultural Centre. The students were attending a film festival and, if it weren't for the women all sheathed in hijab, it could have been a gathering of young movie enthusiasts in New York or Bristol, discussing their favourite foreign film directors. Hollywood films are not shown publicly, but middle-class people with video players get hold of copies the moment they come out in the USA; this group saw *Titanic* before it was released in Britain.

Like other Iranian film-makers, Mona Zaheed's work is oblique and symbolic, personal and not directly political. The film she is working on now features a little girl who protests about the way her father wields power in the family. Zaheed sees herself as the beneficiary of Iran's decade-long awakening from the Iran-Iraq war. "Then we could do nothing. There was just no money. Now much more is possible," she says.

But how much? It would be a mistake to see reformers such as Ebtekar as anything other than Ayatollah Khomeini's heirs. No one is talking of a secular state. President Khatami has said Iran should adopt new technology, but satellite television is banned for all but a select few politicians, journalists and international hotels. The president talks of a "dialogue between civilisations", but Ebtekar is passionate in her hatred of polluting western ideas. "These media have the power to shape people's minds [and the way] societies and nations think . . . it's a new form of occupying a country. Instead of attacking with armed forces you transform the culture. Instead of people going for their national dress, they start wearing jeans."

Young Iranian women have been wearing jeans under the hijab for years. The unanswered question is: will a significant number of them want to throw off the veil completely? No one knows how much change young Iranians want, but an outward show of liberalisation will not be enough. This will prove especially true when the government, as it has promised, allows increased access to the Internet.

The new encouragement of cultural exchanges with the United States also means that middle-class young people will learn more about western society. Indeed, as the old social structures break down under economic pressure, the appeal of foreign ideas will not be limited to the middle class. New suburbs in Iran's sprawling cities have no mosque and no bazaar, the traditional structures for disseminating Islamic values. The split between a cosmopolitan urban society and a conservative, rural Iran where the word of the mullah is never gainsaid seems likely to widen.

PERIODICAL BIBLIOGRAPHY

The following articles have been selected to supplement the diverse views presented in this chapter. Addresses are provided for periodicals not indexed in the *Readers' Guide to Periodical Literature*, the *Alternative Press Index*, the *Social Sciences Index*, or the *Index to Legal Periodicals and Books*.

Lisa Beyer	"The Religious Wars," *Time*, May 11, 1998.
Mark Dow	"'Amiable Visionaries' and the Israeli-Palestinian Conflict," *New Politics*, Summer 1996.
Samira Fellah	"Algeria: Women in the Firing Line," *International Viewpoint*, March 1995.
Marc Gopin	"Carnal Israel: The Future of Jewish Spirituality in the Age of Zionism," *Tikkun*, May/June 1998.
Charles Hirschkind	"What Is Political Islam?" *Middle East Report*, October–December 1997.
Paul Hockenos	"Getting Religion," *In These Times*, April 15–28, 1996.
John Lancaster	"A Fundamental Cooling Down," *Washington Post National Weekly Edition*, April 1–7, 1996. Available from Reprints, 1150 15th St. NW, Washington, DC 20071.
Ira M. Lapidus	"A Sober Survey of the Islamic World," *Orbis*, Summer 1996.
Bernard Lewis	"Islam and Liberal Democracy: A Historical Overview," *Journal of Democracy*, April 1996.
Charles S. Liebman and Asher Cohen	"Synagogue and State," *Harvard International Review*, Spring 1998. Available from University Microfilms, Inc., 300 N. Zeeb Rd., PO Box 1346, Ann Arbor, MI 48106-1346.
Judy Mabro	"Through a Veil Darkly," *Index on Censorship*, May/June 1998.
Taslima Nasrin	"On Islamic Fundamentalism," *Humanist*, July/August 1996.
Abdulaziz Sachedina	"What Is Islam?" *World & I*, September 1997. Available from 3600 New York Ave. NE, Washington, DC 20002.
Emmanuel Sivan	"Why Radical Muslims Aren't Taking Over Governments," *Middle East Quarterly*, December 1997. Available from Middle East Forum, 1920 Chestnut St., Suite 600, Philadelphia, PA 19103.

WHAT ROLE SHOULD THE U.S. PLAY IN THE MIDDLE EAST?

CHAPTER PREFACE

In August 1990, Iraq invaded Kuwait, a small oil-rich nation on the northwestern tip of the Persian Gulf. The ambitions of Iraqi president Saddam Hussein were to procure the wealth needed to pay off debts incurred during the 1980s Iran-Iraq war and to acquire a large harbor on the gulf. Many in the West feared that Iraq's actions imperiled world oil supplies, and American president George Bush dispatched U.S. troops to the gulf to preempt a possible Iraqi invasion of Saudi Arabia. Soon afterwards, the UN imposed economic sanctions on Iraq and authorized the use of force if Iraq did not withdraw from Kuwait by January 15, 1991. Iraq refused to comply, and starting on January 16, U.S. forces led more than a month of allied military assaults on Iraq.

Iraq surrendered in February 1991. However, sanctions against Iraq continued, and in April 1991, the UN passed Resolution 687, requiring Iraq to destroy all of its biological, chemical, and nuclear weapons. The UN formed a Special Commission on Iraq (UNSCOM) to monitor Iraq's compliance with Resolution 687, stipulating that the lifting of sanctions was contingent on Iraq's cooperation with weapons inspectors. Throughout the 1990s, Iraq occasionally barred UNSCOM from inspecting certain sites. Iraq has also continued to be a threat to neighboring nations and to its own ethnic and religious minorities: In 1992, Iraq bombed Shi'ite rebels in the south; in 1994, Iraqi troops again threatened to invade Kuwait; in 1996, Iraqi commandos raided Kurdish areas in the north.

The United States continues to face dilemmas over its support of punitive actions against Iraq. Since the Gulf War, the U.S. has launched missiles into Iraq in response to the attacks on Kurds; the U.S. has also bombed Iraq in retaliation for Hussein's refusal to comply with UN weapons inspectors. Hardliners argue that sanctions and military actions are necessary because Saddam Hussein is ruthless and does not respond to anything but force. Others, however, contend that sanctions and military strikes should end because they harm innocent Iraqi civilians. Still others maintain that the U.S. should focus on bringing Hussein down by assassination or by providing support for Iraqi dissident groups.

In the following chapter, commentators and policymakers present additional debates over the role of the U.S. in Middle Eastern affairs.

| "We as a nation are not comfortable
with the current state of affairs, and
we cannot afford to be complacent."

THE U.S. SHOULD MAINTAIN AN
ACTIVE ROLE IN THE MIDDLE EAST

Robert H. Pelletreau

Robert H. Pelletreau is the assistant U.S. secretary of state for
Near Eastern affairs. In the following viewpoint, Pelletreau argues that the United States must maintain its active role in Middle Eastern affairs. The United States has been responsible for
forwarding the Arab-Israeli peace process and must continue to
ensure the stability of the region by deterring terrorism, containing rogue states, ensuring the free flow of oil, and advancing human rights, Pelletreau maintains. This viewpoint was
originally a speech delivered to the Chautauqua Institution in
Chautauqua, New York, on August 21, 1996.

As you read, consider the following questions:

1. According to Pelletreau, in what way does progress in the
   Arab-Israeli peace process affect the stability of the Middle
   East?
2. In what way did the 1991 Gulf War prove to be a watershed,
   in the author's opinion?
3. According to historian Bernard Lewis, cited by Pelletreau,
   who are the real enemies of peace?

Excerpted from Robert H. Pelletreau's speech, "U.S. Policy Toward the Middle East:
Steering a Steady Course," delivered to the Chautauqua Institution, Chautauqua, N.Y.,
August 21, 1996.

Amerian diplomacy over the years has worked hard to bridge the Arab-Israeli divide, at no time harder and more successfully than during the Clinton Administration. Today, at least part of that divide has been bridged: Israel and Jordan are at peace, as Israel and Egypt before them. The Palestinians and Israel have concluded several agreements on the way to working out the terms of their co-existence, and Syria and Israel have expressed interest in finding a common basis for negotiations. It is fair to say that the core of the Arab-Israeli agenda has moved on from how to make and avoid war to how to make peace and how to make peace bring economic and other benefits for those who have courageously reached agreements across the negotiating table.

ENGAGING U.S. INTERESTS

Everyone in this audience is aware that we live in a time of rapid and fundamental change in world politics. The end of the Cold War has challenged analysts, policymakers, and the American public to make sense of a fluid international situation. Halfway between the end of the Cold War and a new century, Americans are debating such basic questions as how to engage internationally to advance national goals, when to use force to protect our national interests, and how we can best support international institutions like the United Nations and the World Bank.

Finding our bearings in a complex world was not always as difficult as it is today. For more than 40 years, our foreign policy was governed by a single, overriding goal—to contain the Soviet Union's expansionist tendencies. It was never an easy task to contain a massive empire armed with nuclear weapons and the capacity to threaten our interests around the world. During the Cold War, flare-ups in tension regularly occurred, but at least our goals were clear to everyone. Building new security alliances and institutions, forging close ties with other nations, and providing foreign assistance all contributed to this clear purpose.

Today, most current and foreseeable threats to our interests from other nations do not jeopardize the actual survival of the United States. Other nations do not even jeopardize our prosperity except through improvements in their own international economic competitiveness. We have even embarked on a cloudy and still incomplete program of cooperation with our erstwhile Russian opponents. Yet, we as a nation are not comfortable with the current state of affairs, and we cannot afford to be complacent. Terrorism disrupts our tranquility both at home and abroad, and the proliferation of weapons of mass destruction has not been adequately checked. Ethnic conflicts rage on several continents. Global problems of daunting dimensions such as population growth, desertification, disappearance of the rain forests, and global warming are all growing.

A NEW FOREIGN POLICY PARADIGM

When Americans look out over the world, they can take pride in the fact that more people live free and at peace than ever before. But is that enough? Can we be certain that positive trends will continue and negative ones will wither without our active leadership, engagement, and financial underpinning?

These are questions which are driving the restless search for a convincing new paradigm for U.S. foreign policy in [the 1990s]. At the beginning of the [1990s], we heard there was a "new world order" and that America had a free hand to lead the international community in turning back such lawless acts as Saddam Hussein's invasion of Kuwait. We were also told that the "end of history" was at hand, with democracy and the free market triumphing over communism and all other possible forms of human organization.

But then the paradigms took a pessimistic turn. There were lurid predictions of "coming anarchy" in a world where nation-states would collapse under the weight of overcrowded, ungovernable cities and roving bands of lawless thugs. Finally, we heard that we were teetering toward a "clash of civilizations," where traditional fault lines between peoples and cultures would widen and tear apart the fragile political and economic ties that bind the world's nations.

Each of these paradigms is by necessity oversimplified, and each contains important insights into the central question: What are our interests and how do we pursue them? But none so far has provided a convincing answer.

In the Middle East, I would argue, our interests are broadly engaged, no matter what paradigms we apply. Standing threats like aggression by rogue states such as Iraq against our allies and oil supplies loom large as ever. New threats represented by the terrorists who bombed U.S. troops in Saudi Arabia underline the need to maintain a strong and vigilant stance in the region.

THE U.S. STAKE IN THE MIDDLE EAST

Let me be more specific at interests in the Middle East. They include, first and foremost, achieving a just, comprehensive, secure, durable Arab-Israeli peace; helping maintain the security and well-being of Israel; preventing regional conflicts and supporting friendly nations; ensuring the free flow of oil from the Gulf upon which we and the other industrial nations depend for our economic security; enhancing business opportunities for our companies and jobs for our citizens; suppressing terrorism and the spread of weapons of mass destruction; containing rogue regimes in Iran, Iraq, and Libya; advancing respect for human rights, the rule of law, and open and participatory societies; and preserving the deep cultural ties we have to the origins of Western civilization and the birthplace of the great monotheistic religions—Judaism, Christianity, and Islam. All of these give our nation a concrete and lasting stake in the Middle East.

Many of these interests and objectives overlap, and sometimes they cross cut. The peace process, for example, profoundly influences the stability of the entire region. The work of every U.S. ambassador in the region is made easier if there is an active peace process with strong U.S. involvement. Progress in the peace process strengthens governments in Egypt, Jordan, and Saudi Arabia and others which are friendly to the U.S.; it helps isolate Iran and Iraq whose leaders are hostile; and it helps secure our access to Persian Gulf oil. The absence of progress in the peace process, on the other hand, increases tensions and spurs rearmament and violence, endangering our access to oil and undercutting Israeli security. These are only a few examples of the interconnectedness of developments in the Middle East. In general, a successful peace process enhances regional stability, removes a rallying point for fanaticism, and enhances prospects for political and economic development. With so many complex interests at stake, the United States cannot step back from this turbulent and difficult sector of the globe, however tempting it might be at times. Let me now sketch what the United States has been doing to promote Arab-Israeli peace and bring a more peaceful and secure life to the people of Israel and the Palestinians, Syrians, Lebanese, Jordanians, and Egyptians who are their neighbors.

THE LONG QUEST FOR PEACE

The goal of peace between Israel and the Arab world has been a cornerstone of our Middle East policy since the Truman Administration. The Israel-Egypt peace brokered at Camp David by President [Jimmy] Carter was a significant breakthrough. But after that, until the 1990s, progress toward this goal was limited. The climate for peacemaking was poor. Israel and the Arabs shared a profound animosity, suspicion, and sense of vulnerability. Both sides saw themselves as victims; neither side could contemplate compromise on the scale necessary for peace.

For decades, the Middle East was a tinderbox, threatening to embroil us in its deadly wars. This volatility was aggravated by Soviet efforts to gain influence through fueling radicalism and conflict. The Arab-Israeli conflict emboldened radicals, intimidated moderates, and left Israel—except for its friendship with the United States—in a lonely state of siege.

Throughout the long struggle, only one Arab state—Egypt, under the extraordinary leadership of Anwar Sadat—bravely bridged the Arab-Israeli divide to make peace with Israel. For [more than 17] years, that heroic achievement has held strong. Egypt stood nearly alone until 1993, when Israel and the Palestinians signed the Declaration of Principles on the White House lawn and the Arab world began to see that Egypt, its largest and most powerful member, was in reality a pathfinder rather than a pariah.

AMERICA'S COMMITMENT TO PEACE IN THE MIDEAST

America's commitment to peace and security in the Middle East has historically been a bipartisan commitment, stretching from the administrations of Truman and Eisenhower to Bush and Clinton. Because that commitment involves the security of a cherished ally and the vital strategic interests of the United States, our leaders have historically stood together in support of Israel, and shoulder to shoulder with our Arab friends in pursuit of peace. If America is to play its proper role in promoting stability in the Middle East, it is imperative that our leaders now—in the Executive Branch, in Congress, and within the Jewish-American and Arab-American communities—continue to work together on behalf of shared goals.

Madeleine Albright, *Vital Speeches of the Day*, June 1, 1998.

It was not until the Cold War began to wane that new opportunities arose to promote peace. The Gulf War was a watershed. With the United States and its coalition partners working together, Saddam Hussein's invasion of Kuwait and bid to become the dominant power in the Gulf were decisively turned back. Our overwhelming display of power, principle, and leadership during the Gulf War provided us with enhanced influence in the Middle East. It also tilted the regional balance of power toward moderate forces committed to peace and stability. We moved rigorously to seize the historic opportunity for peace in 1990 and 1991 because we know that, in the Middle East, such opportunities do not last very long.

The current peace process was launched in October 1991 in what we generally refer to as the Madrid Middle East peace conference, co-sponsored by the United States and the Soviet Union. As our ambassador to Egypt, I was a member of our delegation. It was a moving experience to see, for the first time in my professional career, Israel, the Palestinians, Jordan, Syria, Lebanon, Egypt, the Europeans, Russia, and the United States together around one table, each saying in his own way, "Let's try to reach a peaceful settlement." The Madrid conference launched a series of bilateral and multilateral talks that proved useful in shattering taboos on political dialogue and helping each side to focus on the practical concerns of the other side. This architecture of mutually reinforcing bilateral and multilateral levels of negotiation has proven both resilient and productive, enabling us to overcome serious obstacles and make some remarkable progress.

BREAKTHROUGH IN 1993

The first real breakthrough after the Madrid conference was the dramatic moment on the White House lawn in September 1993 when Chairman [Yasser] Arafat and Prime Minister [Yitzhak] Rabin reached out and shook hands following the signing of the Israel-PLO [Palestine Liberation Organization] Declaration of Principles. With mutual recognition and a mechanism for resolving differences through negotiation and compromise, the Declaration marked a true turning point in the history of the Israeli and Palestinian communities.

In the . . . years since the signing of the Declaration, Israel and the Palestinians have been engaged in almost continuous negotiations. These talks have resulted in landmark agreements, including the comprehensive Interim Agreement signed in Washington [in] September [1995]. As a result of these agreements, Palestinians now govern themselves throughout Gaza and most cities of the West Bank. Israeli soldiers no longer face the burden of patroling those streets. Where once there was an intifada [Palestinian uprising], Israeli and Palestinian security forces now cooperate to root out the terrorist infrastructure of Hamas and the Palestinian Islamic Jihad.

We have emphasized to the Palestinians that the success of this process will depend on the confidence they engender in their Israeli partners. In response to Hamas suicide bombings in Israel [early in 1996], Chairman Arafat, with strong U.S. encouragement, has taken serious and effective steps against the Hamas infrastructure and has made important progress toward eliminating its terrorist capabilities. Cooperation between Palestinian and Israeli security services has improved. The United States has stressed to Arafat and other Palestinian leaders the need to keep up a comprehensive, sustained, and systematic approach to combating terrorism within the rule of law.

We have also stressed the importance of continuing to make progress on democracy and human rights. We were pleased to see that the Palestinians defied the Hamas call to boycott elections [in] January [1996] and gave Chairman Arafat and the Palestinian leadership a strong mandate to pursue peace. The Palestinian National Council subsequently voted by an overwhelming margin to cancel the anti-Israeli portions of the PLO charter.

TANGIBLE GAINS

These are no small achievements. They are tangible steps toward Arab-Israeli reconciliation and reflect the fundamental desire of the people of the region to secure what President [Bill] Clinton has characterized as the "quiet miracle" of normal life.

For Israel, these agreements with the Palestinians have begun to lift the heavy moral and political burden of ruling a hostile foreign population. Israel's elder statesman, Abba Eban, has pointed out other benefits. They include a bustling economy with Pacific Rim potential, a GNP [gross national product] rating that would delight any major industrial power, and a wider breach than Israel has ever known in the Great Wall of Arab and Moslem hostility. There is also a series of commercial commitments that may still carry the area to an unexpected renewal of its vitality.

With the psychological barrier between Israel and the Palestinians breached, there is a new basis for expanding interaction between Arabs and Israelis. In the past [several] years, Jordan has joined Egypt in signing a peace treaty with Israel. Over 100,000 Israelis have traveled to Jordan, and a large number of Jordanians have visited Israel. In many ways it has become a model peace, a warm peace with numerous sub-agreements being signed and joint exploration of areas of mutual benefit such as civil aviation and transport, trade and tourism, and development of water resources. Beyond Jordan, as many as eight Arab League members have made official visits to Israel, all but three Arab states have participated in some aspect of the peace process, and Israel has exchanged diplomatic offices with Morocco and Tunisia and opened commercial offices in Qatar and Oman. . . .

The U.S. is working with the Netanyahu government to keep up the momentum of Israeli-Arab cooperation across a broad range of issues. Sustaining our momentum requires a viable peace process which offers Arab partners incentives for progress. We are, therefore, encouraged that the Israeli Government has agreed to honor and abide by the agreements reached by its predecessors and has expressed its desire to continue the peace process and build on those agreements. It has recognized that important changes have taken place in the Middle East since the Likud [party] was last in power—new agreements, the beginnings of new relationships with the Arab states, and a new prosperity for Israel which has resulted at least in part from these political developments. . . . We have stressed to the [Israeli] government the key importance of intensifying channels of communication with the Palestinians, and we have cautioned about the harmful effect that major new settlement activity could have on the negotiating process. We have also impressed on Palestinian leaders the need for maximum effort and vigilance to root out and prevent acts of terrorism and respond to Israel's deep-seated security concerns which played such a large role in the [1996] elections. This would accelerate the current gradual relaxation of the tight closure imposed on Gaza and the West Bank and put renewed focus on promoting Palestinian economic development, which the United States strongly supports.

THE EXTREMIST CHALLENGE

Progress on the peace process has not, of course, been free of controversy or pain. With each step forward, there has been a determined challenge from the enemies of peace. The Princeton historian Bernard Lewis, who has viewed regional developments against a 2,000-year continuum of rivalry and conflict, has remarked that:

> The real threat to peace . . . comes from those who see any peace as a betrayal and a surrender. They will continue to use every means to prevent a peaceful end to their various holy wars. The test of all the seekers of peace will be their ability to cope with these forces.

One of the messages we received from Prime Minister [Benjamin] Netanyahu when he visited Washington [in July 1996] was that he is going to take a very determined approach to terrorism while Israel pursues peace with its neighbors.

That approach is certainly an approach we can support, and it is consistent with our own long-standing efforts to rally an international consensus against terrorism, turn off foreign sources of funding for terrorists, and track down and punish the perpetrators of terror, including state sponsors. We recognize that peace and security are indivisible. Waging peace and fighting terrorism are opposite sides of the same coin: You can't pursue peace in isolation, just as you can't deal with terrorism in isolation. You have to do both at the same time.

That is how we approached the suicide bombings in Israel in [early 1996], as well as the crisis involving Israel and Lebanon in April [1996]. Both represented not only human tragedies but serious challenges to security and the peace process.

In both cases, the United States took the initiative to deal with the immediate human crisis, safeguard the peace process, and refocus attention on negotiations. Following the suicide bombings in Israel, President Clinton initiated the Sharm el-Sheikh summit, which brought together leaders from around the world to send a clear message that terrorism from any source must be confronted and beaten.

In the Lebanon crisis, the understanding brokered by Secretary [Warren] Christopher allowed people to return to their homes and will protect civilians on both sides of the Israel-Lebanon border.

The Secretary spent more than a week in the Middle East shuttling seven times between Damascus and Jerusalem to resolve the crisis. It was a grueling exercise. At one point, we had to trade in our Air Force 707 for a C-141 owing to crew rest requirements. At another, we had to enter Lebanon via land convoy across the Bekaa Valley when the air route was judged too dangerous.

Secretary Christopher's work in bringing the parties to closure was one of the finest diplomatic performances I have witnessed. The set of understandings he negotiated to help defuse the conflict between Israel and Hezbollah guerrilla forces improved in several ways upon the U.S.-brokered understandings of 1993. . . .

ISRAEL, SYRIA, AND LEBANON

When Prime Minister Netanyahu was here, he stated that he had been elected to pursue peace with security and not to promote a stalemate. And he emphasized to us he was prepared to work with the U.S. to try to achieve those goals. He and his Foreign Minister have since stated repeatedly that they are prepared to negotiate peace with Syria. The Syrian Government has told us privately and publicly that it, too, is interested in negotiations. The Lebanese Government has been somewhat more reserved in public, but we are convinced that Lebanon also seeks peace. Just how these two tracks, which are separate but clearly linked, can be engaged productively is still being worked out.

We are encouraged by the recent public statements from Jerusalem and Damascus, but we are not under any illusion that achieving peace between Israel and Syria and Israel and Lebanon will be quick or easy. Their conflict has evolved over many years, and the resolution must evolve over time as well. We have long felt that peace between Israel and Syria is essential for closing the circle of peace and producing a comprehensive settlement. We are committed to working toward this goal. The effort must not be put on the shelf just because it is difficult. . . .

The United States stands ready, yes even determined, to facilitate dialogue and act as an honest broker whenever an opportunity for further peace negotiations arises. Let me close by saying that neither U.S. policy nor the U.S. posture has changed. We are actively working with the parties in the region to achieve our long-sought goal of a truly comprehensive and durable Middle East peace.

"[Middle East] states that resist the Pax Americana face economic and political isolation and no longer have a superpower sponsor to turn to for support."

U.S. INTERVENTION DOES NOT BENEFIT THE MIDDLE EAST

Stephen Hubbell

In the following viewpoint, Stephen Hubbell contends that the goal of U.S. intervention in the Middle East is to maintain oil prices at a rate favorable to American interests and to preserve an allegedly strategic alliance with Israeli elites. The United States claims to be concerned with suppressing terrorism, abuses of human rights, and the development of weapons of mass destruction. In actuality, Hubbell argues, the United States favors those nations that advance American strategic and economic objectives regardless of their record on human rights or weapons proliferation. Nations that harbor dissent with U.S. policy face damaging economic sanctions, political isolation, and military intervention, he maintains. Hubbell is an editor of *Middle East Report*, a monthly periodical.

As you read, consider the following questions:

1. In Hubbell's view, what rationalizations for U.S. interventionism arose after the disappearance of the Soviet Union?
2. What is the doctrine of dual containment, according to the author?
3. In Hubbell's opinion, how does the United States define a "rogue state"?

Abridged from Stephen Hubbell, "The Containment Myth," *Middle East Report*, Fall 1998; © MERIP 1998. Reprinted by permission of Blackwell Publishers.

Among those who direct American foreign policy, there is near-unanimity that the collapse of communism represents a kind of zero hour. The end of the Cold War so transformed the geopolitical landscape as to render the present era historically discontinuous from the epoch that preceded it. Policy makers contend that America's mission abroad has had to change to keep pace with these new circumstances.

For more than four decades, American intervention around the world was justified by the need to contain international communism. Containment proved to be a versatile and protean doctrine: it could be applied anywhere and tailored to almost any context. In the Middle East, Soviet expansionism was cited as the rationale behind the 1957 Eisenhower doctrine (which authorized backing for conservative rulers such as King Hussein of Jordan and Camille Chamoun of Lebanon, who were be-sieged by domestic opponents), and for adventures as varied as the overthrow of the Mossadegh government in Iran in 1953, support for Israel in the 1967 and 1973 wars, and the arming of US proxies in the Gulf. It hardly mattered that containment was singularly ill-suited to the specificities of the region. (The Arab states proved to be nearly impervious to Moscow's ideo-logical appeal.) What did matter was Americans' willingness to accept it as a sufficient justification for their government's machinations.

RATIONALIZING INTERVENTIONISM

The sudden disappearance of the Soviet Union compelled the Bush and Clinton administrations to ponder new rationaliza-tions for future interventions abroad. National Security Advisor Anthony Lake voiced the emerging consensus among the for-eign policy elite when he wrote, "[T]he successor to a doctrine of containment must be a strategy of enlargement of the world's free community of market democracies." Commercial and eco-nomic considerations and the promotion of democracy, he sug-gested, would henceforth replace military and political factors in guiding foreign policy.

The collapse of the Soviet empire has indeed wrought sub-stantial changes in the Middle East. . . . Moscow's departure from the world stage has considerably freed the United States to impose its will across the region. States that resist the *Pax Ameri-cana* face economic and political isolation and no longer have a superpower sponsor to turn to for support. Those who persist in challenging Washington's *diktat* can, as always, expect to feel the sting of American military might.

Yet no radical break with the past has occurred in US foreign policy toward the Middle East. What is remarkable is the degree of continuity in Washington's objectives in the region during and after the Cold War. Although circumstances have compelled policy makers to replace containment with a patchwork of contradictory and internally incoherent "doctrines," the chief purpose of the new guidelines—like their Cold War–era counterparts—is to obscure the actual motives of US intervention, which remain largely unchanged.

The twin pillars of American policy since the Gulf War have been the doctrine of dual containment of Iran and Iraq, and support for the now-moribund Arab-Israeli "peace process." In each case, the new policy conceals a surprising continuity with the perennial project of US interventionism: to secure the maximum possible advantage for American capital as it seeks access to markets and resources abroad. In the developing world, this project has necessitated creating and preserving a political environment friendly to the operation of international capital. To accomplish this, the US-led bloc has had to construct and defend an authoritarian order to resist challenges to its domination, while maintaining Israel's military edge over the collective might of Arab armies. (The promotion of democracy . . . was never a goal of US policy in the Middle East, nor is it now.) It is true that the imperatives of globalization and the transnationalization of capital have altered to some degree the form and methods of US intervention. But all available evidence indicates that, whatever doctrine is in favor in the post–Cold War Middle East, the fundamental goals have not changed. . . .

FROM ROLLBACK TO DUAL CONTAINMENT

The doctrine of dual containment was first introduced in 1993, two years after the allied victory in the Gulf War. Conventional balance-of-power theory had held that the region's natural leaders, Iraq and Iran, should be pitted against one another to prevent either from becoming dominant and jeopardizing the flow of oil to the West. By choosing to isolate both nations, however, the Bush administration committed itself to an ambitious program requiring an expanded US military and political presence in the Gulf. Dual containment had two immediate consequences, both of which contradicted the president's putative vision for a New World Order: US military force had to be deployed in the Gulf for an extended period to maintain constant pressure against Iran and Iraq; and Saudi Arabia—heretofore a second-tier proxy behind Washington's ally of the moment—had to be transformed, along with its Gulf neighbors, into a credible military counterweight in its own right. Thus, military force remained as necessary under the new dispensation as it was before. The results have been dramatic. In the three years following the end of the Gulf War, new weapons acquisitions by the Gulf states (Kuwait, Saudi Arabia, Qatar and the UAE) exceeded those of Iran by nearly 30-to-one. Saudi Arabia has emerged as the world's leading arms purchaser, acquiring weapons systems worth $36.4 billion from the United States alone between 1994 and 1997. (Many of these sales are, of course, financed by loans from American banks.) The number of American troops based in the region has swelled to 20,000; US taxpayers spend a staggering $50 billion annually to maintain and equip them. Cooperation between the domestic intelligence services of the US and Saudi Arabia has reached unprecedented levels, particularly following the 1996 Khobar Towers bombing. The US Fifth Fleet is now permanently based in Bahrain. Moreover, the Pentagon announced in 1997 that it was anticipating a 20–50 year deployment of US troops in the Gulf. The goal of this mobilization has been in part to protect the flow of petroleum by intimidating nations that challenge Washington's prerogative to set the terms of trade in the oil market. The maintenance of military expenditures in the region as the Soviet threat vanished is further evidence that, although superpower rivals may come and go, the thirst for oil is eternal.

It would be erroneous, however, to conclude that maintaining the flow of oil at prices favorable to US interests is the sole purpose behind US military mobilization. Of equal significance is Washington's desire to augment the integration of the American and Gulf states' economies. Profits from the sale of petroleum products are increasingly recycled back to the US through arms purchases, as well as through the bank loans such purchases enable.

WHAT IS A "ROGUE STATE"?

Dual containment was premised on the notion that "rogue states" posed the greatest threat to the West following the Soviet collapse. The priority given to containing the rogue states (whose ranks are rarely enumerated publicly, but presumed to include Iran, Iraq, Libya, Cuba, North Korea and, on occasion, Syria and Sudan) supposedly reflects Washington's growing concern about human rights, terrorism and the proliferation of weapons of mass destruction (WMD). The threat posed by the rogues is hardly imaginary: nearly all of them have chemical, biological or nuclear weapons programs and all have poor human rights records. It is clear, however, that their rogue status reflects not the magnitude of their crimes, but the extent of their dissent from US policy. By any rational standard, nations like Israel, Saudi Arabia and Egypt should also be listed among the rogues. Israel's failure to ratify the Nonproliferation Treaty and the 1972 biological and toxic weapons convention, which Iran, Libya and Saudi Arabia have all signed, merits no mention in the Defense Department's annual listing of WMD violators. Nor does Egypt's failure to sign the Chemical Weapons Convention. The bleak climate for human rights in these countries is also ignored. What sets them apart, of course, is their continuing usefulness as regional proxies and enforcers of Washington's strategic objectives.

The main virtue of the rogue state doctrine from the administration's perspective is that it provides a new pretext to "contain" the same countries whose sovereign rights the US routinely violated during the Cold War. The fact that three of the five rogue states are Middle East oil producers, and that two in particular—Iran and Iraq—are clearly the main targets of the doctrine, points to the continuing centrality of oil in American strategic calculations. Iraq's transgression—invading Kuwait in order to boost oil profits to pay off debts from its war with Iran—flagrantly violated the rules set by the US and Saudi Arabia to maintain price stability. Iraq's crime will not soon be forgotten. Moreover, the embargo on Iraqi oil has provided a windfall for regional producers. Saudi Arabia alone is estimated to have earned more than $100 billion as a result. As one oil expert told the Associated Press, "Saudi Arabia would like the embargo on Iraqi oil maintained as long as possible." (US banks, which hold tens of billions of dollars in outstanding Saudi loans, are also deeply concerned about maintaining Saudi profit levels.) The economic collapse in Asia, on which the oil-producing states had placed much hope for future sales, has further increased the necessity of keeping Iraqi oil off-line and thereby forestalling a glut in the market.

MARGINALIZING IRAQ

The brutal sanctions imposed by the US on Iraq are tantamount to a permanent blockade. Because the US has shown little inclination to lift the sanctions, the purpose behind them must be to marginalize Iraq permanently, rather than induce a change in behavior. As Martin Indyk said in his 1993 speech outlining the dual containment policy, "[T]he current regime in Iraq is a criminal regime, beyond the pale of international society and, in our judgment, irredeemable." Iraq's confrontation with Washington in February 1998 was motivated at least in part by Saddam Hussein's desire to force the international community to specify how Iraq could bring itself into compliance with UN Security Council resolutions. Iraqis frequently express fear that the sanctions will not be lifted regardless of what their leadership does.

The isolation of Iran, by contrast, is far weaker. Although the administration imposed sanctions in 1996 on foreign companies investing more than $40 million in Iran and forced the cancellation of a lucrative contract between Conoco and the oil ministry, there is considerable business pressure to lift the embargo. Iran's test on July 22, 1998, of medium-range missiles acquired from North Korea provoked a sharp rebuke from the Clinton administration, but the evidence suggests that the US-Teheran relationship may not be adversely affected. Secretary of State Madeleine Albright has gone out of her way to support the new president, Mohammad Khatami, in his rivalry with Iran's religious leader, Ali Khamenei. The rapprochement with Iran exposes the inadequacies of the rogue state doctrine, and policy makers may eventually have to discard it.

THE "PEACE PROCESS"

The Palestinian-Israeli "peace process" is over. The seductive promise of Oslo [the mid-1990s negotiations between Israel and the Palestinians] has been revealed to be a cruel hoax, a "dying succubus," in Middle Eastern scholar Edward Said's phrase. As one observer wrote: "The Oslo process . . . is less a negotiation between Israelis and Palestinians than an internal Israeli debate about how much territory, authority and sovereignty to offer the Palestinians." It has become clear since September 1997 that, without increased pressure from Washington, the Netanyahu government will continue to stake out a maximalist claim to territory in the West Bank and East Jerusalem. (Gaza is rarely mentioned these days, leaving the impression that Israel regards further withdrawals or "redeployments" of its troops as unnecessary.) Settlement activity continues unabated, as do land seizures, house demolitions, curfews, acts of random violence and the steady, grinding impoverishment of the Palestinian majority. Remarkably, Binyamin Netanyahu's government has flagrantly violated the terms of the accord while managing to preserve the illusion that "peace" is still possible. What accounts, then, for the Clinton administration's tenacious insistence that the interests of the United States, and of the people of the region, are best served by this transparent charade?

[Historians] Phyllis Bennis and Khaled Mansour examine the 50-year history of relations between the two countries and find that the strategic interests of the United States have corresponded neatly with Israel's territorial ambitions for many decades. Ever since Israel proved its prowess in the 1967 Six-Day War, it has been immensely valuable to the US as a "proxy that can fight." Israel provided the front-line troops for the battle against Arab nationalist movements and regimes, whose nationalization programs and advocacy of autarky and import-substitution were anathema to the American business elite. Thus it was thanks largely to rational self-interest that support for Israel became a central tenet of US policy in the region.

Punitive Sanctions

US policy in the Middle East has been particularly cruel toward the Iraqi population, and biased toward Israel. Despite how Middle Eastern leaders sometimes treat their own populations, or the self-destructiveness of the Lebanese and Algerians, few people could tolerate the barbarity of the UN sanctions. Iraq's people have enjoyed much respect in the region for their intellectual attainments and honesty, a feature of the region's history that the US and Britain seem to overlook.

For several years, even Saudi Arabia has called on the US to ease the sanctions against Iraq. Its intransigence, along with almost illegal punitive actions, effectively have lost Washington much of the support it enjoyed only a few years ago.

Barbara Nimri Aziz, *Toward Freedom*, November 1997.

Yet the end of the Cold War has brought about a re-examination of the strategic partnership. Arab nationalism is no longer a threat to US interests, and the International Monetary Fund's ability to impose austerity on the economies of the region is virtually unlimited. One would expect, then, that Israel's diminishing value as a partner might prompt Washington to take a harder line with Netanyahu in his dealings with the Palestinians in the interests of securing regional stability. The reason this is not so, Bennis and Mansour argue, can be explained by the growing influence of non-rational actors—specifically a millenarian movement of Christian conservatives—in the formation of US policy. The Israeli government's success in nullifying existing agreements without any commensurate cost in security terms or serious reproach from the international community has emboldened the Christian right and its allies in Congress. They argue that a continued alliance with

Israel brings greater benefits—both political and spiritual—than would a just settlement of the Palestinian problem. Congressional conservatives, who in decades past were often vulnerable to accusations of anti-Semitism, have realized that demagoguery in defense of Israel will always be rewarded, whereas criticism, no matter how cautiously couched in praise, will always be punished.

THE ERA OF EMPIRE

The Clinton administration, for its part, has adopted a cautious attitude. For the moment at least, it lacks the political capital to oppose forcefully the burgeoning coalition between evangelical Christians, Congress and the Israeli right-wing. The administration is also no doubt aware that the demoralization and disorganization of the Palestinian people will, for the foreseeable future, severely restrict their ability to respond to Israeli aggressions. Thus, there is little pressure on Washington to reconsider its unwavering support of Israel. Moreover, many policy makers view a regional economic order dominated by a conservative, capital-friendly Israeli government as the best long-term prospect for US interests.

As we have seen, during the Cold War era, the formation of US foreign policy was cloaked in mystifying, geopolitical rhetoric. The end of that epoch allows a more candid examination of the nature of US hegemony in the region. Washington now possesses more resources than ever before to enforce its will and to punish those states or movements that seek to "go it alone." Through its predominant influence in international lending institutions such as the IMF [International Monetary Fund], the US can virtually micromanage the economies of developing nations and inflict draconian penalties for nonconformity. Through its influence in multilateral forums such as the United Nations, it can impose crushing economic sanctions. If such methods fail, Washington can announce unilateral trade embargoes and penalize countries that violate them. Lastly, of course, US military might can be summoned to restore "order." The lofty promise of a "multipolar" world to replace the bipolar world of the Cold War era was just a mirage. Whatever the future holds for the countries of the region, as well as for the world's only superpower, it is all too clear that the "era of empire" is still with us.

| "Force can never be the first answer.
| But sometimes, it's the only answer."

U.S. MILITARY STRIKES ON IRAQ ARE JUSTIFIED

Bill Clinton

Throughout the 1990s, the United States has on occasion used military force to keep Iraq from invading neighboring countries and to quell the dangerous and tyrannical ambitions of Iraq's president, Saddam Hussein. In the following viewpoint, Bill Clinton argues that such military intervention in Iraq is justified. In this particular case, Clinton maintains that air strikes may be necessary to diminish the threat of Iraq's weapons-of-mass-destruction program. Clinton is the forty-second president of the United States.

As you read, consider the following questions:

1. When did Saddam Hussein agree to make a total declaration of Iraq's weapons capability?
2. Since the Gulf War, in what ways has the United States responded to Saddam Hussein's threats, according to the author?
3. In Clinton's opinion, what world threats are likely to appear in the twenty-first century?

Excerpted from Bill Clinton's speech "Iraq and the United Nations," delivered February 17, 1998, the Pentagon, Washington, D.C.

This is a time of tremendous promise for America. The super-power confrontation has ended; on every continent democracy is securing for more and more people the basic freedoms we Americans have come to take for granted. Bit by bit the information age is chipping away at the barriers, economic, political and social, that once kept people locked in and freedom and prosperity locked out.

But for all our promise, all our opportunity, people in this room know very well that this is not a time free from peril, especially as a result of reckless acts of outlaw nations and an unholy axis of terrorists, drug traffickers and organized international criminals.

We have to defend our future from these predators of the 21st century. They feed on the free flow of information and technology. They actually take advantage of the freer movement of people, information and ideas.

And they will be all the more lethal if we allow them to build arsenals of nuclear, chemical and biological weapons and the missiles to deliver them. We simply cannot allow that to happen.

There is no more clear example of this threat than Saddam Hussein's Iraq. His regime threatens the safety of his people, the stability of his region and the security of all the rest of us. . . .

I want [the American people] to understand what we must do to protect the national interest, and indeed the interest of all freedom loving people in the world.

Remember, as a condition of the cease fire after the Gulf War, the United Nations demanded—not the United States, the United Nations—demanded, and Saddam Hussein agreed to declare within 15 days—this is way back in 1991—within 15 days his nuclear, chemical and biological weapons and the missiles to deliver them, to make a total declaration. That's what he promised to do.

The United Nations set up a special commission of highly trained international experts called Unscom, to make sure that Iraq made good on that commitment. We had every good reason to insist that Iraq disarm. Saddam had built up a terrible arsenal, and he had used it—not once, but many times, in a decade-long war with Iran; he used chemical weapons against combatants, against civilians, against a foreign adversary, and even against his own people.

And during the Gulf War, Saddam launched Scuds against Saudi Arabia, Israel, and Bahrain.

Now, instead of playing by the very rules he agreed to at the end of the Gulf War, Saddam has spent the better part of the past decade trying to cheat on this solemn commitment. Consider just some of the facts.

BROKEN PROMISES

Iraq repeatedly made false declarations about the weapons that it had left in its possession after the Gulf War. When Unscom would then uncover evidence that gave lie to those declarations, Iraq would simply amend the reports.

For example, Iraq revised its nuclear declarations four times within just 14 months and it has submitted six different biological warfare declarations, each of which has been rejected by Unscom.

In 1995, Hussein Kamal, Saddam's son-in-law, and the chief organizer of Iraq's weapons-of-mass-destruction program, defected to Jordan. He revealed that Iraq was continuing to conceal weapons and missiles and the capacity to build many more. . . .

THE UNITED STATES PREFERS DIPLOMACY

It is obvious that there is an attempt here based on the whole history of this operation since 1991, to protect whatever remains of [Saddam's] capacity to produce weapons of mass destruction, the missiles to deliver them and the feed stocks necessary to produce them.

The Unscom inspectors believe that Iraq still has stockpiles of chemical and biological munitions, a small force of Scud-type missiles, and the capacity to restart quickly its production program and build many, many more weapons.

Now, against that background, let us remember the past here. It is against that background that we have repeatedly and unambiguously made clear our preference for a diplomatic solution.

The inspection system works. The inspection system has worked in the face of lies, stonewalling, obstacle after obstacle after obstacle. The people who have done that work deserve the thanks of civilized people throughout the world.

It has worked. That is all we want. And if we can find a diplomatic way to do what has to be done, to do what he promised to do at the end of the Gulf War, to do what should have been done within 15 days—within 15 days—of the agreement at the end of the Gulf War, if we can find a diplomatic way to do that, that is by far our preference.

WHY FORCE MAY BE NECESSARY

But to be a genuine solution, and not simply one that glosses over the remaining problem, a diplomatic solution must include or meet a clear, immutable, reasonable, simple standard.

Iraq must agree, and soon, to free, full, unfettered access to these sites anywhere in the country. There can be no dilution or diminishment of the integrity of the inspection system that Unscom has put in place. . . .

"Do I look like someone who'd hide unconventional weapons?"

Now, let's imagine the future. What if he fails to comply, and we fail to act, or we take some ambiguous third route which gives him yet more opportunities to develop this program of weapons of mass destruction and continue to press for the release of the sanctions and continue to ignore the solemn commitments that he made?

Well, he will conclude that the international community has lost its will. He will then conclude that he can go right on and do more to rebuild an arsenal of devastating destruction.

And some day, some way, I guarantee you, he'll use the arsenal. And I think every one of you who's really worked on this for any length of time believes that, too. . . .

If Saddam rejects peace and we have to use force, our purpose is clear. We want to seriously diminish the threat posed by Iraq's weapons-of-mass-destruction program. We want to seriously reduce his capacity to threaten his neighbors.

I am quite confident, from the briefing I have just received from our military leaders, that we can achieve the objective and secure our vital strategic interests.

Let me be clear: A military operation cannot destroy all the weapons-of-mass-destruction capacity. But it can and will leave him significantly worse off than he is now in terms of the ability to threaten the world with these weapons or to attack his neighbors.

And he will know that the international community continues to have a will to act if and when he threatens again. Following any strike, we will carefully monitor Iraq's activities with all the means at our disposal. If he seeks to rebuild his weapons of mass destruction, we will be prepared to strike him again.

The economic sanctions will remain in place until Saddam complies fully with all U.N. resolutions. . . .

THE NEED FOR CONSTANT VIGILANCE

Now, let me say to all of you here—as all of you know—the weightiest decision any president ever has to make is to send our troops into harm's way. And force can never be the first answer. But sometimes, it's the only answer.

You are the best-prepared, best-equipped, best-trained fighting force in the world. And should it prove necessary for me to exercise the option of force, your commanders will do everything they can to protect the safety of all the men and women under their command.

No military action, however, is risk-free. I know that the people we may call upon in uniform are ready. The American people have to be ready as well.

Dealing with Saddam Hussein requires constant vigilance. We have seen that constant vigilance pays off. . . . Since the Gulf War, we have pushed back every time Saddam has posed a threat.

When Baghdad plotted to assassinate former President Bush, we struck hard at Iraq's intelligence headquarters.

When Saddam threatened another invasion by amassing his troops in Kuwait along the Kuwaiti border in 1994, we immediately deployed our troops, our ships, our planes, and Saddam backed down.

When Saddam forcefully occupied Irbil in northern Iraq, we broadened our control over Iraq's skies by extending the no-fly zone. . . .

PROTECTING PEACE IN A NEW ERA

Saddam Hussein's Iraq reminds us of what we learned in the 20th century and warns us of what we must know about the 21st. In this [20th] century, we learned through harsh experience that the only answer to aggression and illegal behavior is firmness, determination, and—when necessary—action.

In the next century, the community of nations may see more and more the very kind of threat Iraq poses now—a rogue state with weapons of mass destruction ready to use them or provide them to terrorists, drug traffickers or organized criminals who travel the world among us unnoticed.

If we fail to respond today, Saddam and all those who would follow in his footsteps will be emboldened tomorrow by the knowledge that they can act with impunity, even in the face of a clear message from the United Nations Security Council and clear evidence of a weapons-of-mass-destruction program.

But if we act as one, we can safeguard our interests and send a clear message to every would-be tyrant and terrorist that the international community does have the wisdom and the will and the way to protect peace and security in a new era. That is the future I ask you all to imagine. That is the future I ask our allies to imagine.

If we look at the past and imagine that future, we will act as one together. And we still have, God willing, a chance to find a diplomatic resolution to this, and if not, God willing, the chance to do the right thing for our children and grandchildren.

| "Bombing people into oblivion for no good reason is a descent into barbarism."

U.S. MILITARY STRIKES ON IRAQ ARE NOT JUSTIFIED

Bob Herbert

In the following viewpoint, syndicated columnist Bob Herbert contends that U.S. air strikes on Iraq are not justified. Using military force to diminish the threat of Iraq's weapons of mass destruction would be unsuccessful, Herbert maintains. Furthermore, such actions could result in the deaths of thousands of innocent Iraqi civilians. The United States should focus on bringing down Iraqi president Saddam Hussein rather than resort to inhumane air strikes, Herbert concludes.

As you read, consider the following questions:
1. In Herbert's opinion, why has it become easier for the United States to drop bombs on foreign lands?
2. Why is the resolve to drop bombs on Iraq a badly planned policy, according to Herbert?
3. Why are there no clearly defined strategic goals for a war with Iraq, in the author's opinion?

Reprinted from Bob Herbert, "War Games," The New York Times, February 22, 1998, by permission. Copyright ©1998 by The New York Times.

"War hath no fury like a noncombatant," said C.E. Montague, the writer and veteran of World War I.

Nothing has changed, except now there are more noncombatants than ever. We can all watch the upcoming war on television. No danger there. If it gets boring, we can switch to *Seinfeld*.

Bill Clinton, in charge of whipping up support for the war, has done some of his planning on the golf course. And recently he took time out to party with Democratic fat cats in the luxurious enclosed community of Llewellyn Park in West Orange, N.J. Twenty-five thousand dollars a couple.

"It was lovely," said a Democratic insider. "It didn't even seem like New Jersey."

In the absence of any real sense of danger, any threat to one's personal well-being or way of life, it becomes easier and easier to drop bombs on foreign lands. War becomes a voyeuristic, jingoistic pastime, with the progress discussed at work each day, over coffee. No clearly articulated goal is needed, no long-term perspective, no serious discussion of the moral or ethical implications of the carnage we are so offhandedly unleashing.

THE ARROGANCE OF POWER

Secretary of State Madeleine Albright, in an appearance on NBC's *Today* show, put the matter as plainly as could be. She told Matt Lauer:

"If we have to use force, it is because we are America. We are the indispensable nation. We stand tall. We see further into the future."

Has there ever been a better example of the arrogance of power? We are becoming drunk with the idea that we are the world's only superpower and therefore can do whatever we want to whomever we want.

The case has been made that Saddam Hussein is a menace. No one who is sane can doubt it. He is a warmonger and mass murderer. It is because of him that Iraq is in ruins, and he remains a deadly threat to anyone within his sphere of influence. He has chemical and biological weapons and is mad enough to use them.

So we are sold on the fact that Saddam is a bad guy. The question is what to do about him. The answer, according to the Clinton Administration, is to drop bombs on Iraq to teach him a lesson and "seriously diminish" his threat to others.

But, said President Clinton, the bombing will neither destroy Saddam's stockpiles of chemical and biological weapons nor prevent him from creating new weapons. So after the bombing, according to the Administration's own assessment, Saddam will still be around, he will still have weapons of mass destruction, and he will still be a threat to use them.

This is not a well thought out policy.

"MILITARY FORCE" OR WAR?

Ms. Albright doesn't even think we are contemplating war. She told students at Tennessee State University in Nashville: "We are talking about using military force, but we are not talking about a war. That is an important distinction."

That is an amazing distinction. The G.I.'s who have packed their gear, left their families and headed off to the Middle East are fully aware that they might not come back. They think this is war.

A SETBACK FOR DEMOCRACY

We can only note with great chagrin that any unilateral military action by the United States against Iraq would, in the eyes of many people, constitute a violation of Iraq's national sovereignty, and would, in effect, transform an aggressor nation into an aggrieved one. So, the international sympathy for Iraq following this military action may constitute a setback for the cause of democracy and human rights around the world. And, it would again remind many that the U.S. government is often too willing to be the world's unaccountable gendarme.

Democratic Socialists of America, Policy Statement, February 18, 1998.

The problem in a nutshell is that this war, if it happens, will be fought by professionals but is being planned by amateurs. Bill Clinton is no warrior, nor is Madeleine Albright. That's why there are no clearly stated strategic goals. That's why we ended up with the pathetic spectacle in February 1998 of the nation's three top foreign policy officials being shouted at by protesters while trying to sell the war Oprah-style. And that's why we have so few allies in this adventure.

SACRIFICING INNOCENT CIVILIANS

Poverty-stricken and humiliated Iraqis continue to die by the tens of thousands from the combined effects of Saddam's murderous folly and the unsuccessful attempts to stop him. To kill even more Iraqis without any sort of plan to bring the overall bloodshed to an eventual halt cannot possibly be justified.

I don't believe Americans want to take their cue from Barry Goldwater and bomb Iraq into the Stone Age. But we are in danger of doing just that. In our anger at Saddam, we are willing to needlessly sacrifice the lives of thousands of innocent civilians. And leave him standing.

Either bring down Saddam, or stop the killing.

Bombing people into oblivion for no good reason is a descent into barbarism. In the fury of our righteousness, and from the safety of our living rooms, we are in danger of becoming a nation without a conscience.

| "Both the ancient Iranian civilization
and the new American civilization
can benefit from the flow of ideas
from one to the other."

THE U.S. SHOULD PURSUE A MORE OPEN RELATIONSHIP WITH IRAN

Sandra Mackey

Since 1979, when Shi'ite revolutionaries and clerics gained state power in Iran, relations between Iran and the United States have been strained. In 1997, however, Iranians elected a new president, Mohammad Khatami, a political moderate who appears to be tolerant of Western culture. In the following viewpoint, Sandra Mackey contends that the United States should pursue a more open and relaxed relationship with Iran. By taking up Khatami's call for a cultural dialogue between Iran and the United States, the political relationship between the two nations can improve, Mackey concludes. Mackey is the author of *The Iranians: Persia, Islam, and the Soul of a Nation*.

As you read, consider the following questions:

1. According to Mackey, what are the three identities that comprise Iranian culture?
2. In what ways does Mohammad Khatami hope to lead the Islamic Republic of Iran to prosperity, according to the author?
3. Who should participate in a cultural exchange between Iran and the United States, in Khatami's view?

Reprinted from Sandra Mackey, "A Culture, More Than a State, Reaches Out," *Los Angeles Times*, January 9, 1998, by permission of the author.

On the medium of global television, Mohammad Khatami came before the American people on January 7, 1998, bearing 2,500 years of Iranian history. In an unprecedented act of diplomacy, the president of the Islamic Republic of Iran packaged his message in terms of culture, not politics. And it is only in terms of culture that America can understand what is happening in Iran and what it means to U.S. interests.

IRAN'S COMPLEX CULTURE

Iran possesses an old, complex culture composed of three competing yet interlocking identities. The first strand of that identity stretches back to the 4th century BC when Cyrus the Great built the mighty Persian empire. Into the soil of its heartland were planted the seeds of intellectual inquiry, artistic excellence, tolerance and assimilation. For almost a thousand years, this culture survived all challenges hurled at it.

In the 7th century AD, the Iranians acquired a second identity when they embraced Islam. Although Persia, the nation, had fallen to Arab conquest, Persian culture fed Islam's great intellectual achievements. By the 16th century, the Iranians had found in Shiism, Islam's dissenting sect, the vehicle that allowed them to preserve their unique Persian identity while remaining professing Muslims. Essentially Persianized Islam, Shiism wrapped an Islamic cloak around Persian culture. Under it, the legacies of ancient Persia and Shia Islam intertwined to create what we now know as the Iranian nation.

In the 19th century, the Iranians gathered in the political ideas of the West. As a result, representative government and the rule of law embedded themselves into Iranian culture to form yet a third strand of Iranian identity.

Over the centuries, Iran functioned best when the various parts of Iranian identity maintained balance. But over most of the 20th century, that vital balance has tipped in one direction and then the other. Before 1979, Shah Mohammed Reza Pahlavi pushed the Iranians to the extreme of their Persian identity, and after 1979, Ayatollah Ruhollah Khomeini pushed them to the extreme of their Islamic identity. Neither leader achieved the internal peace and the external security the nation required. Just as the shah attempted to break the powerful Iranian cultural pattern composed of Persia, Islam and Western political liberalism, the imam enforced his own aberration of Iranian culture. It is Mohammad Khatami who now, in the interest of the nation, seeks to instill the delicate balance between the Iranians' three identities. This is why the United States must take seriously what he says.

MOHAMMAD KHATAMI'S INFLUENCE

Khatami is first and foremost a nationalist. Unlike Khomeini and those who continue to follow his line, Khatami sees the interests of the nation exceeding the interests of Islam. Peering through an Iranian lens ground by a thousand years of experience, he recognizes that if Iran is to achieve prosperity, security and social order, the Islamic Republic must change course. But this change cannot be simply political. It must also be cultural. Thus into the inflexible frame of political Islam, Khatami is placing the tolerance of Persia. And into the vitriolic anger of the revolution, he is pouring the oil of Persian assimilation that embraces the Western concept of civil society and the rule of law.

AN INTERCHANGE WITH IRAN

We should take up President Mohammad Khatami's suggestion and encourage as much interchange with Iran—media, scholars, commerce, and diplomatic—as Iran will allow. That probably will not be much, because its distrust of the United States reaches back to the CIA's 1953 overthrow of the Mossadegh government. We need direct and accurate information about Iran, and we must deal with our side of the mutual demonology that has characterized U.S.-Iran relations for so long.

Arthur T. Downey, *Commonweal*, February 27, 1998.

In his call for internal reform and external accommodation, Khatami is not exercising the caprice of a leader engaged in an internal power struggle. Rather he is responding to the life force of ancient Iranian culture which is reasserting itself after two decades of rigid Islamic rule. This is precisely why Khatami spoke to the American people about a dialogue between cultures in which the old civilization of the East engages the new civilization of the West. Praising both American and Iranian cultures and acknowledging the hurts that Iran and the U.S. have inflicted on each other, Khatami's remarks in the CNN broadcast in January 1998 were intended to spin the first thread of understanding between equals.

PURSUING IMPROVED RELATIONS

In the face of Khatami's bold and studied gesture, the Clinton administration cannot stay mired in the same worn formula concerning improved relations between the United States and Iran. That formula, restated by the State Department's official response to the Iranian president, maintains that improved relations between the two countries can begin only with official government-to-government engagement.

At the moment, President Khatami understands perhaps better than President Clinton that Iran and the United States have demonized each other so long that neither government is in a position politically or emotionally to embrace the other. That is why what Khatami terms "the crack in the wall" must be expanded by scholars, traders, artists and tourists. This is something that Americans, as eager entrepreneurs and highly successful exporters of popular culture, can understand. So must the American government.

In an extraordinary way, Mohammad Khatami has opened the door to a new relationship between revolutionary Iran and its Great Satan. The United States must walk through that door by accepting the cultural dialogue that Iran's president seeks. Both the ancient Iranian civilization and the new American civilization can benefit from the flow of ideas from one to the other. That in turn will result in the government-to-government relationship that the United States demands.

| "The United States cannot afford to undertake a one-sided détente with Iran."

THE U.S. SHOULD NOT PURSUE A MORE OPEN RELATIONSHIP WITH IRAN

James Phillips

In January 1998, Iran's newly elected president called for a cultural exchange between Iran and the United States in hopes of easing the strained relationship between the two nations. In the following viewpoint, James Phillips argues that the United States cannot yet pursue a more relaxed relationship with Iran. In fact, Phillips contends, the United States must maintain sanctions against Iran until the Iranian government agrees to stop supporting international terrorism, fomenting Islamic revolution, and pursuing efforts to amass weapons of mass destruction. Phillips is a senior policy analyst at the Heritage Foundation, a conservative think tank.

As you read, consider the following questions:

1. In Phillips's opinion, what would happen if the United States were to relax its economic sanctions against Iran?
2. What have been the benefits of the U.S. dual containment policy toward Iran and Iraq, according to the author?
3. In Phillips's view, what would be an appropriate response to Mohammad Khatami's "peace offensive"?

Excerpted from James Phillips, "Press Iran's Khatami to Follow Words with Deeds," *The Heritage Foundation Backgrounder*, #1152, January 23, 1998. Reprinted by permission of The Heritage Foundation.

I ranian President Mohammad Khatami's January 7, 1998, interview on CNN has raised hopes for a détente in Iranian-American relations. Close examination of Khatami's statements, however, reveals no evidence that the Iranian government is willing to halt the hostile policies that have generated bilateral tensions: Iran's support of terrorism, export of Islamic revolution, clandestine efforts to develop weapons of mass destruction, and violent opposition to Arab-Israeli peace efforts. Moreover, Khatami rejected government-to-government talks, advocating instead a vague dialogue between peoples. Such a "warm and fuzzy" dialogue, bereft of meaningful policy exchanges, would undermine long-standing American efforts to contain Iran and would advance Tehran's goal of obtaining European investment without ending its efforts to export terrorism and subversion. The Clinton Administration must not let Khatami's soothing words distract it from Iran's hostile policies, which continue unabated.

THE U.S. SHOULD KEEP UP ITS GUARD

The United States cannot afford to undertake a one-sided détente with Iran that allows Tehran to benefit from Western aid, trade, and investment while continuing to subvert its neighbors, sponsor terrorism, and acquire weapons of mass destruction. If the Clinton Administration rewards cosmetic rhetorical changes in Tehran's foreign policy by relaxing U.S. economic sanctions against Iran, America's allies in Western Europe and Japan are likely to join Russia and China in a stampede to ingratiate themselves with Tehran and gain a share of Iran's import market and oil investment opportunities. Such an outcome would vindicate the views of the hard-liners who dominate Iranian foreign policy by allowing them to exploit Western loans and investment to bolster Iran's faltering economy and prop up their regime without abandoning their dangerously hostile policies.

The United States should not let down its guard in dealing with Iran. The Clinton Administration should not repeat the mistakes of the Carter and the Reagan Administrations, both of which sought to reach out to Iranian "moderates" who proved unwilling or unable to moderate Iran's rabidly anti-American foreign policy. This is not the time to relax economic pressure on Iran: Economic pressure helped to pave the way for Khatami's upset victory over the hard-line Speaker of Iran's Parliament, Ali Akbar Nateq-Nouri, in Iran's May 1997 presidential elections. And it undoubtedly was a motivating factor behind Khatami's call for a dialogue with the American people.

Some critics of the Clinton Administration's dual containment policy toward Iran and Iraq have jumped to the conclusion that the policy has failed and should be abandoned. Since Iraqi dictator Saddam Hussein has outmaneuvered the Clinton Administration repeatedly, they argue, the United States should drop its containment policy against Iran and seek to include Tehran in the anti-Iraq coalition. This ignores the fact that working out a *modus vivendi* with Iran will take years of effort, during which Tehran could not be considered a reliable ally against Baghdad. In the meantime, Iran will continue to build weapons of mass destruction and to pose subversive, terrorist, and military threats to the United States and its allies, particularly those in the Persian Gulf. And because Iran, unlike Iraq, is not constrained by United Nations sanctions, it will be better positioned to cause mischief and possibly destabilize one or more of the Arab Gulf states. Moreover, if the United States tilts toward Iran, many of these Arab emirates will be tempted to improve relations with Iraq as a counterweight to Iran, thereby weakening the coalition against Saddam Hussein.

BENEFITS OF THE DUAL CONTAINMENT POLICY

Critics should not underestimate the benefits of the U.S. dual containment policy. Although containment has not compelled Iran and Iraq to abandon their hostile policies, it has deprived both of scarce hard currency, forced them to scale back their ambitious military buildups, and whittled away their ability to threaten their neighbors. Economic sanctions, moreover, have helped spark a debate in Iran about the need for an opening to the West and helped to prompt President Khatami's overture to the "Great American People." Washington should not discard its containment policy just when it appears to be on the brink of succeeding.

To respond prudently to President Khatami's peace offensive, therefore, the Clinton Administration should:

• *Press Khatami to back his temperate words with concrete actions to prove that he is willing and able to end Iran's hostile policies.* The United States has been disappointed by the abortive outcomes of several previous efforts to improve U.S.-Iran relations since the 1979 Islamic revolution. Washington should ask Khatami to prove his good faith by undertaking specific actions to reduce tensions. Three verifiable benchmarks that could be used to establish whether Khatami is serious about altering Iran's international behavior would be a halt to Iranian surveillance of U.S. officials overseas, an end to Iran's cooperation with Iraq in smuggling

Iraqi oil in violation of United Nations economic sanctions against Iraq, and the public withdrawal of the death threats against British author Salman Rushdie, condemned by Ayatollah Ruhollah Khomeini in 1989 for allegedly writing a blasphemous novel. [In 1998, Iran retracted Khomeini's condemnation of Rushdie.]

Rob Rogers reprinted by permission of United Feature Syndicate, Inc.

- *Reach out to the Iranian people.* The rule of the ayatollahs is increasingly unpopular in Iran. The U.S. should emphasize the heavy price that Iranians pay for their rulers' anti-Western policies and support the development of a genuine democracy in Iran by moving quickly to establish a Radio Free Iran with the $4 million that Congress appropriated for that purpose in November 1997.
- *Push patiently for government-to-government talks on outstanding issues.* Iran has the only government in the world that refuses to talk to the U.S. government. The people-to-people dialogue advocated by Khatami advances Iran's goal of weakening international support for sanctions against Iran without requiring that Tehran give an inch on other issues. A genuine thaw in the Iran-U.S. cold war requires official government contacts to discuss outstanding policy issues, not merely an exchange of "professors, writers, scholars, artists, journalists, and tourists" as Khatami has suggested.
- *Maintain the strongest possible economic sanctions against Iran.* This will

give Tehran a powerful incentive to abandon its hostile foreign policy and give self-professed reformers like President Khatami strong political arguments against the radical policies advocated by their hard-line rivals. Khatami's interview with CNN is a sign that the American sanctions policy is working and should be maintained, not abandoned. The Clinton Administration should make it clear that the United States will not lift its economic sanctions against Iran until Tehran has halted (1) its support for terrorism, including its assassination campaign against Iranian exiles; (2) its violent attempts to overthrow secular and moderate Muslim governments; and (3) its clandestine efforts to obtain weapons of mass destruction.

Periodical Bibliography

The following articles have been selected to supplement the diverse views presented in this chapter. Addresses are provided for periodicals not indexed in the *Readers' Guide to Periodical Literature*, the *Alternative Press Index*, the *Social Sciences Index*, or the *Index to Legal Periodicals and Books*.

Madeleine Albright	"The Middle East Peace Process," *Vital Speeches of the Day*, June 1, 1998.
Barbara Nimri Aziz	"A Separate Peace," *Toward Freedom*, November 1997.
George Bush	"Why We Didn't Remove Saddam," *Time*, March 2, 1998.
John Deutch	"How Best to Oust Hussein?" *New York Times*, February 22, 1998.
Arthur T. Downey	"What to Do About the Middle East?" *Commonweal*, February 27, 1998.
Adam Garfinkle	"The U.S. Imperial Postulate in the Mideast," *Orbis*, Winter 1997.
Paul B. Henze and S. Enders Wimbush	"A New Policy for a New Middle East," *Wall Street Journal*, January 31, 1997.
Michael C. Hudson	"To Play the Hegemon: Fifty Years of U.S. Policy Toward the Middle East," *Middle East Journal*, Summer 1996.
Tarek E. Masoud	"Misreading Iran," *Current History*, January 1998.
Anthony E. Mitchell	"Iran May Be Our Best Hope Against Iraq," *Wall Street Journal*, January 29, 1998.
Richard W. Murphy and F. Gregory Gause	"Democracy and U.S. Policy in the Muslim Middle East," *Middle East Policy*, January 1997. Available from 1730 M St. NW, Suite 512, Washington, DC 20036.
Progressive	"The Case Against War," March 1, 1998.
Robert Satloff	"New Nuances," *New Republic*, July 13, 1998.
George Stephanopoulos	"Why We Should Kill Saddam," *Newsweek*, December 1, 1997.
Tikkun	"Strategy of the Israeli Right: Keep the U.S. Out," July/August 1998.

CHAPTER 4

HOW COULD PEACE BE ADVANCED IN THE MIDDLE EAST?

CHAPTER PREFACE

The Middle East is the birthplace of three world religions: Judaism, Christianity, and Islam. Jerusalem, the capital of Israel, illustrates this religious variety with its numerous sites that are sacred to Jews, Christians, and Muslims. For example, Muslims believe that a mosque-like structure atop a stony outcropping at the center of the city—the Dome of the Rock—commemorates the place from which the prophet Muhammad ascended into heaven. This same spot is also referred to as the Temple Mount— the site of the first and second Jewish temples and the place where some Jews and Christians believe that a third temple must be built to usher in the reign of God. These rival interpretations of geography, many argue, reflect the lack of consensus and compromise that has brought political instability and war to Israel and Palestine. As history professor Hassan S. Hassad writes: "The problem of Palestine is becoming more complex and dangerous because it is regarded as holy not only by one group but by three. . . . The chances for continued strife have tripled, and the chance for a peaceful solution has all but vanished. . . . Two groups identify one hill as the most sacred place on earth and are willing to fight and die for it. . . . Jerusalem is the . . . fuse that will ignite the fury of an extensive war in the future."

German theologian Hans Küng, on the other hand, contends that religion could provide an opportunity for peace in the Middle East. He points out that that Judaism, Christianity, and Islam have much in common because all three trace themselves back to the same progenitor, Abraham of the Old Testament. These faiths also share a "fundamental prophetic ethos: humane demands for justice, honesty, loyalty, peace and love—justified as the demands of God Himself." Were the followers of these faiths to reflect on their common origin, Küng maintains, they could engage in dialogue and "clarify the misunderstandings, dissolve the stereotyped, dehumanising images which each side holds of the 'enemy,' [and] reduce the mutual hatreds."

Such a dialogue would, of course, require a willingness among Jews, Christians, and Muslims to learn more about each other by participating in a kind of cultural détente. This idea is one of the several suggestions for advancing Middle East peace discussed in the following chapter.

| "The scourge of sanctions on the people of Iraq must come to an immediate and unqualified end."

UN SANCTIONS AGAINST IRAQ SHOULD BE LIFTED

Rick McDowell

The United Nations began imposing economic sanctions on Iraq after its unsuccessful 1990 invasion of Kuwait. These sanctions have continued throughout the 1990s as part of a plan to thwart the aggressive ambitions of Iraq's government. In the following viewpoint, Rick McDowell contends that these sanctions should be lifted because they have caused years of suffering for the Iraqi civilian population. Shortages of food, clean water, and medicine have led to massive starvation and outbreaks of disease, McDowell reports. Upholding human rights requires ending such cruel and destructive sanctions, he concludes. McDowell is a member of Voices in the Wilderness, a campaign to stop the UN sanctions against Iraq.

As you read, consider the following questions:

1. According to the UN Food and Agriculture Association, how many Iraqis have died as a result of the UN-imposed economic sanctions?
2. Why is the UN's "oil for food" resolution a failure, according to McDowell?
3. According to the author, what are the average monthly wages for public sector employees in Iraq?

Reprinted from Rick McDowell, "Economic Sanctions on Iraq," Z Magazine, November 1997, by permission of Z Magazine.

Years of the most comprehensive sanctions in modern history have reduced Iraq and its people to utter destitution. United Nations Security Council's economic sanctions, invoked only ten times since the inception of the United Nations, and applied eight times since the end of the Cold War, constitute an extension of the devastating allied bombing campaign of 1991.

For the sixth time since January 1996, a delegation from Voices in the Wilderness, a campaign to end the U.S.-supported UN economic sanctions against Iraq, traveled to Iraq in May 1997 in public violation of U.S. law. The delegation visited hospitals in Baghdad and the southern port city of Basrah. Members met with UN and relief officials, doctors, government workers, religious leaders, and Iraqis from all walks of life. Our findings of increasing suffering, death, and desperation throughout Iraq are confirmed by recent UN reports.

The UN Food and Agriculture Organization (FAO) reported in December 1995 that more than one million Iraqis have died—567,000 of them children—as a direct consequence of economic sanctions. UNICEF reports that 4,500 children under the age of 5 are dying each month from hunger and disease. An April 1997 nutritional survey, carried out by UNICEF with the participation of the World Food Program (WFP) and Iraq's Minister of Health, indicated that in Central/Southern Iraq, 27.5 percent of Iraq's 3 million children are now at risk of acute malnutrition.

A PUBLIC HEALTH CRISIS

To date, more children have died in Iraq than the combined toll of two atomic bombs on Japan and the ethnic cleansing of former Yugoslavia. The UN's Department of Humanitarian Affairs reports that Iraq's public health services are nearing a total breakdown from a lack of basic medicines, life-saving drugs, and essential medical supplies. The lack of clean water—50 percent of all rural people have no access to potable water—and the collapse of waste water treatment facilities in most urban areas are contributing to the rapidly deteriorating state of public health.

Air borne and water borne diseases are on the rise, while deaths related to diarrheal diseases have tripled in an increasingly unhealthy environment. The World Health Organization (WHO) reports a sixfold increase in the mortality rate for children under five, an explosive rise in the incidence of endemic infections, such as cholera and typhoid, and a markedly elevated incidence of measles, polio, myelitis, and tetanus. Malaria has reached epidemic levels. The WHO further states that the majority of Iraqis have subsisted on a semi-starvation diet for the past several years.

The use of Depleted Uranium (DU) during the Gulf War—a possible contributing factor to Gulf War Syndrome—may also be linked to increases in childhood cancers and leukemia, Hodgkin's disease, lymphomas, and increases in congenital diseases and deformities in fetuses, along with limb reductional abnormalities and increases in genetic abnormalities throughout Iraq.

The vaunted oil for food resolution (UN Resolution 986) is a failure—its promise of food and medicine having proved to be too little, too late. According to the WFP, by the end of May 1997, Iraq had exported 120 million barrels of oil and received 692,999 metric tons of food, 29 percent of what had been expected under the deal. Of the 574 contracts submitted to the Sanctions Committee for exports of humanitarian supplies to Iraq, 331 were approved, 191 placed on hold, 14 blocked, and 38 were awaiting clarification.

DEVASTATING SANCTIONS

Several years of the most severe Security Council sanctions in history have failed to dislodge the regime of President Saddam Hussein. These sanctions, however, have had a devastating impact on the most vulnerable sectors of Iraqi society, especially children. Numerous studies by United Nations agencies and independent groups, including an April–May 1996 survey conducted by the Center for Economic and Social Rights, have documented dramatic increases in malnutrition and disease, leading to the deaths of hundreds of thousands of children under the age of five since 1991. Yet there has been an astonishing lack of public debate over the moral and legal implications of a policy that imposes such enormous costs on a civilian population.

Roger Normand, *Middle East Report*, July–September 1996.

Of the $2 billion in Iraqi oil revenue authorized for a six-month period, 30 percent is designated for war reparations; 5 to 10 percent for UN operations; 5 to 10 percent covers maintenance and repair of the oil pipeline; and 15 percent is earmarked for humanitarian supplies for the Kurdish population in Northern Iraq. About $800,000 is available for Central/Southern Iraq or approximately 25 cents per person per day for food and medicine.

Regardless, UN Resolution 986 does not provide for critically needed spare parts to repair Iraq's water, sanitation, and medical infrastructure, which was devastated during the Gulf War. Importing such basic items as chlorine, fertilizers, and pencils is prohibited.

Lacking spare parts and materials needed to repair and maintain their water and sewage treatment facilities, the condition of many Iraqis is scarcely improved by the food they receive. The untreated water is contributing to disease and death. Without hard currency, the economy of Iraq, estimated to have the second largest oil reserves in the world, has collapsed. Average public sector wages, for the few who have employment, have fallen to less than $5 a month, while hyper inflation has caused the price of goods to rise astronomically. The Iraqi dinar, worth $3 prior to sanctions, was worth $.000625 in May 1997. Skilled workers, including doctors and engineers, have deserted their jobs to become taxi drivers or to sell cigarettes. Iraqi professionals are leaving the country in increasing numbers. With an estimated 80 percent of Iraqis affected by the sanctions, families are selling household and personal possessions to purchase food and medicine. As the population struggles for survival, the social fabric of Iraq is disintegrating, as witnessed by the widespread rise in begging, street children, crime, and prostitution.

The people of Iraq have been on a roller coaster of hope and despair for several years and seem to have settled on the rung of despair. Frial, the manager of a small hotel, asked us to go home and tell our government to bomb Iraq for 42 more days and get it over with for, she says, "We are all dying a slow and painful death under sanctions." A young doctor at a Baghdad hospital said, "Our life is over." Another doctor, who has practiced for 8 years and is forced to play God with the few available life-saving drugs, makes 3,000 dinar a month, or $2, while a bottle of milk for his children costs 3,500 dinar. He asks, "What does your country gain from our suffering?"

Children born since the Gulf War and hardly involved in the politics of sanctions suffer in silence, often without access to pain killers, drugs, antibiotics, or hope. Some childhood cancers realized an 80 percent cure rate prior to sanctions. Now, without cancer fighting drugs, the survival rate for children with these same cancers is 0 percent.

The UN, chartered to protect civilian populations from the ravages of war, is instead engaged in a war of collective punishment, a war of mass destruction directed at the civilian population of Iraq.

Considering the suffering and death in Iraq, the lack of public debate over the UN/U.S. participation in this massive violation of human rights is astonishing. The scourge of sanctions on the people of Iraq must come to an immediate and unqualified end.

2

| "[Sanctions deny] Saddam one of his
most urgent objectives: to regain
control of Iraq's revenue so he can
reconstitute his ability to threaten
his neighbors."

UN SANCTIONS AGAINST IRAQ SHOULD CONTINUE

Madeleine K. Albright

The United States must take decisive action to help destroy Iraq's capacity to threaten neighboring nations, argues Secretary of State Madeleine K. Albright in the following viewpoint. Such action includes the possible use of military force and continued support of the UN-imposed economic sanctions against Iraq. Albright maintains that these sanctions are necessary to ensure the disarmament of Iraq and to impede the dangerous aspirations of Iraq's president, Saddam Hussein. This viewpoint was originally written in August 1998, during one of the occasions when Iraq temporarily blocked investigations by UN weapons inspectors.

As you read, consider the following questions:

1. According to Albright, why does Saddam Hussein occasionally "rattle his cage"?
2. In Albright's opinion, why has Saddam Hussein claimed that the UN weapons inspectors are biased?
3. How does the "oil for food" arrangement benefit Iraqi civilians, according to the author?

Reprinted from Madeleine K. Albright, "The U.S. Will Stand Firm on Iraq, No Matter What," The New York Times, August 17, 1998, by permission. Copyright ©1998 by The New York Times.

At the end of the 1991 Persian Gulf war, conventional wisdom had it that Saddam Hussein would not last six months. Unfortunately, conventional wisdom was wrong and we have had to deal with the consequences ever since. For seven years, we have successfully contained Saddam by maintaining the toughest multilateral sanctions in history, while the United Nations special commission on arms inspections, or Unscom, has managed to destroy much of Saddam's stockpiles of missiles and weapons of mass destruction.

Periodically, Saddam rattles his cage, hoping that by provoking a crisis he can wear down the will of the international community, while we spend our precious defense dollars dispatching and recalling our forces. We will keep our eye on the ball: the threat to our national interests posed by Iraq. We control the timetable and will decide how and when to respond to Iraq's actions, based on the threat they pose to Iraq's neighbors, to regional security and to America's vital interests.

Our assessment will include Saddam Hussein's capacity to reconstitute, use or threaten to use weapons of mass destruction. We have ruled nothing out, including the use of force. We have reconfigured our forces in the gulf so that we can react swiftly and forcefully when necessary.

TAKING DECISIVE ACTION

In the meantime, Saddam's decision to suspend cooperation with the International Atomic Energy Agency and U.N. special commission is a violation of the agreement he reached with Secretary General Kofi Annan early in 1998 and is a direct challenge to the authority of the Security Council. This is a confrontation between Iraq and the United Nations. It is up to Mr. Annan and the Security Council to make sure that Saddam reverses course and cooperates with Unscom. And if they fail to persuade him to back down, we will have laid the foundation for taking our own decisive action.

Supporting Unscom is at the heart of our efforts to prevent Saddam Hussein from threatening his neighborhood, and we are proud to be its strongest backer. Because the U.N. special commission has been so effective in disarming Iraq, despite Iraq's elaborate efforts to hide and lie about its weapons of mass destruction, Saddam has sought to discredit the organization as provocative and biased. While this is patently untrue, some in the Security Council have lent support to this effort.

We have taken the opposite approach, staunchly defending Unscom and its chairman, Richard Butler. We have supported his conduct of intrusive inspections while seeking to insure that Saddam was not able to exploit this effort to the disadvantage of the U.N. inspection team in the Security Council. Since the January 1998 crisis, Unscom has in fact been very effective. It has carried out a range of inspection activities, turning up very serious evidence that Saddam has still not accounted for many undeclared chemical warheads and demonstrating that Iraq had "weaponized" deadly VX gas. This directly contradicts Foreign Minister Tariq Aziz's claims to have fully disclosed Iraq's weapons-of-mass-destruction programs.

FOCUSING ON IRAQ'S DEFIANCE

In the summer of 1998, Unscom had intended to follow up with some particularly intrusive inspections, which we supported. However, when Iraq suspended all inspections on Aug. 3, 1998, we understood that Saddam had done something which even his backers in the Security Council could not defend. It was in that context that I consulted with Mr. Butler, who came to his own conclusion that it was wiser to keep the focus on Iraq's open defiance of the Security Council. Had Unscom gone ahead with the intrusive inspections, they would have been blocked anyway. But some in the Security Council would have muddied the waters by claiming again that Unscom had provoked Iraq.

Our purpose now is to get the Security Council to face up to

Wiley Miller/*San Francisco Examiner*. Reprinted by permission.

its responsibilities to the U.N. special commission and the International Atomic Energy Agency. These organizations have been clearly mandated by the Security Council to carry out the necessary measures to disarm Iraq. If the Council fails to persuade Saddam to resume cooperation, then we will have a free hand to use other means to support Unscom's mandate.

THE NEED FOR SANCTIONS

Let's be clear: what Saddam really wants is to have sanctions lifted while retaining his residual weapons-of-mass-destruction capabilities. We will not allow it. As long as Saddam refuses to comply with the Security Council resolutions, the comprehensive sanctions on Iraq will remain in place. This denies Saddam one of his most urgent objectives: to regain control of Iraq's revenue so he can reconstitute his ability to threaten his neighbors. His lack of cooperation with Unscom may delay the day when Iraq is fully disarmed. But it will also help us insure that the sanctions regime is maintained, thereby doing much to prevent Saddam from rearming.

Some will argue that this imposes an inhumane burden on the Iraqi people who are not to blame for Saddam's behavior. But the Iraqi people are benefiting from the expansion of the "oil for food" arrangements which now insure that every Iraqi receives a daily ration basket equivalent to the recommended caloric intake of the average American. Under this arrangement, however, Saddam is denied access to this oil revenue. The money is put in escrow in a U.N. account, and released only for supplies approved by the U.N. sanctions committee.

In short, Saddam may be rattling his cage again, but he has no way to break out of it. Through his latest actions he has in fact thrown away the key and only helped us to keep his cage in place. One way or another, his latest effort to blackmail the international community into accepting his false claims of compliance will not be allowed to succeed.

> "Clear majorities of Arabs and Israelis finally are prepared to live with one another on the basis of reasonable compromises."

ARAB-ISRAELI NEGOTIATIONS WILL FOSTER PEACE

Rami G. Khouri

In January 1997, Israeli and Palestinian leaders signed the Hebron agreement, considered by many to be the first significant Mideast peace negotiation since the Oslo accords of 1993 and 1995. In the following viewpoint, Rami G. Khouri argues that these negotiations will lead to peace because they emphasize practical concessions that are supported by the majority of Arabs and Israelis. Rather than continuing to fight ideological and territorial battles, Khouri maintains, Arabs and Israelis are ready to live together in peace. Khouri is an internationally syndicated columnist based in Amman, Jordan.

As you read, consider the following questions:

1. What significant new elements characterize the Hebron accord, in Khouri's opinion?
2. According to the author, what compromise will enable the Arab world to live in peace with Israel?
3. In Khouri's view, how are the final status negotiations between Israelis and Palestinians likely to proceed?

Reprinted from Rami G. Khouri, "Learning to Share Both Land and Respect," Los Angeles Times, January 22, 1997, by permission of the author.

The agreement between Palestinians and Israelis to resume the Israeli military redeployment and withdrawal in the city of Hebron and subsequently throughout the West Bank may prove to be more important for its political symbolism in the Middle East than for its limited territorial disengagement.

The Hebron agreement marks the beginning of a new era of Arab-Israeli peace-making in which the momentum for success among people and leaders alike is likely to promote continued compromises and pragmatism.

The Hebron accord is characterized by several important new elements: This was the first formal agreement signed between a Palestinian political authority and a Likud-led Israeli government; the first time Likud agreed to return to the Palestinians lands it considers part of "biblical Israel"; and the first major Israeli-Palestinian diplomatic process in which Arab intervention impacted the outcome as much as American and other third-party mediation, something highly significant for Israelis who yearn for continued, gradual acceptance in this predominantly Arab and Muslim region.

The most dramatic Arab intervention was the 11th-hour helicopter-hopping that Jordan's King Hussein undertook. His calls on Palestinian Authority President Yasser Arafat and Israeli Prime Minister Benjamin Netanyahu resulted in a compromise package.

Arab public opinion also played a powerful role in pressuring the parties to agree. In the two Arab states that have signed peace agreements with Israel—Jordan and Egypt—public opinion toward the Netanyahu-led government has been hostile.

A sudden deterioration in Israel's ties with Egypt and Jordan, combined with a virtual freeze on nascent ties between Israel and Arab states such as Oman and Qatar, must have frightened thoughtful Israelis who had believed that the Jewish state was finally being accepted in the Middle East.

The message to Israel from many quarters in the Arab world was: We agree to live in peace with Israel, but only to the extent that Israel accepts coexistence with a Palestinian state.

The Hebron accord signals the continuing emergence of a pragmatic, pan-Semitic Middle Eastern political center comprising Arabs and Israelis who are prepared to drop absolutist principles to achieve meaningful political gains. Thus, a Likud-led Israeli government withdraws from "biblical Israel" and gradually accepts the emergence of a Palestinian entity that enjoys the basic trappings of sovereign statehood. The Palestinians have little choice but to signal their willingness to live with the continued presence of Israelis (protected by the Israeli army) in their midst, whether in downtown Hebron or in Jewish settlements throughout the West Bank and Gaza.

Both sides are hinting about innovative arrangements for Jerusalem that satisfy their desire to claim the holy city as their capital. Both sides seem to be saying that they care more about security and sovereignty than they do about exclusivist territorial claims. Thus, the separation of Israelis and Palestinians portends longer-term arrangements in which both populations and sovereignties will be meshed together in a complex manner.

The post-Hebron Israeli withdrawals and the final status negotiations between Israelis and Palestinians are likely to proceed within the same emotional and political framework that we have witnessed since the Oslo accords were signed: Each side will present maximalist positions, public opinion on both sides will harden, pressures will build on the political leaderships to compromise, and a last-minute accord will be reached that fully satisfies neither side.

Such accords, Hebron teaches us, will sacrifice ideological purity and territorial exclusivism for the more pragmatic mode of conflict resolution and intertwined sovereignties that we have just seen validated in Hebron.

Steve Kelley/Copley News Service. Reprinted with permission.

Minority voices on both sides will complain and accuse their governments of selling out. But the silent, accommodating majorities on both sides will get on with the business of addressing the broader problems.

Arabs and Israelis are facing enormous pressures on a combination of economic and environmental fronts that can be alleviated only through regional cooperation. Arabs and Israelis face similar internal divisions between secular and religious components of their populations, and the Arab world is deeply scarred, distorted and burdened by its consequences of its autocratic governance systems.

The Hebron agreement suggests that in 1997, exactly 100 years after the idea of a modern Jewish state and political Zionism was born, clear majorities of Arabs and Israelis finally are prepared to live with one another on the basis of reasonable compromises, instead of at the expense of one another's rights and lands. A century of confrontation and conflict can be a long time, but also an emphatic teacher. The lesson of the century in Palestine and Israel is that the land will be shared. Hebron was its first, shaky test.

"*What Israel offered was land for peace. The exchange it got instead was land for terror.*"

ARAB-ISRAELI NEGOTIATIONS WILL NOT FOSTER PEACE

Jeff Jacoby

In October 1998, Israeli and Arab leaders signed the Wye Memorandum, a document that releases some Israeli-occupied territory to Palestinian authorities in exchange for Arab promises to combat terrorism. In the following viewpoint, Jeff Jacoby argues that this agreement will not lead to peace. In previous negotiations, Jacoby points out, Israel has offered Palestinians "land for peace" and received hatred and terrorism in return. Because the Wye accord does not ensure Palestinian compliance and security for Israel, it could lead to disaster, the author concludes. Jacoby is a columnist for the *Boston Globe*, a daily newspaper.

As you read, consider the following questions:

1. How has Yasser Arafat benefited from the Israeli-Palestinian peace negotiations, in Jacoby's opinion?
2. According to the author, why did Palestinian Authority police arrest six Arabs in the village of Waladja?
3. According to the Center for Palestine Research, what percentage of the Palestinian public supports acts of violence against Israel?

Reprinted from Jeff Jacoby, "The Disastrous Wye Accord," *Boston Globe*, October 29, 1998, by permission of the author.

Yasser Arafat signed his first peace agreement with Israel (the Oslo accord) in September 1993. He signed a second peace agreement (the Gaza-Jericho accord) in May 1994. He signed a third peace agreement (Oslo II) in September 1995. He signed a fourth peace agreement (the Hebron accord) in January 1997. And in October 1998 he signed the document negotiated at the Wye Plantation, his fifth peace agreement with Israel in five years.

ARAFAT'S BOUNTY

Arafat has reaped a rich bounty from this peace process. He rules his own quasi-state, the Palestinian Authority. Nearly all of Gaza is his, as is every major town on the West Bank—and more land is to come. He enjoys international deference and prestige. He has a well-armed police force and millions of dollars. He controls Palestinian newspapers, radio and TV. He is immune from prosecution for his many crimes, which include the murder of children. He has been awarded the Nobel Prize.

All through the years of peacemaking with Israel, Arafat has repeatedly made clear just how far his vision of coexistence extends. He made it clear again on Oct. 22, 1998.

Even as the negotiations were under way in Maryland, Palestinian Authority police were arresting six Arabs from the village of Waladja, near Bethlehem on the West Bank. They were seized for engaging in behavior that is forbidden in Arafat's kingdom: They had paid a condolence call on the family of Itamar Doron, a 25-year-old Israeli Jew murdered a few days earlier while bathing in the stream at Moshav Ora. Other residents of Waladja protested. The six, they said, had no right to visit the grieving family "in the name of all the village." Arafat's Fatah organization announced that while murder should be condemned, there must be no condolence calls by Palestinians to Israeli homes.

Such is the nature of peace in Arafatland.

LAND FOR TERROR

The road from Oslo has led to calamity. What Israel offered was land for peace. The exchange it got instead was land for terror: More Israelis have been blown up and gunned down by Palestinian terrorists in the five years of "peace" than in the previous 15 years.

Israel has exchanged land for threats: Farouk Kaddoumi, head of the Palestine Liberation Organization's political bureau, vowed on Oct. 14, 1998, that the Palestinians will follow up their declaration of a state in May 1999 by launching "the battle against Israeli forces" to eradicate "the Israeli presence on Palestinian lands." Kaddoumi is seen by many as Arafat's most likely successor.

Israel has exchanged land for anti-Semitism: The largest newspaper in the Palestinian Authority, *Al-Hayat Al-Jadida*, writes that Hitler's persecution "was a malicious fabrication by the Jews." That "Jewish control over the mass media has . . . put a pleasant face on the vile image of Jews." That "Jews spread prostitution as a means of plunging the world into decadence, abomination, and corruption."

© Peter Steiner. Reprinted with permission.

Israel has exchanged land for incitement: Fiery sermons in Palestinian mosques preach jihad [holy war] against the Zionists. Schoolbooks exhort children to "gather for war with red blood and blazing fire" and assign essays on the question, "Why must we fight the Jews and drive them out of our land?"

Land for peace? Israel surrendered land and was paid back in hatred. The Center for Palestine Research reported in October 1998 that 51 percent of the Palestinian public supports acts of violence against Israel. If those are the sentiments of Israel's peace partners, how must its enemies feel?

A DANGEROUS AGREEMENT

The accord that Benjamin Netanyahu brought back from Wye is worse than the deals negotiated by Yitzhak Rabin and Shimon Peres. Not just because Arafat will again be paid in land for promises he has broken over and over. Not just because the language is so full of fuzz and loopholes that it makes a farce of the "reciprocity" Netanyahu insisted would be his irreducible minimum.

What is most alarming about this agreement is that there is no Likud Party to oppose it. Netanyahu and his foreign minister, Ariel Sharon, have acquiesced in an accord that would have had them screaming had it been signed by their predecessors.

Peres was deposed as prime minister because most Israelis didn't trust him to keep them safe. Now Netanyahu has agreed to terms that even Peres never swallowed—for example, letting the Clinton administration, not the Israeli government, be the sole judge of Palestinian compliance. The administration that couldn't stand up to Saddam Hussein, that had no idea India was about to go nuclear, that was stunned when North Korea launched a missile over Japan, that has lurched from empty threat to empty threat in Kosovo—this administration is now going to crack down on Arafat's violations?

The language of the Wye Memorandum is plain. It does not say, contrary to media reports, that the Palestinian charter calling for Israel's destruction is to be annulled. It does not say that Arafat's police force is to be reduced. It does not say that terrorist murderers will be extradited to Israel or imprisoned by the Palestinian Authority.

The only sure consequence of Wye is that Israel will yield more land and Arafat will demand still more. Eventually Israel will refuse to give, but by then the state of Palestine—with its Arab allies—will be ready to take. For the fifth time in five years, a peace agreement has been signed that brings war closer. There is a reason Arafat wore battle fatigues to the signing ceremony.

| "The current vindictiveness of Jew against Jew must be brought to an end."

JEWISH UNITY WOULD FOSTER PEACE

Stanley K. Sheinbaum

In the following viewpoint, Stanley K. Sheinbaum contends that unity among Israelis and among the international Jewish community would enhance the prospects for peace in the Middle East. Infighting among Israelis could endanger Israel if the Arab world sees these tensions as a vulnerability, he maintains. Moreover, the distancing of American Jews from Israel undermines Jewish cultural identity and threatens the important alliance between Israel and American Jewry. Jews should work together to ensure peace in Israel and the Middle East, insists Sheinbaum. Sheinbaum is the publisher of New Perspectives Quarterly, a journal of social and political thought.

As you read, consider the following questions:

1. Which Israeli groups have been pitted against each other in recent years, according to Sheinbaum?
2. According to the author, why has American Jewish support for Israel diminished?
3. What are the "mixed messages" that Benjamin Netanyahu has been sending to the American Jewish constituency, in Sheinbaum's opinion?

Reprinted from Stanley K. Sheinbaum, "A House Divided Cannot Heal Itself," Los Angeles Times, January 12, 1998, by permission. Copyright ©1998 by the Los Angeles Times.

As an American Jew, I am intensely concerned about achieving peace in the Middle East. I had an Orthodox service to become a Bar Mitzvah in 1933, 15 years before the United Nations granted statehood to Israel. With the Holocaust as background, the significance of a Jewish homeland was enormous. Israel offered an essential shelter as well as an identity for me and my people.

As the years passed, my pride in the Jewish state grew. Not only was it military strength but also the social and spiritual achievements that made seemingly indelible marks. Time and again, surrounding Arab nations tried to beat back those achievements, always unsuccessfully.

ISRAELI VERSUS ISRAELI

Peace, I always thought, had to be the first priority. Only through peace with the Palestinians and the surrounding Arab nations would terrorism wane and Israel blossom into its fullest potential.

But today in Israel, there is a force making peace only the remotest possibility. That is the pitting of Israeli against Israeli with an intensity that is relatively new; the religious versus the secular; the Sephardim versus the Ashkenazim; the left versus the right; the rich versus the poor; and the Ethiopian Jews and the Russian Jews both feeling alienated. It is a new Israel and it is being torn asunder by Jews against each other.

A less cohesive Israel will be further endangered if the surrounding Arab world senses the weakness. The current vindictiveness of Jew against Jew must be brought to an end.

DIMINISHING SUPPORT FROM JEWS

Then the question arises about the attitude of American Jews toward Israel. What has become clear . . . is that support for Israel is diminishing. An almost steady flow of articles in the mainstream and Jewish press tell of a significant reduction in American Jewish contributions.

Several factors are at work. In addition to the concern about the divisiveness in Israel, there is the intense reaction on the part of Reform and Conservative Jews to the conversion issue.

No doubt the trend toward assimilation in the U.S. has confused the loyalty of American Jews at the same time the Israeli state is losing its meaning for many. And then occasionally someone in Israel even comments that Israel no longer needs U.S. support or even its aid. This wounds American Jews who have long supported Israel. American Jews see U.S. government aid as objective evidence that they continue to support Israel in an increasingly trying time for the Jewish state—even though their personal money is being withheld. So go figure out political psychology.

MIXED MESSAGES

Lastly, there is the factor of Prime Minister Benjamin Netanyahu, who is anything but popular in the U.S. Oslo [the mid-1990s peace negotiations between Israelis and Palestinians] meant much to Americans and to American Jews. It seemed that finally a solution to the peace dilemma was in process. Yet Netanyahu sends mixed messages about where he stands on this important agreement. Sometimes he appears against it. Other times, he sends the message that he is locked in by the radical right, thus placing his own political survival above the need for peace. And sometimes, he sends the confusing message that what his predecessor agreed to in Oslo is OK, but it needs basic change. He has alienated not only President Bill Clinton and Secretary of State Madeleine Albright but especially the American Jewish constituency which is losing its confidence in him.

Horsey. Reprinted by permission of North America Syndicate.

In the final analysis and regardless of American Jewish attitudes, the intensifying lack of unity among Israelis is in and of itself perhaps the most disturbing phenomenon about Israel.

That divisiveness is clearly a serious impediment to achieving peace. At the same time the manifest distancing of the American Jews from Israel leaves us without the confidence of our identity.

Yes, perhaps we all should have made *aliyah* [moved to Israel] and become more a part of Israel's struggle. Hardly a Jew has not carefully weighed that possibility. Regardless, Israel cannot be without the support of its closest and strongest allies—American Jewry.

"For Israel to remain a Jewish state, both morally and demographically, it needs a Palestinian state."

THE ESTABLISHMENT OF A PALESTINIAN STATE WOULD FOSTER PEACE

Shimon Peres

The establishment of a separate Palestinian state would foster peace in the Middle East, argues Shimon Peres in the following viewpoint. Now that Israel has come to accept the necessity of Palestinian self-rule, the land between the Mediterranean Sea and the River Jordan should be fairly divided between Israelis and Palestinians, Peres contends. This division of land into two states should be perceived as an opportunity for profitable collaboration, industrialization, and commerce for both Israel and Palestine, he maintains. Peres is a former prime minister of Israel.

As you read, consider the following questions:

1. What was the result of the Oslo negotiations, according to Peres?
2. In Peres's view, what would happen if a binational state were established?
3. Why have borders between states lost their significance, in the author's opinion?

Reprinted from Shimon Peres, "Israel Needs a Palestinian State," *World Press Review*, July 1998 (originally in *Le Monde Diplomatique*, May 1998), by permission of The New York Times Syndicate.

When Theodor Herzl, the founder of Zionism, spoke of "a people without a land" looking for "a land without a people," he was not aware of the Arab population in Palestine or its future evolution. His vision, a utopia unlike anything else in the Middle East, led to an independent state that surpassed anything he could have dreamed of.

Jews, a people dispersed, almost lost, came together to be reborn. They returned to their historic homeland and infused it with new life; they revived their historic tongue and transformed it into a living language; they created new forms of life (such as the kibbutz); they formed a state in which democratic freedoms were observed, even in wartime; they put in place industry, agriculture, and services as advanced as those of the most developed nations. Israel became the only compensation, if compensation there could be, for the Holocaust, the Shoah, which the Jewish people suffered under the Nazis.

But a central objective has not yet been achieved: a global peace with the Arab countries. Still unresolved, the Palestinian question—the pretext for attacks on Israel—remains the principal danger to its security. Its solution would make the Palestinian problem assume its own natural dimensions, but its non-resolution risks lighting a fire that could go far beyond the geographical dimensions of the problem.

THE OSLO ACCORDS

At Oslo [the mid-1990s peace negotiations], we began reconciliation between Israelis and Palestinians. We negotiated regarding recognition of the Palestinian entity and the necessity of making it possible for the Palestinians to achieve independence. It was no longer a question of an agreement on something that already existed: Something new was born at Oslo.

It was decided that the Palestinians would win recognition of their national dignity, and Israel would be freed of a moral weight on its historic conscience. Israel would no longer control the destiny of another people, which is contrary to our historic conception and has outraged the Palestinians.

In fact, for Israel to remain a Jewish state, both morally and demographically, it needs a Palestinian state. Today, 4.7 million Jews and 4 million Arabs live between the Mediterranean and the River Jordan. Without two separate states, a binational state will come into being, to the great frustration of the two peoples. A binational tragedy would ensue which, in the course of time, would force Israel to stay armed against the Palestinians, whose bitterness could lead once more to terrorism.

LAND AND ECONOMICS

At the same time, dividing the land between the two peoples is not easy. There are more than 9,000 square miles between the Mediterranean and the Jordan. Today, 9 million people live on this land. In 20 years, the population will double, reaching 20 million, of whom half (if not more) will be Arabs and the other half (or less) will be Jews. Whether the Arabs receive most of the land that they are claiming (about 20 percent of the land lying between the Mediterranean and the Jordan) or whether Israel keeps the greater part of it, the two peoples will suffer from great pressure on the land that they have. Paradoxically, it will be Israel's concern to see that the Palestinians have a modern economy providing their population with a fair income.

THE GOAL OF THE PALESTINIAN PEOPLE

I would like to call upon all of you, from this place [the UN General Assembly], the source of international legitimacy and peacemaking, the guardian of freedom, security and stability, and the source for the achievement of justice and prosperity for humankind, to stand by our people [the Palestinians], especially as the five-year transitional period provided for in the Palestinian-Israeli agreements will end on 4 May 1999 and our people demand of us to shoulder our responsibilities and wait [for] the establishment of their independent state. I assure you that our people will continue to pursue and protect the peace of the brave in the Middle East. We appeal to you to continue your support for us, as has always been the case in the decisive moments of history, the present and the future of our people. Help us to achieve the national goal of our people.

Yasser Arafat, statement before the 53rd session of the UN General Assembly, September 28, 1998.

We must not allow two different economies to develop: a poor Arab economy offering cheap labor and a rich Israeli economy profiting from that labor. Such a divergence would risk prolonging the conflict and transforming a national conflict into a socioeconomic one. To ensure a fair future, we need two states and a modern economy built on the basis of cooperation between two separate states.

THE QUESTION OF BORDERS

There is the question of borders. The nature of these borders can make the task of drawing them easier or more complicated. But in reality, these days, borders between states have lost much of their value. A border cannot protect us from economic flows because the economy is now global. Markets are more important than states, and being a player in these markets means competition that has no respect for national borders. Borders can no longer stop an armed attack since they make no impression either on missiles or on terrorism. Maginot lines are useless when a chemical, biological, or even nuclear weapon is following a ballistic trajectory.

So putting land mines on borders is pointless. It is better to transform them into opportunities for cooperation and build airports, hotels, and industrial parks. Meetings between peoples are the best alternative to a possible clash of their armies; hotels on borders could be a better guarantee of peace than military bases.

Peace is not the pursuit of war by other means. Peace consists of putting an end to the red ink of past history and starting anew in a different color so that the next generation can rejoice in a fresh landscape with a new taste for life and look forward to long years ahead.

| "Fighting intolerance . . . means
  encouraging broader education."

EDUCATION AND CULTURAL EXCHANGE WOULD FOSTER PEACE

Ben Barber

The fear of terrorism from Islamic radicals is as strong in Muslim nations as it is in the West, Ben Barber points out in the following viewpoint. To help curb terrorism, Westerners should learn more about the economic, educational, and religious differences among the various Muslim peoples, he contends. Furthermore, government leaders and theologians should encourage academic and cultural exchanges between the Islamic world and the West. Such exchange would foster the tolerance that leads to peace, Barber maintains. Barber is a correspondent for the *Washington Times*, a daily newspaper.

As you read, consider the following questions:

1. How were Muslim attitudes toward the West influenced by the media, in Barber's opinion?
2. Why have some Muslim elites encouraged anti-Western sentiments, according to the author?
3. Why do Islamic fundamentalists reject today's Jews and Christians, according to Barber?

Reprinted from Ben Barber, "Finding the Door to Islamic Peace," *The Washington Times*, October 15, 1998, by permission of *The Washington Times*; © News World Communications, Inc.

The West is not the only place Islamic terror and fanaticism is feared. It's feared and despised back home in Islamic nations as well. From Morocco to Algeria to Egypt, from Turkey to Jordan to Pakistan. Moderate, educated people are trembling at the rage and furor and ignorance sprouting in the streets.

Under the green banners of Islamic radicalism sprouts a virulent mob psychology. Intolerant, destructive, hateful of all who disagree with its views. The standoff between Iran and Afghanistan is partly about who is more radical as a Muslim. If it was not so dangerous for millions of people on both sides of the barren, stone-strewn desert border between Mashed and Herat, the irony of the two Islamic intolerants going at each other might be laughable.

For certain, it is not laughable.

Yet there are things that can be done by the West and by the East to defuse this time bomb—this ideological virus that has already seized control in Iran, Afghanistan and Sudan and threatens to win power in a half dozen other capitals.

THE ELITE AND THE STREET

First of all, the roots of this movement must be examined. Thirty years ago, the Islamic world was, as today, divided into the elite and the street. The elite sent their children to Oxford and Harvard, and they welcomed any chance to get involved in Western fashion, technology and even the Cold War rivalry.

The street ploughed the fields, recited Koran and lived in a timeless poverty that did not know the extent of its own deprivation.

Yes, there was pain and hunger and early death. But there was balance and tradition and respect and a sense of location.

Much of that changed as traditional Islamic governments were toppled and replaced by populist dictators not simply satisfied with ruling—they also wanted to be loved for their wisdom. Men like Gamal Nasser, Moamar Khadafy, Saddam Hussein, Hafez Assad. Then came the explosion in media, allowing the street to view the external reality of Europe and America— the short skirts, the divorce, the booze and drugs, the crime, the pornography. But the street rarely understood the internal reality of the West—the universal, secular education, the impartial justice and police, the responsible, objective news media, the accountability of elected governments from the school board to the head of state.

This left the street with a superficial, jaundiced view of the West easily manipulated by dictators to disparage Western con-

197

cepts of democracy. Through that open gate marched the fundamentalists.

Over Saudi-funded radio broadcasts and at the Friday mosque
sermons from Marrakesh to Karachi, fundamentalists rode the
coat tails of the dictators' rejection of Western politics, calling
for rejection of the West's tolerance and secular government.

PROMOTING RELIGIOUS TOLERANCE

[The U.S. State Department's Advisory Committee on Religious
Freedom Abroad] has sponsored and funded programs to promote religious liberty and tolerance. Some of these programs are
specifically targeted at the issue [of religious intolerance], while
others are broader in scope but still impact positively on the
problem. For example, [U.S. embassy] posts in Arab countries
have sent clerics, journalists, politicians and academics to the
United States to participate in an annual International Visitor
program on "Religion in America," in which they meet with
American Christian, Muslim, Jewish and ecumenical groups to
discuss ways to promoting religious tolerance. Participants have
returned impressed with the extent of religious freedom in the
U.S. and the possibilities for cooperative relationships among
people of different faiths. Through the National Endowment for
Democracy we are funding several programs to support tolerance and secularism; for example, a project to enable an independent literary journal to organize debates on religion and
democracy among theologians, historians, and lawyers, and another project to translate into Arabic and publish important
works on democracy, tolerance and pluralism.

Steven Coffey, testimony before the Senate Foreign Relations Subcommittee on
the Middle East, May 1, 1997.

The bitter irony is that in countries such as Pakistan, where
senior figures told me in the summer of 1998 they are in fear of
the demons of fundamentalism—calling it a disease—the elites
once welcomed anti-Western rhetoric. It was a way to keep the
feudal masses down. The rhetoric served to explain why millions of dollars were budgeted for the army and to send the elite
children to foreign universities but 75 percent of the street
could not read and write and had no clean water or medicine.

The rejection of the West as a model also served to keep lower
class women in the bondage of illiteracy, forced confinement,
multiple wives, reduced legal status and no access to birth control.

Now these same elites are trembling each time America or Israel bombs a terrorist base, such as the U.S. attack on Osama bin

Laden's Afghanistan redoubts in August 1998. The leaders of the mobs respond by taking over the street with demands for Islamic law, cutting ties with the West and drawing closer to fundamentalist regimes.

ALLIANCES WITH ISRAEL

The third leg of the fundamentalist platform—after political dictatorship and the inflammatory media—was Israel's military victory in 1967 against Egypt, Jordan and Syria. I recall being in a Turkish cafe near Adana around June 8 that year, asking to search for news of the war on the owner's radio for a moment. Permission granted, I found an Israeli broadcast that said Israel was winning and had taken Jerusalem's old city.

The Turks asked what it said and I explained, translating into rudimentary Turkish.

"Good," said the cafe owner with a smile. "The Israelis work hard. They deserve to win."

Today Turkey is drawing ever closer to Israel and possibly Jordan in an alliance aimed at blocking Islamic terrorism and fundamentalism. The split between Turkey and the radicals, the Iranians and the Afghans and other diverse Islamic trends is one key to defusing the Green bomb that a small minority of the world's Muslims are seeking to construct.

UNDERSTANDING THE ISLAMIC REVIVAL

What the West needs to know about the Islamic revival in order to channel its volatile energy in a positive direction is:

• Economic, educational and class differences within Islamic nations are an essential element. The poor are manipulated and incited because of their anger at being left out of the wealth they now can view on television.

• Each Islamic nation has a unique tradition and they often hate each other as much as they hate the West. Afghan mujahideen with whom I traveled during the war against the Soviets expressed contempt for the "Wahabis"—the Saudi volunteers who insisted their style of prayer was superior to that of the Afghans. Each country's Islamic practice also has its own rules dealing with foreigners, women, education, alcohol, marijuana, militancy and tolerance.

• Ignorance is the single biggest asset to the fundamentalist revival. Lacking objective instruction in science, history, geography and other basics, everything is recast as propaganda, as part of the cultural, religious war that the extremists are preparing for. The hundreds of thousands of Pakistani youths enrolled in religious schools often go because they can find no public schools to attend.

• Ignorance also means lack of human contact with other cultures. Gone are the days when each valley held its own tribe with its own world view. It had been hoped that modern economies and transport would produce a flourishing global marketplace of goods and ideas that would enlighten the world and produce the kind of tolerance seen in modern Europe—where different languages, religions and cultures are tolerated, and political and economic barriers melt away.

This is not happening in many Islamic countries where the street is too poor to travel, dictators and fundamentalists control the media and foreign visitors are few. Instead intolerance is growing.

Islamic fundamentalists totally reject Buddhism and Hinduism as idol worship that must be extirpated. They also believe that Jews and Christians are not real Jews and Christians because their texts have been altered. As such they are not even entitled to Islamic protection accorded to "people of the book" who follow the Old or New Testaments but do not accept Mohammed. This is a dangerous concept.

WHAT SHOULD BE DONE

So what needs to be done to counter intolerant and violent Islamic fundamentalism?

Nourish Western contacts with mainstream Islamic thinkers and opinion leaders. Using government and academic exchange programs, bring them to visit the United States. And send to Islamic countries religious and political figures. Hold forums to exchange ideas with leaders of the Al Ahzar Islamic center in Cairo and other senior Islamic institutions. Even if Christian, Jewish and Muslim theologians disagree, by listening to each other they will open the door to humanization of the other—to the understanding that tolerance does not mean one agrees with another, only that one understands the other's right to hold differing views.

Fighting intolerance also means encouraging broader education for the street. But that requires that the elites divert resources from their walled compounds, cell phones and foreign education towards their maids and drivers. It also requires that education be firmly vetted to teach as objectively as possible about the real world.

What the Israelis and the Sri Lankans and the Indians have learned after decades fighting terrorism is that the mailed fist is unable to win a final victory. Education, human contact, intellectual exchange, ping-pong diplomacy, wrestling teams and the openness to debate and learn from each other stand the best chance of creating a world climate of understanding in which even the most orthodox, strict Islamic people would find respect and fulfillment in peace.

PERIODICAL BIBLIOGRAPHY

The following articles have been selected to supplement the diverse views presented in this chapter. Addresses are provided for periodicals not indexed in the *Readers' Guide to Periodical Literature*, the *Alternative Press Index*, the *Social Sciences Index*, or the *Index to Legal Periodicals and Books*.

Barbara Nimri Aziz   "Dashed Hopes," *Toward Freedom*, November 1998.

Stanley Cohen   "No Time for Reconciliation," *Index on Censorship*, September/October 1996.

Christopher Hitchens   "Iraq and the Visitations of Empire," *Nation*, March 16, 1998.

Michael C. Hudson   "Obstacles to Democratization in the Middle East," *Contention*, Winter 1996. Available from Journals Manager, Indiana University Press, 601 N. Morton St., Bloomington, IN 47404.

David Makovsky   "We Might Surprise Ourselves," *U.S. News & World Report*, May 4, 1998.

New York Times   "Arafat and Netanyahu in Pact on Next Steps Toward Peace; Modest Deal to 'Rebuild Trust,'" October 24, 1998.

Roger Normand   "Iraqi Sanctions, Human Rights, and Humanitarian Law," *Middle East Report*, July–September 1996.

Daniel Pipes   "On Arab Rejectionism," *Commentary*, December 1, 1997.

Peter W. Rodman   "Mideast Burnout," *National Review*, August 3, 1998.

Debra Rosenberg et al.   "The Deal Makers," *Newsweek*, November 2, 1998.

Edward W. Said   "The Poverty of Nationalism," *Progressive*, March 1998.

Uri Savir   "Why Oslo Still Matters," *New York Times Magazine*, May 3, 1998.

John V. Whitbeck   "Palestine Already Is a State," *Los Angeles Times*, March 3, 1997. Available from Reprints, Times Mirror Square, Los Angeles, CA 90053.

Stephen Zunes   "Hazardous Hegemony: The United States in the Middle East," *Current History*, January 1997.

FOR FURTHER DISCUSSION

CHAPTER 1

1. Rachelle Marshall argues that right-wing Jewish extremism is to blame for tensions between Israel and Palestine, while Mortimer B. Zuckerman maintains that the intransigence of Palestinian Islamic fundamentalists is Israel's main source of conflict. What evidence does each author present to support his or her argument? Which author's use of evidence do you find more convincing? Explain.

2. The authors in this chapter discuss several causes of tension and potential conflict in the Middle East. After reading this chapter, what do you believe is the predominant source of conflict in the region? Support your answer with evidence from the viewpoints.

CHAPTER 2

1. Martin Kramer contends that fundamentalist Islam's drive for power often mobilizes its adherents for violent conflict. Muhammad M. El-Hodaiby argues that a Muslim who participates in violence is committing a sin because Islamic tenets explicitly reject violence. Kramer is the director of a Middle Eastern studies program at an Israeli university; El-Hodaiby is a leader of the Muslim Brotherhood in Egypt. Does knowing their backgrounds influence your assessment of their arguments? Explain your answer.

2. Uri Regev claims that orthodox Judaism threatens religious freedom and democracy in Israel, while Tom Bethell contends that secular Israelis are intensifying Israel's cultural war. Which viewpoint do you agree with, and why?

3. Abraham Cooper argues that terrorism in Israel is partly the result of Muslim leaders' refusal to publicly rebuke suicide attacks against Israelis. Ahmad Yusuf maintains that Muslim attacks of Israelis are a retaliatory response to Israel's terrorism against Palestinians. Do you agree with Yusuf that the Israeli government is terrorist? Why or why not? Explain your answer, using evidence from the viewpoints.

4. Donna M. Hughes contends that Iranian women are not likely to find increasing support for women's rights within an Islamic republic. Scott MacLeod and Lindsey Hilsum argue that women are slowly making gains in Iran and are challenging the Islamic government to change some of its restrictive poli-

cies. Evaluate each author's opinion, then formulate your own argument describing the nature of feminism in Iran.

CHAPTER 3

1. Robert H. Pelletreau and Stephen Hubbell disagree about the aims of U.S. intervention in Middle Eastern affairs. In each viewpoint, try to find two supporting arguments that you agree with. Why do you agree with them?

2. Bill Clinton maintains that if necessary, air strikes on Iraq are justified to prevent the growth of Saddam Hussein's weapons-of-mass-destruction program. Does Bob Herbert's viewpoint effectively refute Clinton's argument? Why or why not?

3. Sandra Mackey argues that the United States should participate in a cultural dialogue with Iran. James Phillips maintains that such a dialogue could subvert U.S. efforts to deter Iran from terrorism and revolutionary violence. What evidence does each author use to bolster his or her argument? Whose use of evidence is more persuasive? Explain.

CHAPTER 4

1. Rick McDowell uses health surveys and statistics, as well as the testimony of Iraqi civilians, to support his contention that the UN-imposed economic sanctions against Iraq should be lifted. Madeleine Albright discusses the strained relationship between Saddam Hussein and UN weapons inspectors as part of her argument that sanctions against Iraq should continue. In your opinion, which author's rhetorical technique is more effective? Why?

2. Rami G. Khouri maintains that the Arab-Israeli negotiations will eventually succeed because the majority of Arabs and Israelis are ready to live together in peace. Jeff Jacoby argues that Palestinian anti-Semitism and terrorism continue to undermine any prospects for peace in the Middle East. In your opinion, which of these viewpoints presents the most likely scenario for the future of Arab-Israeli relations? Explain.

3. This chapter lists several recommendations for advancing peace in the Middle East. Consider each recommendation and then list arguments for and against each one. Note whether the arguments are based on facts, values, emotions, or other considerations. If you believe a recommendation should not be considered at all, explain why.

CHRONOLOGY OF EVENTS

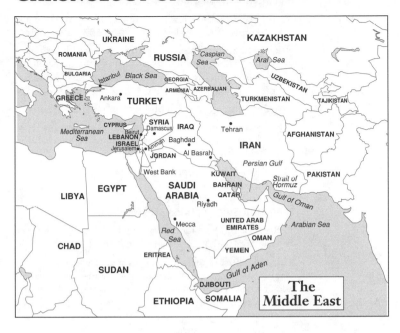

The Middle East

1897   Theodor Herzl convenes First Zionist Congress, which designates Palestine as an appropriate Jewish homeland. Less than 10 percent of Palestine's population is Jewish.

1914–1918   World War I. Arab nationalists cooperate with Britain against Turkey. Turkey's Ottoman Empire collapses.

1917   British foreign secretary A.J. Balfour declares Britain's support for a national homeland for the Jewish people in Palestine, a declaration that conflicts with promises to the Arabs.

1920–1948   Britain rules Palestine under agreement with the League of Nations. The British mandate approves limited immigration for Jews.

1921   Military officer Reza Khan rules Iran after a coup and begins a secularization campaign that abolishes many Islamic customs. Faisal I, with British support, is made king of Iraq, which is composed of three former Ottoman Empire provinces.

1922   At the Uqair Conference, the modern borders of Iraq, Saudi Arabia, and Kuwait are drawn by representatives of the British government.

1927–1938   Oil is discovered in commercial quantities in northern Iraq, Bahrain, Saudi Arabia, and Kuwait.

1928   The Muslim Brotherhood is established in Egypt as a movement of fundamentalist reform among Sunni Muslims.

1929–1939	Arabs rebel against British rule; Arabs fight Jews for the right to live in Palestine.
1939–1945	World War II. Six million Jews are killed by Nazi Germany. Jewish population in Palestine swells to 608,000 by 1946.
1941	British and Soviet forces, concerned that Reza Khan is allied with Adolf Hitler, invade Iran and depose the monarch, replacing him with his son, Muhammed Reza Khan Pahlavi.
November 1943	Lebanon achieves independence, with government posts given to members of each of the main religious groups.
November 29, 1947	UN General Assembly votes to partition Palestine into Jewish and Arab states with Jerusalem being an international city. Arabs refuse.
May 14, 1948	David Ben-Gurion proclaims the state of Israel, which is immediately attacked by five Arab states. Israel defeats the coalition, and takes more land than originally assigned. More than 500,000 Palestinians flee Israel.
1952	Officers of the Egyptian army overthrow King Farouk and replace him with their leader, Gamal Abdel Nasser.
1953	U.S. and British intelligence forces organize a coup against democratic reformer Muhammed Mossadeq that restores the Shah of Iran, Muhammed Reza Pahlavi, to power. He allows a consortium of foreign companies to operate Iran's oil industry.
July 1956	The U.S. and Britain refuse to support a loan to Egypt to build the Aswan High Dam; in retaliation, Nasser seizes control of the Suez Canal. After Britain freezes Egyptian assets held in England, Egypt closes the canal.
October 1956	The Israelis, with military aid from Britain and France, invade Egypt. They take the Gaza Strip and the Sinai Peninsula, which they later return in a peace settlement.
1958	Faisal II, who had succeeded Faisal I as king of Iraq, is assassinated. Abdul Karim Kassem installs himself as military dictator of Iraq.
August 1959	Jordan offers citizenship to all Palestinian refugees.
January 1961	Iran, Iraq, Kuwait, and Saudi Arabia found the Organization of Petroleum Exporting Countries (OPEC).
May 1964	Palestine Liberation Organization (PLO) is established.
May 1967	Nasser orders UN emergency forces to withdraw from the Sinai, declares a state of emergency in the Gaza Strip, and closes the Strait of Tiran to shipping to and from Israel. Israel and the U.S. warn Egypt to remove the blockade.
June 5–10, 1967	Six-Day War. Israel attacks Egypt, Jordan, and Syria and captures the Sinai, Gaza Strip, West Bank, and Golan Heights.
November 22, 1967	UN Security Council Resolution 242 calling for peace in the Middle East is adopted. The resolution asks that Israel return land acquired in the Six-Day War and that Arabs respect Israel's boundaries.

1969	Yasser Arafat and Fatah (the largest Palestinian group) take over the PLO and give it a more assertive role.
1970	Nasser dies and Vice President Anwar Sadat takes over leadership of Egypt.
1970–1971	Jordanian civil war. King Hussein crushes Palestinian guerrillas and invading troops. Palestinians move offices from Jordan to Beirut, Lebanon.
October 6, 1973	Yom Kippur War. Egypt and Syria launch a two-front surprise attack on Israeli forces in the Sinai Peninsula and the Golan Heights.
October 18, 1973	First day of five-month Arab oil embargo cutting off or sharply curtailing oil exports to countries that support Israel.
November 11, 1973	Egypt and Israel agree to a cease-fire.
October 1974	The UN grants the PLO observer status and allows it to participate in debates on the status of Palestinian refugees.
April 1975	In Lebanon, Christian Phalangists attack Palestinians, touching off large-scale confrontations between Christians and Muslims. Syria participates on the side of the Muslims.
November 1977	Sadat makes the first visit of an Arab leader to Israel to promote renewed peace talks. In exchange for peace, Israel offers to return Sinai to Egypt and allow limited Palestinian self-rule in the Israeli-occupied areas of the West Bank and Gaza Strip.
September 1978	Camp David summit meeting between U.S. president Jimmy Carter, Israeli prime minister Menachem Begin, and Sadat leads to an Egyptian-Israeli peace agreement and accords on the Palestinian question. Under the agreement, Israel returns all of Sinai to Egypt by 1982. Most of the Arab states, the Soviet Union, and the PLO denounce the agreements.
February 1979	After months of unrest, the government of Iran is overthrown. The Shah is replaced by Shi'ite Muslim fundamentalists led by Ayatollah Ruhollah Khomeini.
July 1979	Saddam Hussein seizes power in Iraq.
November 4, 1979	Militants storm the U.S. embassy in Tehran, Iran, and hold fifty-two Americans hostage for the next fourteen months.
September 1980	Iran makes air attacks on Iraqi towns. A few weeks later, Iraq invades Iran, beginning the eight-year Iran-Iraq war.
1981	Jewish settlements and housing construction on the West Bank begin.
June 1981	Israel bombs a nuclear reactor in Iraq "to prevent another Holocaust." The U.S. refuses to deliver promised military equipment to Israel.
October 1981	Sadat is assassinated by members of the Egyptian army. Vice President Hosni Mubarak takes over the government.
December 1981	Israel annexes the Golan Heights in Syria. The UN Security

	Council declares the annexation "null and void." Israel refuses to withdraw.
February 1982	Syrian leader Hafez Assad's troops crush a Muslim Brotherhood uprising in the city of Hama, killing more than ten thousand people.
June–September 1982	Israel invades Lebanon; it occupies Beirut and demands that the PLO leave the city. U.S. Marines help oversee the PLO evacuation. The PLO establishes its headquarters in Tunisia.
April 18, 1983	Sixty-three people are killed in the bombing of the U.S. embassy in Beirut.
May 17, 1983	Lebanon and Israel sign an agreement to withdraw Israeli forces from Lebanon. Israel refuses to withdraw completely until Syria also withdraws.
October 23, 1983	A pro-Iranian suicide bomber drives an explosives-laden truck into U.S. Marine headquarters in Beirut, killing 241 people.
January 1984	The administration of U.S. president Ronald Reagan officially lists Iran as a supporter of international terrorism and cuts arms sales to Iran.
May 16, 1985	Journalist Terry A. Anderson is kidnapped and held hostage in Lebanon. He becomes the longest-held American hostage of the eighteen kidnapped by various Islamic groups in Lebanon between 1982 and 1991. Of these eighteen hostages, three died or were killed in captivity, one escaped, six were released before 1987, two were released in 1990, and the remaining six were released in 1991.
June 1985	Shi'ite gunmen hijack TWA flight 847 and hold its 153 passengers hostage. They kill a U.S. Navy passenger. Most passengers are released except for 39 Americans, who are taken to Beirut. Iranian officials help negotiate freedom for the Americans.
October 7, 1985	Four Palestinians hijack the Italian ship *Achille Lauro* and hold 400 hostages. They kill Leon Klinghoffer, an elderly American Jew.
April 14, 1986	Reagan, arguing that Libyan leader Muammar Qaddafi supports anti-American terrorism, orders the bombing of Libyan cities Tripoli and Benghazi. Dozens of Libyans die as many homes are hit, including Qaddafi's.
November 1986	The U.S. government reveals that it covertly sold arms to Iran and diverted profits to the Nicaraguan Contra resistance in Central America. The scandal becomes known as the Iran-Contra affair.
December 1987	Four Palestinians are killed when an Israeli army truck rams their car after they attempt to run a military roadblock in Gaza. During their funeral, Israeli troops clash with mourners. The event marks the beginning of the widespread Palestinian uprising that comes to be called

the *intifada*. Hundreds of demonstrators are killed over the next five years in clashes between Israelis and Palestinians.

July 3, 1988	U.S. Navy ship patrolling the Persian Gulf accidentally shoots down Iranian commercial airliner, killing 290.
August 1988	Iran and Iraq accept UN peace terms and announce a cease-fire. The eight-year war leaves more than one million casualties. 100,000 Kurds flee to Turkey amidst reports that Iraq is attacking them with poison gas.
November 1988	Palestine National Council (PNC) meets in Algiers and votes to accept UN Security Council Resolutions 242 and 338, which call for Arab recognition of Israel and Israeli withdrawal from territories occupied since 1967. Jordan severs legal and administrative ties to the West Bank. Responsibility for the West Bank's economic and municipal functions shifts to the PLO.
December 1988	The U.S. establishes a "diplomatic dialogue" with the PLO after Arafat renounces terrorism and states that he accepts the right of "Palestine, Israel, and other neighbors" to exist in peace.
February 1989	Iranian leader Khomeini calls for Muslims to execute Indian-born British author Salman Rushdie, whose novel *The Satanic Verses* Khomeini calls blasphemous.
June 3, 1989	Iranian leader Khomeini dies in Tehran.
April 2, 1990	Iraqi president Saddam Hussein claims Iraq possesses advanced chemical weapons and threatens to destroy half of Israel if it launches any preemptive strike against Iraq.
August 2, 1990	Iraq invades Kuwait. The emir of Kuwait flees to Saudi Arabia. The UN Security Council passes Resolution 660 condemning the invasion and demanding Iraq's unconditional withdrawal from Kuwait.
August 6, 1990	The UN Security Council passes Resolution 661, which imposes a trade embargo and economic sanctions on Iraq.
August 7, 1990	U.S. president George Bush, after consulting with the leaders of Great Britain, the Soviet Union, Japan, Egypt, and Saudi Arabia, sends U.S. forces to Saudi Arabia to protect it from a potential Iraqi invasion.
November 29, 1990	The UN Security Council passes Resolution 678 authorizing the use of "all necessary means" to force Iraq from Kuwait if Iraq does not withdraw before January 15, 1991.
January 16, 1991	Allied coalition forces launch massive air attacks on Iraq. Israel declares a state of emergency and imposes a curfew in the occupied territories.
January 18, 1991	Iraq attacks Israel with Scud missiles, causing light casualties. The U.S. responds by sending troops to operate Patriot anti-missile systems in Israel.
February 23, 1991	The U.S.-led multinational coalition launches a ground offensive against Iraqi troops.

February 27, 1991	Bush declares victory over Iraq and announces the liberation of Kuwait.
April 1991	The UN Security Council passes resolutions establishing a formal cease-fire between Iraq and the UN coalition and condemning Iraq's suppression of Kurds and Shi'ites. It also passes Resolution 687, requiring Iraq to destroy its weapons of mass destruction. A Special Commission on Iraq (UNSCOM) is formed to monitor Iraq's compliance with Resolution 687.
July 4, 1991	After four days of clashes around Sidon, Lebanon, the PLO agrees to withdraw from its only military base near Israel.
October 30, 1991	International Middle East peace conference is convened in Madrid, Spain. The event marks the first open and direct negotiations between Israel, Syria, Jordan, Lebanon, and the Palestinians. No treaties or agreements are signed. The participants agree to meet for further talks.
July 1992	Yitzhak Rabin is elected prime minister of Israel. He pledges to promote peace and to limit construction of new Jewish settlements in the occupied territories.
August 1992	The UN Security Council establishes "no-fly" zones in northern and southern Iraq in response to continued Iraqi air strikes on Shi'ite rebels. The areas are patrolled by U.S.-led UN troops.
February 1993	Israeli and Palestinian officials begin secret talks in Oslo, Norway. Israel agrees to withdraw from most of Gaza and the West Bank city of Jericho. Arafat's Palestinian Authority is to administer these areas. The final status of the occupied territories is to be determined over the next several years.
February 26, 1993	The World Trade Center in New York City is bombed, leaving six dead and thousands injured. A group of Middle Eastern Islamic militants, later convicted of the bombing, claim the attack was in revenge for U.S. support of Israel.
July 25, 1993	Israel begins a week-long air and artillery assault on 70 villages in southern Lebanon, killing more than 100 Lebanese and driving 300,000 refugees northward. The assault is in retaliation for rocket attacks on Israeli settlements by the pro-Iranian Hezbollah militia, stationed in Lebanon.
September 1993	Rabin and Arafat sign letters proclaiming that the PLO recognizes the right of Israel to exist in peace and security and that Israel acknowledges the PLO as the representative of the Palestinian people. In Washington, D.C., Rabin and Arafat officially sign the historic peace accords agreed to at Oslo.
1994	The Palestinian National Authority (PNA) is formed to govern the semi-autonomous Palestinian state. Violence breaks out as Jewish settlers resist efforts to turn land over to the PNA.

October 1994	54,000 U.S. troops are sent to the Middle East after Iraq again threatens to invade Kuwait. Iraq subsequently withdraws its troops from the Kuwaiti border.
September 1995	The Israeli-Palestinian Oslo II interim agreements are signed. Oslo II divides the West Bank into three areas: one section that is to be governed by the PNA, another section that is granted limited Palestinian self-rule, and a third area to remain under Israeli rule.
November 1995	A car bomb explodes outside an army training building in Riyadh, Saudi Arabia, killing five Americans and two Indians. The Saudi government captures and executes Muslim terrorists implicated in the bombing.
November 4, 1995	Yitzhak Rabin is assassinated by an ultra-right Israeli extremist. Shimon Peres takes over as Israel's prime minister.
May 1996	Benjamin Netanyahu is elected prime minister of Israel.
June 25, 1996	A truck bomb explodes outside a military apartment building in the Khobar Towers complex in Dhahran, Saudi Arabia, killing 19 U.S. airmen and injuring hundreds. Shi'ite terrorists are suspected in the bombing.
September 1996	Violence breaks out in Jerusalem after Israeli authorities open a tunnel near a Muslim holy site. More than 70 people die as a result of clashes involving protestors, Palestinian police, and Israeli soldiers. The U.S. launches 44 cruise missiles into Iraq in response to Iraqi attacks on Kurds in the north. The UN extends the southern no-fly zone closer to Baghdad.
January 1997	Israeli and Palestinian officials sign the Hebron agreement, in which Israel agrees to withdraw its forces from most of the West Bank city of Hebron and to resume Israeli military redeployment throughout the West Bank.
February 1997	Netanyahu announces the beginning of massive construction of Israeli settlements in the West Bank. Violent clashes occur between Palestinian protestors and Israeli troops, stalling peace negotiations.
October 1997	Iraq orders U.S. members of the UN weapons-inspection team to leave the country and threatens to shoot down any U.S. spy planes used for inspections. The remaining UNSCOM team leaves Iraq in support of their U.S. colleagues. After Russian diplomats intervene, the inspectors are allowed to return in November.
January 1998	Iranian president Muhammad Khatami, a political moderate, invites the U.S. to engage in a cultural dialogue and exchange with Iran.
August 7, 1998	U.S. embassies in Nairobi, Kenya, and Dar es Salaam, Tanzania, are simultaneously bombed, killing 257 and injuring thousands. Investigators suspect Osama bin Laden, a Saudi Arabian dissident said to be residing in Afghanistan.

	Bin Laden is also possibly linked to the 1993 World Trade Center bombing and bombings in Riyadh, Saudi Arabia.
August 22, 1998	The U.S. launches military strikes on suspected terrorist-related facilities in Afghanistan and Sudan in retaliation for the August 7 embassy bombings.
October 1998	At the Wye River Conference Center in Maryland, U.S., Israeli, and Arab leaders sign the Wye Memorandum, in which Israel grants Palestinians more control over the West Bank in exchange for guarantees of security and antiterrorism measures from Palestinian authorities.
December 1998	The Palestinian National Council revokes clauses in its founding charter that call for Israel's destruction.
December 15, 1998	In response to repeated Iraqi threats to suspend cooperation with UN weapons inspectors, the U.S. launches four days of air strikes on Iraq. At the end of the operation, Saddam Hussein permanently terminates cooperation with weapons inspectors.
February 7, 1999	King Hussein of Jordan dies. His son, Abdullah, takes the throne.

ORGANIZATIONS TO CONTACT

The editors have compiled the following list of organizations concerned with the issues debated in this book. The descriptions are derived from materials provided by the organizations. All have publications or information available for interested readers. The list was compiled on the date of publication of the present volume; the information provided here may change. Be aware that many organizations take several weeks or longer to respond to inquiries, so allow as much time as possible.

American Jewish Congress
15 E. 84th St., New York, NY 10028
(212) 879-4500 • fax: (212) 249-3672
e-mail: pr@ajcongress.org • website: http://www.ajcongress.org
The congress is dedicated to combating bigotry by lobbying for improved laws and legislation. It also supports the Middle East peace process through education and political activism. Its publications include the magazine *Congress Monthly* and the newsletter *Radical Islamic Fundamentalism Update*.

Americans for Middle East Understanding (AMEU)
475 Riverside Dr., Room 245, New York, NY 10115-0245
(212) 870-2053 • fax: (212) 870-2050
e-mail: ameu@aol.com • website: http://members.aol.com/ameulink
AMEU's purpose is to foster a better understanding in America of the history, goals, and values of Middle Eastern cultures and peoples, the rights of Palestinians, and the forces shaping U.S. policy in the Middle East. AMEU publishes *The Link*, a bimonthly newsletter, as well as books and pamphlets on the Middle East.

Anti-Defamation League (ADL)
823 United Nations Plaza, New York, NY 10017
(212) 885-7700 • fax: (212) 867-0779
website: http://www.adl.org
The Anti-Defamation League is a human relations organization dedicated to combating all forms of prejudice and bigotry. It publishes a wide range of materials on Israel, the Middle East, and the Arab-Israeli peace process, including *The Israel Accord* and *Towards Final Status: Pending Issues in Israeli-Palestinian Negotiations*. The ADL also maintains a bimonthly on-line newsletter, *Frontline*.

Center for Middle Eastern Studies
University of Texas, Austin, TX 78712
(512) 471-3881 • fax: (512) 471-7834
e-mail: cmes@menic.utexas.edu
website: http://menic.utexas.edu/menic/cmes

The center was established by the U.S. Department of Education to promote a better understanding of the Middle East. It provides research and instructional materials and publishes three series of books on the Middle East: the Modern Middle East series, the Middle East Monograph series, and the Modern Middle East Literatures in Translation series.

Foundation for Middle East Peace

1763 N St. NW, Washington, DC 20036
(202) 835-3650 • fax: (202) 835-3651
website: http://www.fmep.org

The foundation assists the peaceful resolution of the Israeli-Palestinian conflict by making financial grants available within the Arab and Jewish communities. It publishes the bimonthly *Report on Israeli Settlements in the Occupied Territories* and additional books and papers.

Institute for Palestine Studies (IPS)

3501 M St. NW, Washington, DC 20007
(202) 342-3990 • fax: (202) 342-3927
website: http://www.ipsjps.org

The Institute for Palestine Studies is a private, nonprofit, pro-Arab institute unaffiliated with any political organization or government. Established in 1963 in Beirut, the institute promotes research, analysis, and documentation of the Arab-Israeli conflict and its resolution. IPS publishes quarterlies in three languages and maintains offices all over the world. In addition to editing the *Journal of Palestine Studies*, the institute's U.S. branch publishes books and documents on the Arab-Israeli conflict and Palestinian affairs.

Jordan Information Bureau

2319 Wyoming Ave. NW, Washington, DC 20008
(202) 265-1606 • fax: (202) 667-0777
website: http://www.jordanembassyus.org/jordanInfo.htm

The bureau provides political, cultural, and economic information on Jordan. It publishes fact sheets, speeches by Jordanian officials, government documents, and the bimonthly *Jordan Issues and Perspectives*.

Middle East Policy Council

1730 M St. NW, Suite 512, Washington, DC 20036-4505
(202) 296-6767 • fax: (202) 296-5791
e-mail: general@mepc.org • website: http://www.mepc.org

The Middle East Policy Council was founded in 1981 to expand public discussion and understanding of issues affecting U.S. policy in the Middle East. The council is a nonprofit educational organization that operates nationwide. It publishes the quarterly *Middle East Policy Journal* and offers workshops for secondary-level educators on how to teach students about the Arab world and Islam.

Middle East Research and Information Project (MERIP)
1500 Massachusetts Ave. NW, Washington, DC 20005
(202) 223-3677 • fax: (202) 223-3604
website: http://www.merip.org

MERIP is a nonprofit, nongovernmental organization with no links to any religious, educational, or political organizations in the United States or elsewhere. MERIP feels that understanding of the Middle East in the United States and Europe is limited and plagued by stereotypes and misconceptions. The project strives to end these limitations by addressing a broad range of social, political, and cultural issues and by soliciting writings and views from authors from the Middle East that are not often read in the West. Its newsletter, *Middle East Report*, is published four times a year, and MERIP offers an extensive list of other Middle East Internet resources.

United Nations Commission on Human Rights (UNCHR)
United Nations, New York, NY 10017
website: http://www.unhchr.ch

UNCHR works with the international community and promotes human rights as the foundation of freedom, justice, and peace in the world. Some of its many resources include fact sheets about human rights, a searchable Middle East database on its website, and a human rights study series.

Washington Institute for Near East Policy
1828 L St. NW, Suite 1050, Washington, DC 20036
(202) 452-0650 • fax: (202) 223-5364
e-mail: info@washingtoninstitute.org
website: http://www.washingtoninstitute.org

The institute is an independent organization that produces research and analysis on the Middle East and on U.S. policy in the region. It publishes numerous position papers and reports on Arab and Israeli politics and social developments. It also publishes position papers on Middle Eastern military issues and U.S. policy, including "The Future of Iraq" and "Building for Peace: An American Strategy for the Middle East."

Bibliography of Books

Lila Abu-Lughod, ed.   *Remaking Women: Feminism and Modernity in the Middle East.* Princeton, NJ: Princeton University Press, 1998.

Karen Armstrong   *Jerusalem: One City, Three Faiths.* New York: Knopf, 1996.

Mordechai Bar-On   *In Pursuit of Peace: A History of the Israeli Peace Movement.* Washington, DC: United States Institute of Peace Press, 1996.

Joel Beinen and   *Political Islam: Essays from Middle East Report.* Berkeley
Joe Stork, eds.   and Los Angeles: University of California Press, 1997.

Boutros Boutros-Ghali   *A Diplomat's Story of the Struggle for Peace in the Middle East.* New York: Random House, 1997.

Dale F. Eichelman and   *Muslim Politics.* Princeton, NJ: Princeton University
James Piscatori   Press, 1996.

Laura Zittrain   *Negotiating Arab-Israeli Peace.* Bloomington: Indiana
Eisenberg and   University Press, 1998.
Neil Caplan

Yaron Ezrahi   *Rubber Bullets: Power and Conscience in Modern Israel.* New York: Farrar, Straus, and Giroux, 1997.

Sattareh Farman   *Daughter of Persia: A Woman's Journey from Her Father's*
Farmaian   *Harem Through the Islamic Revolution.* New York: Anchor, 1993.

Samih K. Farsoun with   *Palestine and the Palestinians.* Boulder, CO: Westview
Christina E. Zacharia   Press, 1997.

Sydney Nettleton Fisher   *The Middle East: A History.* New York: McGraw-Hill, 1997.

Adam Garfinkle   *Politics and Society in Modern Israel: Myths and Realities.* Armonk, NY: M.E. Sharpe, 1997.

Martin Gilbert   *Israel: A History.* New York: Morrow, 1998.

Yvonne Yazbek Haddad   *Islam, Gender, and Social Change.* New York: Oxford
and John L. Esposito,   University Press, 1998.
eds.

Fred Halliday   *Islam and the Myth of Confrontation: Religion and Politics in the Middle East.* New York: I.B. Tauris, 1996.

William Harris et al.   *Challenges to Democracy in the Middle East.* Princeton, NJ: Markus Wiener, 1997.

Dilip Hiro   *The Middle East.* Phoenix: Oryx Press, 1996.

Mehran Kamrava   *Democracy in the Balance: Culture and Society in the Middle East.* Chappaqua, NY: Chatham House, 1998.

Deniz Kandiyoti, ed. *Gendering the Middle East: Emerging Perspectives.* Syracuse, NY: Syracuse University Press, 1996.

Ilana Kass and Bard O'Neill *The Deadly Embrace: The Impact of Israeli and Palestinian Rejectionism on the Peace Process.* Lanham, MD: University Press of America, 1997.

Geoffrey Kemp and Robert E. Harkavy *Strategic Geography and the Changing Middle East.* Washington, DC: Brookings Institution Press, 1997.

Rashid Khalidi *Palestinian Identity.* New York: Columbia University Press, 1997.

Martin Kramer *Arab Awakening and Islamic Revival.* New Brunswick, NJ: Transaction, 1996.

Rose Wilder Lane with Imad-ad-Dean Ahmad *Islam and the Discovery of Freedom.* Beltsville, MD: Amana, 1997.

Bernard Lewis *The Middle East: A Brief History of the Last 2000 Years.* New York: Scribner, 1996.

Staughton Lynd, Sam Bahour, and Alice Lynd, eds. *Homeland: Oral Histories of Palestine and Palestinians.* New York: Olive Branch Press, 1994.

Bruce Maddy-Weitzman and Efraim Inbar *Religious Radicalism in the Greater Middle East.* London: Frank Cass, 1997.

Judith Miller *God Has Ninety-Nine Names: Reporting from a Militant Middle East.* New York: Simon & Schuster, 1996.

Mahmood Monshipouri *Islamism, Secularism, and Human Rights in the Middle East.* Boulder, CO: L. Rienner, 1998.

Benjamin Netanyahu *A Place Among Nations: Israel and the World.* New York: Warner Books, 1999.

Augustus Richard Norton, ed. *Civil Society in the Middle East.* New York: Brill, 1995.

Amos Oz *Israel, Palestine, and Peace.* Farmington, PA: Plough Books, 1997.

Shimon Peres *Battling for Peace: A Memoir.* New York: Random House, 1997.

Daniel Pipes *The Hidden Hand: Middle East Fears of Conspiracy.* New York: St. Martin's Press, 1996.

Saeed Rahnema and Sohrab Behdad *Iran After the Revolution.* New York: I.B. Tauris, 1996.

Glenn E. Robinson *Building a Palestinian State: The Incomplete Revolution.* Bloomington: Indiana University Press, 1997.

Edward Said *Covering Islam: How the Media and Experts Determine How We See the Rest of the World.* New York: Vintage Books, 1997.

INDEX